McGUIRE'S IRISH PUB

COOK BOOK

Our Brewery Bar.

McGUIRE'S IRISH PUB

COOK BOOK

Jessie Tirsch

Foreword by
McGuire and Molly Martin

PELICAN PUBLISHING COMPANY
Gretna 2005

First printing, April 1998
Second printing, June 2002
Third printing, March 2005

Library of Congress Cataloging-in-Publication Data

Tirsch, Jessie.
    McGuire's Irish pub cookbook / Jessie Tirsch; foreword by McGuire
and Molly Martin.
        p.   cm.
    Includes index.
    ISBN 9781565542990 (hardcover : alk. paper)
    1. Cookery, Irish. 2. McGuire's Irish Pub (Pensacola, Fla.)
I. Title.
TX717.5.T56 1998
641.59417—dc21   97-44575
                                                                    CIP

Photographs by Marilee Martin

Printed in Singapore
Published by Pelican Publishing Company, Inc.
1000 Burmaster Street, Gretna, Louisiana 70053

Contents

McGuire's son, Jim Martin, now serves as vice-president of operations for the family-owned business. A certified executive chef, Jim not only chose but personally developed many of the recipes in our book.

Foreword

My wife, Molly, and I opened McGuire's Irish Pub in Pensacola, Florida in May of 1977. It's almost a wonder that we did, considering the experience that I had when I was a wee lad. One Sunday afternoon while I was in my grandmother McGuire's saloon in West Philadelphia, I wandered into the back room and was horrified to see it filled with nuns and priests, in their habits and Roman collars, casually imbibing alcohol. I was convinced that I would be damned to hell for witnessing this sin. Little did I know what my destiny would be!

For the first five years, McGuire's was a small neighborhood pub in a shopping center on the wrong side of town, with me doing the cooking and tending bar and Molly waiting tables and greeting customers. The menu featured "Kosher" deli-style sandwiches served on paper plates. But even in those early days, we insisted on the finest ingredients. There was live Irish entertainment on the weekends and Molly was a featured performer.

When Molly received her first tip—one dollar—she tacked it behind the bar for good luck. A few days later, the local magistrate and his cronies were sitting at the bar and noticed the bill on the wall. As they sipped another round of Irish whiskey, the gentlemen decided to add their dollars to the wall. The wise judge suggested that they write their names on the dollars, so if the pub failed, they could recoup their investments. Thus, a tradition was born!

Whenever a guest signs a dollar and staples it up, he or she is greeted with bells and sirens and presented with an Official Irishman card. And woe to the prankster who takes a few dollars as a souvenir or on a dare. Over the years we have pressed charges against anyone caught stealing the bills. Among the culprits have been two California men who said they were collecting souvenirs, a Coast Guard officer who claimed intoxication, college students from Louisiana who tried to buy seventy-five dollars worth of pizza with the marked bills, and a young lady who tried to pay the cover charge—on Saint Patrick's Day—at another nightspot using our unique "wallpaper."

Fortunately for us, before long McGuire's came to be known all along the Gulf Coast as a comfortable bar with good food and a warm and friendly atmosphere and we quickly outgrew our location. We purchased Pensacola's charming, original 1927 Old Firehouse and in November of '82 moved to the new location lock, stock, barrel, and dollar bills. The day we moved, a team of CPAs verified the tally of dollar bills, and the treasure was safely transported to the new pub by armed Brinks guards.

The old "firehouse" look of McGuire's has become a true landmark in downtown Pensacola. Inside the pub, a turn-of-the-century, New York Irish saloon theme reigns. The hand-burnished, solid-wood tables are set with polished, yet sensible, silverware and crisp, white linen napkins. At night, rosy-pink lighting bathes diners with a warm, welcoming glow while during the day, exterior windows and stained-glass skylights let in the warm Florida sunshine.

Throughout the pub we have created a decor that adds to the fun. The walls and ceilings are papered with more than 500,000 dollar bills, all signed and hung by Irishmen of every nationality. The lobby features bills and photographs signed by international celebrities who have dined at our famous Pensacola pub. An interesting note: every year we hire an accounting firm to count the bills and we pay the appropriate taxes.

As the restaurant continued to grow, wings were added that now contain the Notre Dame Room, the Piper's Den (originally known as the Rugby Room), the Irish Links Room, the wine cellar, and the brewery. Today McGuire's Irish Pub is a 400-seat, 20,000-square-foot landmark with a staff of over 200 friendly, fun-loving employees, and during Pensacola's peak tourist season, more than 2,500 guests visit us every day!

We're a perennial winner of the *Florida Trend* magazine Golden Spoon Award—naming us one of Florida's top twenty restaurants. We're also proud of receiving *Wine Spectator* magazine's Award of Excellence, recognizing our wine list as one of the finest in the world.

Visitors can't fail to notice the more than 5,000 beer mugs hanging from the ceiling and stored on shelves along the walls. These green and white ceramic steins belong to members of the "McGuire's Family Mug Club," who use them when they visit. Each mug is personalized with the name, nickname, alma mater, or favorite saying of the customer. Some of the mugs date back to the seventies and bear battle scars caused by spirited imbibery. Patrons who have been gone for years often return looking for their long-lost mugs. With a bit of Irish luck and leprechaun's magic (and modern computer technology), the mugs are often located, a bit dusty, but still at the pub.

Just a few of the 500,000 dollar bills hanging on the walls and ceilings.

Then Vice-President Gore signed this dollar bill and posed with Molly for a picture. This photo along with those of many other famous people who have visited, such as Sugar Ray Leonard, Sen. John McCain, our own Florida governor Jeb Bush, Sen. Sam Nunn, Janet Jackson, Reba McEntire, and David Copperfield, just to name a few, adorn the walls of McGuire's Irish Pub.

The Notre Dame Room is a museum of posters, artwork, and memorabilia. It was home to the Notre Dame Club of Pensacola until the club outgrew the room. Every Notre Dame student, alumnus, or fan who comes to town is sure to stop by to raise a pint to the Fighting Irish.

Many people are curious as to why we have twelve moose heads on the walls. As legend goes, in fifth-century Ireland, when leprechauns tilled the earth and druids lurked in forests, moose were very common. They overran this tiny realm until there was little room for the wee folks, not to mention druids or peasants. Now, these were not the diminutive 1,200-pound moose that live today—they were the direct descendants of the prehistoric monsters of the Ice Age. The moose, being confirmed vegetarians, were devouring all of the flora. It was such

Seamus, the Irish water buffalo, is one of the many antique animal heads that decorate the pub. Most of the animals were killed and their heads mounted before animal rights and conservation became issues. We assure our guests that we are sensitive to the environment and do not condone killing endangered species. The hippo head at the pub is really a prop from the movie Arthur, starring Dudley Moore (the scene ended up on the cutting-room floor).

a widespread catastrophe that there were no longer forty shades of green in Ireland; there were only twelve recognizable hues of green left.

Fortunately, a young priest known as Patrick had just been sent to Ireland to embark on an evangelistic mission. Realizing that the country's greenery—specifically, its shamrocks—was necessary for the conversion of pagans, Patrick took swift action. He broke off a bare branch of a blackthorn tree (the leaves having been eaten by moose), creating the first shillelagh. He used this makeshift weapon to beat the moose on their hindquarters, driving them westward into the Irish Sea and across the Atlantic Ocean to the shores of Maine.

Thanks to the soft Irish rains and the organic fertilizer left by the moose, in a few short seasons Eire was once again adorned with forty shades of green. In honor of Saint Patrick and his brave and selfless deeds, twelve moose heads adorn the walls of the many dining rooms at McGuire's Irish Pub, symbolizing those twelve tenacious shades of green.

A new tradition was created the night we hung "Moosehead McGuire" over the stage. Then, as now, one of our audience-participation songs was "Tim Finnegan's

The bronze bust in the main bar (as seen from the lobby) was cast to commemorate Cousin Nathan's term as mayor of Chicago, 1932-42.

Cousin Nathan.

This plaque commemorates Cousin Nathan's amazing hole in one, when Arnold Palmer was his caddy.

Wake." If a guest messed up and clapped after the chorus ended, he or she was urged to chug a drink. We were concerned about overindulgence and changed the rules of the game—now people who can't keep time with the music have to kiss the moose! And if it's your birthday, anniversary, first visit to the pub, or any occasion at all, by all means, kiss the moose!

Also displayed in the pub, to amuse and delight with a sense of blarney, are the racing silks of McGuire's mythical "Cousin Nathan," a crafty leprechaun with a sense of adventure. He played football with Knute Rockne, took Ernest Hemingway big-game fishing in Key West, taught Arnold Palmer how to sink a championship putt, was Bing Crosby's voice instructor, handicapped the Irish Sweepstakes, acted as wine steward to the Rothschilds, performed as pipe major at the queen's coronation, and even showed Michael Jackson how to moonwalk! When the beer's too warm or the soup too cold you can always blame Cousin Nathan. When Molly's keys are missing or a waitress drops a tray it probably had something to do with Cousin Nathan. And when the Notre Dame football team recaptures the national championship, you can bet that Cousin Nathan will be on the sidelines, calling the plays!

One of his great claims to fame and his most enduring practical joke involves the signs on the rest-room doors. When you visit our pub, take an extra moment to read the signs carefully or you may end up with some unexpected companions! Included in our lore is the tale of the couple who met in the rest room one Friday night and ended up as husband and wife.

This oil painting of Cousin Nathan's first wife shows a lovely, Rubenesque (if slightly vain) lady. Patrons who are good-naturedly charged with "bad attitudes" during the entertainment are frequently sent to kiss the shamrock tattoo that graces her posterior.

Bing Crosby stands proudly with his Irish Sweepstakes winner, who was trained by Cousin Nathan.

Cousin Nathan's practical joke on the rest-room doors often invites unwary patrons into the wrong water closet.

Conspicuous among our collectibles is Bridget McGuire's dusty, yellowed skeleton in a wood and glass case. As legend goes, as she was walking one evening, she encountered two sailors from the Royal Navy. They were on shore leave and were fairly inebriated. Apparently they made some inappropriate comments, which caused the young Irish lass to take matters into her own hands (so to speak). She was apprehended, charged with murder, and brought before the magistrate for sentencing. Being a loyal subject of Great Britain, he ordered that Bridget be put to death by hanging, using her own undergarments in place of the hangman's noose. According to folklore:

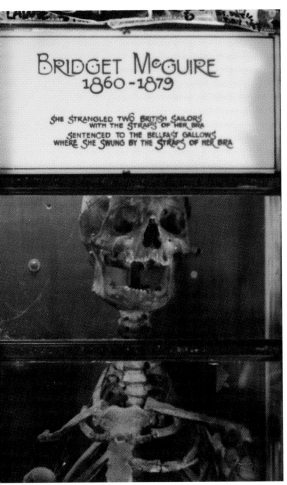

Bridget McGuire, 1860-79.

*She strangled two British sailors
with the straps of her bra
Sentenced to the Belfast gallows
where she swung by the straps of her bra*

We have also dedicated a whole hallway at the pub to the honoring and lampooning of notorious Southern "Good Ole Boy" politicians. Among those enshrined is the Florida state senator who in 1971 was charged with frequenting an illegal gambling place, in 1979 was charged with fraudulent banking practices, and in 1990 was convicted of tax evasion and laundering drug profits. There is also the candidate for state representative who was convicted for the 1975 "Clay Pit Scheme," where he sold the same pit twice, the second time to the County Commission.

It is oft said that when you gather a group of politicians in one room, you can never be certain of the outcome. With this truism in mind, the Irish Politicians Club was founded—a group of Pensacola's movers, shakers, and town characters who lease a private club room from us. They are businesspeople and professionals (some politicians, some not, some behind the scenes, some in the scenes) who are active members of this community. They are people who make things happen and who are sometimes considered to be rather colorful personalities in their own right. Membership in the Irish Politicians Club is limited to 100 active members (give or take a few). All members must be sponsored and unanimously approved by the Charter Masters, the governing body of this illustrious organization, although members are permitted to bring guests.

Who knows what liaisons have been formed, deals made, or trysts conducted behind the green velvet curtains that seclude some of the private tables in the Irish Politicians Club? Naturally, our staff would never disclose the secrets of the members.

Each year the IPC hosts the Northwest Florida Politician of the Year Banquet and presents the Bob Sikes "He-Coon" Trophy to a deserving local politician. Congressman Sikes represented the Panhandle of Florida for more than thirty

The Bob Sikes "He-Coon" Trophy is kept in the Irish Politicians Club.

years. Past recipients include U.S. Cong. Joe Scarborough, Florida State Sen. W. D. Childers, and Florida State Cong. Buzz Ritchie.

And speaking of politicians, one of the most popular side items on our menu is a steaming bowl of Senate Bean Soup. This is the same recipe that has been served in the U.S. Senate for years. We've been selling this wonderful homemade soup for eighteen cents a bowl since 1977. The Senate cafeteria has raised its price to ninety-seven cents, but we all know that Washington can't control costs.

Our Piper's Den is dedicated to the award-winning McGuire's Bagpipe Band—the "Irish Show Band of the South"—a band that we sponsor that has played at all of the major Highland Games and Celtic festivals from North Carolina to Louisiana. Formed in 1988 under the leadership of Pipe Major Jack Dasinger, the group has played for the vice-president of the United States, the secretary of the navy, and many other visiting dignitaries. It has even been featured on an

In memory of Pipe Major Jack Dasinger, who formed McGuire's Pipe Band and served from 1988 to 2003.

ESPN broadcast of the Emerald Coast Classic Golf Tournament. The pipes and drums of this colorful ensemble are also popular in parades. In their striking tartan kilts and traditional Balmorals or pith helmets, they are a crowd favorite. The band is often escorted by one of our two green double-decker buses or our hand-painted 1929 GMC brewery wagon. In 1996 it released a recording, *McGuire's Irish Pub Pipe Band and Friends,* featuring traditional tunes such as "Scotland the Brave," "Amazing Grace," and "Highland Cathedral" as well as unique arrangements of "Danny Boy," "Dixie Land," and even "When the Saints Go Marching In"!

Our gift shop features collectibles, glassware, jewelry, and clothing, with many of the items imported from Ireland. Some of the best-selling pieces are sixteen-ounce ceramic beer mugs like the ones in our Family Mug Club and *Molly McGuire & Friends: Live at McGuire's*, a collection of Irish drinking songs and ballads performed by the Best Irish Entertainers South of Boston.

A leprechaun seated on a stump is our logo and it is displayed throughout the pub, on our gift-shop items, and wherever you see our name. This stained-glass window is surrounded by our Golden Spoon Awards.

During a night of feasting and imbibery at the pub, Jeff MacNelly drew these cartoons. The price? One moose head and one German helmet.

Our craft-brewed ales.

In 1988, we opened Florida's first micro-brewery, at the restaurant. The custom-built brewhouse—a wonder of rich oak and shiny copper—produces award-winning, craft-brewed ales, stouts, and porters in the Old World tradition. We even brew our own root beer on the premises, using only the purest natural ingredients and genuine sassafras root. This is the real thing (alcohol: 0 percent)! We also boast a full-service bar that pours premium brands, a grand array of Irish whiskeys, and a remarkable selection of single-malt Scotch and small-batch bourbons.

In 1996, we added a new wing to the restaurant: an impressive wine-cellar dining room complete with burnished oak casks from

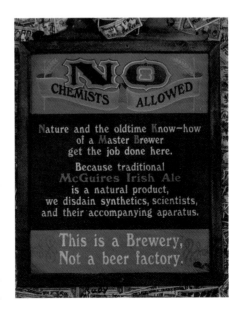

Pronounced "Kaid Meal Falcha," this sign means "A Hundred Thousand Welcomes." It appropriately greets guests at the front door.

Pensacola's Bartel's winery (circa 1925-75) and a gas fireplace, which help to create the warm ambience of an ancient European monastery. When we purchased the contents of Bartel's winery, the 3,200-gallon fermentation barrels still contained 500 gallons of aged scuppernong and muscadine wine. Twenty years in the oak barrels turned it into sherry-wine vinegar, which we bottled and sold in our gift shop!

   Flanking the fireplace in the adults-only room are two twelve-foot-high stained-glass windows that once graced a Masonic hall in Philadelphia. The

The wine racks in our cellar can accommodate more than 8,000 bottles.

granite walls were quarried from Stone Mountain, Georgia. Illuminating the room from the vaulted ceiling is a hand-crafted iron and copper chandelier from a Quebec abbey. Other prizes from the abbey's ruins are the three sixteen-foot-high, rose-tinted windows that line the adjoining hallway. The antique wine press in the loft was used in the 1930s and 1940s in one of Napa Valley's oldest vineyards.

The wine racks behind the display glass are designed to accommodate more than eight thousand bottles. We carefully maintain the temperature behind the glass at an optimum range of fifty-five to sixty degrees, with a constant humidity of 75 percent, to assure preservation of the many priceless bottles.

You could visit McGuire's many times without seeing

This 1935 Peugeot motorcycle was ridden by legendary Cousin Nathan while he was smuggling diamonds into Cairo during Rommel's desert campaign.

The antique, fully operational meat locker just off the lobby.

Don't be concerned by our antique poor box. Our bartenders and servers are well rewarded for their warm and friendly service.

or doing it all. You might miss, for instance, a potent green drink aptly named an "Irish Wake" (limit two per customer); the antique, fully operational meat locker just off the lobby, where you can gaze fondly at steaks, loins, ribs, chops, and other sexy cuts of USDA Prime meat; and lots more. McGuire's Pub is a happy stew of great food and drink, lively entertainment, fascinating legend, and good-natured silliness. The neon sign in the kitchen sums up the attitude of the employees—If You're Not Proud of It Don't Serve It! We hope you will cook these recipes, come visit our pub, and enjoy an unforgettable experience.

McGuire & Molly

McGuire and Molly Martin

Acknowledgments

I offer my hearty thanks to the many people who worked so hard to make this book happen: executive chef Jim Martin, consulting chef Sharan Sheppard, and photographer Marilee Martin; Susi Lyon, Keeper of the Lore and Legends; and Sherry Davis, Keeper of the Pot o' Gold. But most of all, I thank Molly and McGuire, without whom none of it would have been possible.

This neon sign hangs in the kitchen and sums up the attitude of all our employees.

Introduction

One would never dream of traveling in Ireland without visiting the pubs. It's almost unthinkable. It could be said that, after the church, the "publick house" is the soul of Ireland—the center of its people's social, political, and cultural worlds. Whether rural or urban, the pub is the place where ideas are exchanged, pints imbibed, and food enjoyed.

In the cities of Ireland, pub settings are apt to be fairly sophisticated and teeming with activity—some of it raucous. But in a small village you might find a pub tucked into the corner of a grocery store, where the drinking, eating, and convivial fellowship take place among the rows of canned goods and piles of produce. There, tales are woven and deals negotiated.

In times past, anything a customer might get to eat in an Irish tavern was considered secondary—an alibi for the whiskey. But today, food is an important element, and in many pubs it's the main attraction, carefully and creatively prepared, and proudly served. The cooking in these places has become bolder, while reflecting the generosity of the people and the simplicity of Irish fare over the ages.

In America, the pub is loosely modeled around its Irish cousin. Here it is very much the place to meet—old friends, new friends, and sometimes new lovers. The first pubs in this country probably sprang up in Boston, where the great majority of Irish immigrants originally clustered. These cozy retreats—where pilgrims could go for a pint, a meal, and companionship—helped them through their adjustment to strange surroundings and soothed their pervasive homesickness and loneliness.

Eventually, as the Irish dispersed throughout the United States, so did the concept of the Irish pub, and today this popular setting for eating, drinking, and socializing abounds in cities and towns across the country. Though drink is still king and conversation its consort, the habitué knows he will also get honest, satisfying food at his local pub.

One of the best known nationally is McGuire's Irish Pub. Visitors to Pensacola, Florida—whether from Boston, Los Angeles, Chicago, Memphis, or Wherever, U.S.A.—gravitate to the joyful sounds of Irish folk songs, the taste on the tongue of brewery beer, and the good food that are synonymous with McGuire's. *Florida Trend* Magazine Hall of Fame member, dubbing it one of the state's "Top Twenty Restaurants," and recommended by the *Mobil Travel Guide,* McGuire's Irish Pub is famous for its traditional pub fare as well as its plump burgers and thick, juicy steaks.

McGuire's is an ongoing celebration—a never-ending family party filled with Irish music, singing, dancing, warmth, and laughter. But best of all, according to McGuire's huge and loyal following, is the food, which—like the music—is hearty, fun, and tasty. Crocks of cheese-crusted onion soup, bowls of Irish stew, platters piled high with sizzling meat or fish, trays of rich, tempting desserts—they're all a part of the experience.

In this book you will find pub food—some of it swell enough for the fanciest dinner party, some of it more traditional Irish food, updated to suit the contemporary palate. Not every dish in this book is on the menu at McGuire's Irish Pub—yet. But at the restaurant you will always be able to enjoy USDA Certified Prime steaks, fresh Gulf seafood, classic Irish pub fare, and a bona fide McGuire's special—Senate Bean Soup (although the Senate cafeteria in the Capitol Building in Washington, D.C. has raised the price of their signature soup to ninety-seven cents, McGuire's has held the line at eighteen cents). And if you write to them and tell them which are your favorite recipes in the cookbook—who knows?—they might wind up on the menu.

Many of the dishes in this book are laced with wines, liqueurs, whiskey, and beer, blissfully wedded to the food for some astoundingly delicious results. Molly, McGuire, and their staff hope you enjoy them all and wish you a hearty appetite—"bain taitneamh as do bhéile!

ABBREVIATIONS

STANDARD

tsp.	=	teaspoon
tbsp.	=	tablespoon
oz.	=	ounce
qt.	=	quart
pt.	=	pint
lb.	=	pound

METRIC

ml.	=	milliliter
l.	=	liter
g.	=	gram
kg.	=	kilogram
mg.	=	milligram

STANDARD-METRIC APPROXIMATIONS

⅛ teaspoon	=	.6 milliliter		
¼ teaspoon	=	1.2 milliliters		
½ teaspoon	=	2.5 milliliters		
1 teaspoon	=	5 milliliters		
1 tablespoon	=	15 milliliters		
4 tablespoons	=	¼ cup	=	60 milliliters
8 tablespoons	=	½ cup	=	118 milliliters
16 tablespoons	=	1 cup	=	236 milliliters
2 cups	=	473 milliliters		
2½ cups	=	563 milliliters		
4 cups	=	946 milliliters		
1 quart	=	4 cups	=	.94 liter

SOLID MEASUREMENTS

½ ounce	=	15 grams		
1 ounce	=	25 grams		
4 ounces	=	110 grams		
16 ounces	=	1 pound	=	454 grams

McGUIRE'S
IRISH PUB

SALUTE TO 46TH GALWAY OYSTER FESTIVAL

Galway Bay Oysters on the Half Shell with Mignonette, Lemon-Tabasco Sauce,
Scallion-Lime Sauce, and Beluga Caviar

Twice-Baked Truffled Potatoes with Pancetta and Asiago Cheese

Irish Salmon on Potato Gaufrettes with Chive Crème Fraîche and Golden Caviar

Pickled Oysters with Marinated Fennel and Goat Cheese on Artichoke Petals

Morel and Roasted Garlic Potato Crostini

Schramsberg Blanc de Noirs / McGuire's Irish Stout

Savory Oyster Custard with Woodland Mushroom Consommé
Robert Mondavi Napa Chardonnay 1998

Candy-Striped Oyster Ravioli w/Tomato-Basil Beurre Blanc & Braised Savoy Cabbage
Kenwood Reserve Sauvignon Blanc 1997

Rack of Lamb w/Oyster Dressing, Portobello Wine Sauce & Roasted Root Vegetables
Leasingham Shiraz 1997

Potato-Crusted Salmon with Bushmills Black Mustard Sauce, Onion Tart, and Field Greens
Gallo Sonoma Laguna Ranch Chardonnay 1997

Chocolate Oyster Shells with Bailey's Irish Cream and White Chocolate Mint Sauce
Irish Coffee

The above menu was served at the James Beard House in New York City by Executive Chef Jim Martin and his staff at McGuire's Irish Pub. It is a very prestigious honor to be invited to the James Beard House, where some of the country's finest chefs have prepared meals.

M^cGUIRE'S
IRISH PUB
COOK
BOOK

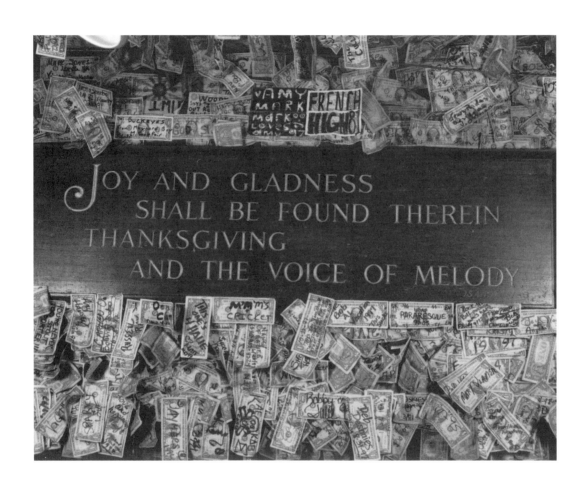

Good Mornings:

Bread and Brunch

Nothing brings hearth and home to mind as quickly as the smell of baking bread. Although dense, heavy loaves of barley or oats helped keep the Irish alive in hard times, the soda breads for which they are best known are relatively new. The Irish Soda Bread recipe here easily produces a perfect example of the popular bread with the X on top.

In this chapter you'll find some new wrinkles on traditional Irish loaves—Barmbrack, Irish Buttermilk Bread, and Oatcakes, as well as novelties such as Bloody Mary Bread, Mrs. O'Hara's Focaccia, and No-Rise Swiss-Cheese Applesauce Bread. There are also baked goods that create the foundations for other dishes and treats: variations of Puff Pastry Twists for parties, Basic Pizza Crust for Vegetable Cheese Pizza Pie, and Onion Rye Rolls, Potato Buns, and Dill Bread to make sandwiches and burgers or to accompany soup.

Bread is such a popular item in the morning and early afternoon that when the savory Bacon Bread created a natural segue into brunches—Bacon Bread Irish Toast with "Hair o' the Dog" Syrup—I decided to combine the two categories into one chapter.

From Blackberry Muffins with Lemon Glaze to Barney's Brioches, Gingerbread Waffles with Irish Coffee Syrup and Ginger Sugar to Beer-Battered Oysters with Muenster Cheese Grits, you'll find more than enough hearty breads and hospitable brunches to feed a hungry mob.

BACON BREAD

This is the bread that comes to breakfast or brunch as Bacon Bread Irish Toast with "Hair o' the Dog" Syrup and as Dublin Eggs Bacondict. For a super lunch, serve it with Onion, Leek, and Mushroom Soup (see index). Or spread a slice of Bacon Bread with Orange Irish Whiskey Marmalade.

1 tsp. vegetable oil
4 cups all-purpose or bread flour, plus more for the pans
¼ lb. bacon
1 cup whole-wheat flour
2 pkg. dry yeast

2 tsp. salt
¼ tsp. ground coriander
½ cup nonfat milk powder
2 cups hot water (130 degrees)
¼ cup packed brown sugar
1 large egg

1. Using the oil and a handful of white flour, grease and flour 2 medium (8" x 4") loaf pans. Shake out the excess.

2. Cook the bacon in a heavy skillet until crisp. Reserve 2 tbsp. of the drippings. Drain and crumble enough bacon to equal ⅓ cup.

3. In a large bowl, combine the whole-wheat flour, 3 cups of the white flour, yeast, salt, coriander, dry milk, hot water, and the 2 tbsp. reserved bacon drippings. Using an electric mixer, blend at low speed for 30 seconds.

4. Beat in the brown sugar, egg, and crumbled bacon. Increase the mixer speed to high and beat for 3 more minutes.

5. Use a wooden spoon to blend in the remaining 1 cup white flour. Scrape down the sides of the bowl, cover with plastic wrap, and leave at room temperature until the dough has doubled in volume, about 45 minutes.

6. Preheat the oven to 375 degrees.

7. Remove the plastic wrap and, using 2 wooden spoons, transfer the dough to the prepared loaf pans. Cover the pans with plastic wrap and allow the dough to rise to the edge of each pan, about 30 minutes.

8. Remove the plastic wrap and place the loaf pans on a heavy baking sheet. Bake until the loaves are brown and a metal skewer inserted into the center of each comes out clean and dry, about 30 to 40 minutes.

9. Remove the bread from the pans and cool on a wire rack before slicing.
Makes 2 medium loaves.

BLOODY MARY BREAD

If you love drinking a Bloody Mary, now you can eat it—and have almost as much fun! Bloody Mary Bread makes a wonderful sandwich, especially with Leeky Brie and Cherry Tomatoes (see index).

2 pkg. dry yeast

1 tbsp. granulated sugar

1 tsp. salt

3 tbsp. warm water (115 to 120 degrees)

1 cup plus 2 tbsp. commercial Bloody Mary mix

1 tbsp. unsalted butter, plus more for the bowl and the baking sheet, room temperature

1 tbsp. Worcestershire sauce

1 tbsp. vodka

2 to 3 dashes hot sauce

3 to 3½ cups bread flour, plus more for kneading

1 tbsp. celery seed, divided

½ cup peeled, seeded, and chopped tomatoes

1 large egg, beaten

1. Combine the yeast, sugar, and salt in a custard cup or small bowl. Add the water and allow the mixture to sit and the yeast to activate, 3 to 5 minutes.

2. Heat the Bloody Mary mix in a small saucepan over medium-low heat, until it bubbles or a thermometer inserted in the pan reads 120 degrees, 5 to 6 minutes. Stir in 1 tbsp. butter, the Worcestershire, vodka, and hot sauce, and cook, stirring, until the butter has melted and all of the ingredients are incorporated, 3 to 4 minutes. Remove from the heat and allow to cool slightly.

3. In a large bowl, combine 1 cup of the flour with ½ tsp. celery seed. Stir in the Bloody Mary mixture and the yeast mixture, and beat 50 strokes with a wooden spoon. Continue adding the flour ½ cup at a time, beating 50 strokes after each addition to incorporate it thoroughly into the dough. Add only enough flour to make the dough smooth. Beat in the chopped tomatoes. If the dough seems too dry and is cracking or crumbling, add more Bloody Mary mix 1 tsp. at a time, until the problem is corrected.

4. Turn the dough out on a lightly floured surface and knead until it becomes smooth, shiny, and elastic, about 10 minutes (see index for kneading techniques). Grease a bowl with butter and place the dough in the bowl. Cover with a dish towel and set in a warm place until the dough has doubled in volume, about 1 hour. Grease a baking sheet with butter.

5. Turn the dough out again onto a lightly floured work surface, pat down, and divide in half. Press each piece into a long, thin shape, and roll out until you have

2 loaves measuring 18" long by 2½" wide. Place the loaves on the greased baking sheet, cover loosely with wax paper, and set in a warm place to rise again until double in size, about 45 minutes. After 30 minutes, preheat the oven to 375 degrees.

6. Remove the wax paper, brush the loaves with the beaten egg, and sprinkle with the remaining celery seeds. Bake until the bread is golden brown and gives off a hollow sound when tapped, about 20 minutes. Remove from the oven and allow the bread to sit until cool enough to handle, about 5 minutes. Slice and serve.

Makes 2 loaves.

DILL BREAD

This delicious bread perfectly complements Smoked Salmon Bisque.

1 tsp. melted unsalted butter, divided

1 cup cottage cheese, room temperature

2 tbsp. sugar

1 tbsp. grated fresh onion

1 tbsp. chopped fresh dill

¼ tsp. baking soda

2 large eggs, room temperature

1 pkg. (2 tsp.) active dry yeast

1½ tsp. salt, divided

2½ cups bread flour

1. Grease a 1½-qt. casserole with ½ tsp. of the butter, and set aside.

2. Heat the cottage cheese in a small saucepan over low heat until it is warm to the touch (110 degrees). Turn the warmed cottage cheese into a bowl and stir in the sugar, onion, dill, baking soda, eggs, yeast, and 1 tsp. of the salt. Mix well.

3. Beat in the flour ½ cup at a time, beating well after each addition. Cover the bowl with plastic wrap and place it in a warm spot in the kitchen to rise until double in volume, about 1 hour.

4. Remove the plastic wrap from the bowl and, using a wooden spoon, beat the dough 20 strokes. Turn the dough into the buttered casserole dish, cover with plastic wrap, and leave to rise until it has doubled again, about 45 minutes.

5. About 15 minutes before the dough is finished rising, preheat the oven to 350 degrees.

6. Remove the plastic wrap and bake the bread until deep brown and crusty, about 35 to 45 minutes. Remove from the oven and immediately brush the top of the bread with the remaining ½ tsp. butter. Sprinkle the remaining ½ tsp. salt over the top.

Serves 6-8.

FRECKLE BREAD

This wonderful potato bread gets just the right touch of sweetness from raisins (its freckles). It makes great toast and spectacular bread pudding.

1½ cups water
¾ cup peeled, cubed potatoes
2 to 3 cups bread flour, divided
1 pkg. dry yeast
3 tbsp. granulated sugar
½ tsp. salt

1 large egg, room temperature
¼ cup unsalted butter, melted and
    cooled to room temperature
½ cup raisins
Vegetable oil spray

1. Bring the water to a boil in a small saucepan. Add the potatoes and cook until tender, about 20 minutes. Measure off ¾ cup of the boiling water. If there isn't enough potato water, add warm tap water to make ¾ cup.

2. Mash the potatoes in a bowl. Add ¾ cup of the flour, the yeast, sugar, and salt. Stir in the potato water with a wooden spoon, and continue stirring until the mixture forms a smooth batter. Cover with a dish towel and set in a warm place until the dough doubles in volume, 1 to 1½ hours.

3. Whisk the egg until frothy. Stir the egg, butter, and raisins into the batter. Start adding flour ½ cup at a time, mixing well after each addition, until you have a soft dough.

4. Preheat the oven to 375 degrees.

5. Turn out the dough on a lightly floured work surface. Divide the dough in half with the side of your hand, and allow it to rest for 5 minutes.

6. Roll the dough into 2 cylinders, each about 9" long. Grease a 9" x 5" loaf pan with the vegetable oil spray, and place the dough cylinders side by side in the pan. Cover with a towel and set in a warm place to rise again until double in size, about 45 minutes.

7. Remove the towel and bake the bread until light brown (it should sound hollow when tapped), about 20 minutes.

Makes 1 loaf.

IRISH BUTTERMILK BREAD

This hearty peasant bread is delicious eaten warm and smeared with soft butter or cream cheese.

2 cups bread flour
1 tsp. granulated sugar
½ tsp. baking soda
½ tsp. cream of tartar

¼ tsp. salt
1 tbsp. unsalted butter, room
   temperature
¾ cup buttermilk

1. Preheat the oven to 375 degrees.
2. In a bowl, sift together the flour, sugar, baking soda, cream of tartar, and salt. Cut in the butter with a fork until the mixture resembles cornmeal. Slowly add the buttermilk, a little at a time, blending well until you have a sticky dough.
3. Turn the dough out onto a lightly floured work surface and pat into a round loaf about 8" in diameter. Place the loaf on a baking sheet and use the edge of a knife to mark an *X* in its center.
4. Bake until golden brown, 25 to 30 minutes. Serve warm with butter.
Makes 1 small loaf.

IRISH FLAG BREAD

This unusual tricolor bread pays homage to the Irish flag. The three layers of dough are stacked one atop the other, rolled up jelly-roll style, and baked. The bread is exceptionally pretty when sliced, and even better, it's delicious when eaten.

WHITE DOUGH

1 pkg. dry yeast
½ tsp. salt
½ tsp. granulated sugar
⅔ cup plus 1 tbsp. hot water (130 degrees)
1¾ cups bread flour, plus more for kneading, divided

1 large egg, room temperature
1 tbsp. unsalted butter, plus more for greasing, room temperature
2 tbsp. milk, room temperature

GREEN DOUGH

Same as above except:
4 additional tbsp. milk, divided

One 15-oz. pkg. frozen spinach, thawed and squeezed to remove excess liquid

RED DOUGH

Same as for white dough

1 cup canned tomato sauce

1. To prepare the white dough, combine the yeast with the salt, sugar, and 1 tbsp. hot water in a cup or small bowl. Mix well and allow the mixture to sit for 3 to 5 minutes.

2. Measure 1 cup of the flour into a large bowl. Make a well in the center of the flour and add the egg, butter, yeast mixture, and the remaining ⅔ cup hot water. Stir with a wooden spoon until thoroughly blended, about 75 strokes. Mix in the remaining flour ½ cup at a time, alternating with small additions of the milk, and mixing well after each addition, until you have a smooth dough.

3. Turn the dough onto a lightly floured surface and knead (see index) until it is smooth and elastic, 8 to 10 minutes.

4. Grease a large bowl with butter and place the dough in the bowl. Cover the bowl and place it in a warm, draft-free spot. Allow the dough to rise until almost double in volume, about 45 minutes.

5. To prepare the green dough, place 4 tbsp. milk and the drained spinach in a food processor and puree. Set aside. Follow steps 1 through 4, above, adding the spinach puree to the well in the flour in step 2.

6. To prepare the red dough, follow steps 1 through 4, adding the tomato sauce to the well in the flour in step 2.

7. To assemble the loaf, transfer the three mounds of dough to a lightly floured work surface. Divide each color in half and allow the 6 pieces of dough to rest for 5 minutes.

8. Flatten each piece of dough and roll it out with a rolling pin into a rectangle measuring 15" x 7" and about ¼" thick. Place the white dough sections side by side on the work surface. Place the green sections on these, and top with the red dough. From the long side of each rectangle, roll up the dough like a jelly roll, tuck the ends under, and pinch to seal. Place the loaves on a baking sheet in a warm place. Cover and allow the dough to rise until double in size, about 30 minutes.

9. About halfway through this rising time, preheat the oven to 375 degrees. Bake the loaves until they give off a hollow sound when they're tapped, about 15 minutes.

Makes 2 loaves.

ONION RYE BREAD

This is a hearty and delicious twist on an old favorite. Rye flour is used for flavor and texture, but its gluten provides little elasticity, so a larger proportion of wheat flour must be included.

2 tbsp. vegetable oil, divided
¾ cup minced onions
1¼ cups white bread flour, divided
¾ cup rye flour, divided
1 tbsp. granulated sugar
1 tsp. salt

1 pkg. dry yeast
½ cup milk, room temperature
¼ cup hot water (130 degrees)
1 tbsp. caraway seeds
2 tbsp. unsalted butter, softened

1. Heat 1 tbsp. oil in a small skillet over medium-high heat. Add the onions and cook, stirring often, until the onions are tender and light golden, 4 to 5 minutes. Turn the onions into a small bowl or dish to cool.

2. In a bowl combine ¾ cup white bread flour and ¼ cup rye flour. Add the sugar, salt, and yeast and mix well. Make a well in the center of the dry ingredients and add the milk, water, and remaining 1 tbsp. oil. Blend the mixture lightly with a wooden spoon. Stir in the cooled onions and the caraway seeds.

3. Gradually stir in the remaining rye flour, then stir in the remaining white flour ¼ cup at a time, and mix until you have a very stiff dough.

4. Turn the dough out on a lightly floured work surface. Knead with a push-and-fold motion (see index) for 8 minutes, dusting the dough lightly with more flour if it's too sticky.

5. Grease a bowl with 1 tbsp. of the softened butter, and turn the dough into the bowl. Cover the bowl and set in a warm place until the dough has doubled in volume, 1 to 1½ hours.

6. Preheat the oven to 375 degrees. Grease a 9" x 5" loaf pan with the remaining 1 tbsp. butter.

7. Uncover the bowl and punch the dough down. Turn the dough onto the work surface and allow it to rest for 5 minutes. Shape the dough into a smooth oval, fold it in half, and pinch the edges together. Tuck in the ends and place in the loaf pan, seam side down. Cover, set in a warm place, and let the dough rise again until double in size, about 45 minutes.

8. Place the pan in the oven and bake until brown (it should sound hollow when tapped), 25 to 35 minutes.

Makes 1 loaf.

IRISH SODA BREAD

Although there are dozens of variations on the traditional Irish soda bread, they all have two things in common: they're all made with buttermilk, and they all have a cross cut into the top to keep the dough from splitting while it bakes. Quick and easy to make, soda bread is totally irresistible when slathered with sweet, creamy butter or Orange Irish Whiskey Marmalade.

3 cups all-purpose flour
¼ cup sugar
1 tbsp. baking powder
1 tsp. baking soda
½ tsp. salt

4 tbsp. (¼ cup) unsalted butter
2 tbsp. caraway seeds (optional)
1 cup raisins
1 cup buttermilk
1 egg

1. Set a rack in the middle of the oven and preheat the oven to 400 degrees.
2. In a mixing bowl, combine the flour, sugar, baking powder, baking soda, and salt. Stir to mix well.
3. Add the butter and rub in until the butter disappears into the dry ingredients.
4. Stir in the caraway seeds, if used, and the raisins.
5. In a small bowl, whisk the buttermilk and egg together. Mix into the dough mixture with a rubber spatula.
6. Turn the dough out on a floured work surface and fold it over on itself several times, shaping it into a round loaf. Transfer the loaf to a cookie sheet or jelly-roll pan covered with parchment or foil and cut a cross in the top. Bake for 15 minutes, then reduce the heat to 350 degrees and cook for about 15 to 20 minutes more, until well colored and a toothpick plunged into the center emerges clean. Cool the soda bread on a rack.

BARMBRACK

This traditional Irish loaf, whose name means speckled yeast bread, is enjoyed year round. But at Halloween various symbols are baked into the loaves, each signifying the fortune of the individual who gets it. A button means a man will remain a bachelor and a thimble portends spinsterhood for a woman. But a ring found in a slice predicts marriage within a year. A dried pea signifies poverty, but a coin forecasts wealth. Gather some of your own charms and have fun with this at a party.

1½ cups golden raisins
½ cup mixed candied fruit
1 tbsp. brandy
1 tbsp. orange-flavored liqueur, such as Grand Marnier or Triple Sec
2 pkg. dry yeast
¼ cup warm water (115 to 130 degrees)
½ cup granulated sugar

2 tsp. salt
2 large eggs, room temperature
½ cup (1 stick) unsalted butter, melted
½ cup milk
½ cup water
4 to 5 cups bread flour
Vegetable oil for greasing

1. Combine the raisins and candied fruit in a small bowl. Sprinkle with the brandy and orange liqueur and toss. Set aside to macerate while you prepare the dough.

2. In a large bowl, dissolve the yeast in the warm water, and allow the mixture to sit for 5 minutes. Stir in the sugar and salt and mix well. Beat in the eggs and melted butter with a wooden spoon. In a small bowl or cup, combine the milk with the ½ cup water.

3. To the egg-yeast mixture, add the flour in 3 increments, alternating with the milk, mixing thoroughly after each addition and working with your hands until you have a cohesive ball of dough. Add 4 to 5 cups of the flour, stopping when you have the desired consistency.

4. Turn the dough onto a lightly floured work surface. Knead (see index) until the dough is stiff and elastic, about 5 minutes.

5. Lightly oil a large bowl and place the dough in it. Cover the bowl and place it in a warm part of the kitchen. Allow the dough to rise until it has doubled in bulk, about 1 hour.

6. Turn the dough out onto the work surface and flatten it into an oblong (about 1" thick) with your hands. Spread the raisin and fruit mixture on the center of the flattened dough, leaving about a 2" border all the way around. If you

would like to add charms to your barmbrack, do it now, using clean, heat-resistant items. Knead the fruit into the dough, pushing back any pieces that pop out as you go. Shape the dough into a loaf approximately 9" x 3" and place it in a lightly oiled 11½" x 5½" loaf pan. Cover and place in a warm spot to rise until doubled in volume, about 1 hour.

7. About 15 minutes before the dough has finished rising, preheat the oven to 375 degrees. Uncover the loaf pan and bake until the loaf is a dark golden brown and sounds hollow when tapped, 60 to 65 minutes. Remove the bread and cool on a wire rack before slicing.

Makes 1 large loaf.

NO-RISE SWISS-CHEESE APPLESAUCE BREAD

This tangy-sweet bread makes terrific sandwiches. My favorite is Smoked Chicken Salad (see index) piled high on thick slices of the bread and served for lunch.

Vegetable oil for greasing
½ cup (1 stick) unsalted butter, room temperature
⅓ cup granulated sugar
3 tbsp. honey
3 tbsp. maple syrup
2 large eggs

1 cup whole-wheat flour
1 cup all-purpose flour
1 tsp. baking powder
½ tsp. baking soda
½ tsp. salt
1 cup unsweetened applesauce
½ cup grated Swiss cheese

1. Preheat the oven to 350 degrees. Oil a 9" x 5" loaf pan.
2. In a large bowl with an electric mixer on medium speed, cream together the butter and sugar until smooth and creamy, 2 to 3 minutes. Beat in the honey, maple syrup, and the eggs—one at a time.
3. In another large bowl, combine the wheat and all-purpose flours with the baking powder, baking soda, and salt. Slowly stir the flour mixture into the wet mixture, and beat until just blended. Stir in the applesauce and cheese.
4. Pour the batter into the oiled loaf pan. Bake until the top of the bread is golden and a knife comes out clean, about 1 hour. Cool the bread on a rack before slicing.

Makes 1 loaf.

OATCAKES

These chewy bread-cakes have been fed to children in Ireland for many years, in the belief that vigorous chewing would strengthen their young jaws. Today's children like them because they're fun to eat. And because they are low in fat and high in fiber, they are definitely healthful. The loaf is cut in quarters, or "farls," before it is baked.

2 cups uncooked, old-fashioned
   rolled oats (not instant)
1¼ cups buttermilk
2½ cups sifted bread flour

1 tsp. baking soda
½ tsp. baking powder
1 tsp. salt
Vegetable oil spray

   1. A day ahead, combine the oats and buttermilk in a small bowl. Blend thoroughly, cover, and refrigerate overnight.

   2. The next day, preheat the oven to 350 degrees. Remove the oat mixture from the refrigerator.

   3. Combine the bread flour, baking soda, baking powder, and salt in a large bowl. Slowly add the oat mixture and stir with a wooden spoon 20 to 30 times, or until you have a smooth dough.

   4. Grease a baking sheet with the oil spray. Turn the dough onto the baking sheet, and use your hands to form a round, cake-shaped loaf, about 1" thick. Use a sharp knife or pizza cutter to cut the dough into 4 quarters. Move the quarters apart slightly, but keep them in the original round shape.

   5. Bake until the cakes are light golden brown and firm to the touch, 30 to 35 minutes. Cool slightly on a rack, and serve with butter and jam or preserves.

   Makes 1 quartered loaf (4 farls), serving 4-8.

ONION RYE ROLLS

These rolls are great with hamburgers but I really love them best under open-face Corned Beef with Horseradish Cabbage Confit (see index).

3½ cups bread flour, divided
1½ cups rye flour, plus more for
    kneading and shaping
2 tbsp. granulated sugar
2 tsp. salt
1 pkg. dry yeast

1 cup milk
½ cup hot water
2 tbsp. vegetable oil, plus more for
    greasing
¾ cup minced onions
2 tbsp. caraway seeds

   1. In a large bowl, combine 1½ cups of the bread flour with ½ cup of the rye flour, the sugar, salt, and yeast.

   2. In a small saucepan, heat the milk just to the boiling point, and remove it immediately from the heat. Lightly grease another large bowl.

   3. Make a well in the center of the dry ingredients in the bowl, and pour in the scalded milk, hot water, and oil. Stir to combine the wet with the dry ingredients, then work the mixture with your hands until everything is thoroughly incorporated. Add the onions and caraway seeds and continue to work the mixture. Add the remaining bread and rye flours and knead the dough for 4 to 5 minutes until smooth.

   4. Shape the dough into a ball, place it in the greased bowl, and cover. Place the bowl in a warm spot and allow the dough to rise until doubled in volume, about 1 hour. Lightly grease a baking sheet.

   5. Punch the dough down and turn it out onto a lightly floured surface. Divide the dough into 6 equal portions and gently shape each into a ball. Flatten each ball to a circle roughly 1" thick and 5" in diameter. Place the circles on the baking sheet, cover with a dish towel, and allow the dough to rise until doubled in size, about 30 minutes. About halfway through, preheat the oven to 375 degrees.

   6. Remove the dish towel and bake the rolls until they are brown on the bottom and firm on top, 20 to 25 minutes. Remove from the oven and cool slightly. Split and toast before using for hamburgers. Or just butter and enjoy.

   Makes 6 large rolls.

POTATO BUNS

Potato breads are commonly served in Ireland with what is alternately called "Irish fry" or "Ulster fry," which is a traditional dish of bacon, sausages, eggs, black or white pudding, and soda bread. Although this is a larger breakfast than most Americans are accustomed to, I think these soft, flavorful buns would definitely be a pleasing addition to whatever you're serving for breakfast.

2 pkg. active dry yeast
¼ cup warm water (115 degrees)
1 cup warm mashed potatoes, processed through a ricer or food mill
1 cup lukewarm potato water (reserved from boiling the potatoes)
½ cup unsalted butter, cut into ½" pieces

1½ tsp. salt
¼ cup granulated sugar
6 to 7 cups all-purpose flour, plus more for kneading
2 tsp. olive oil
1 tsp. cornmeal
1 large egg, beaten
½ cup poppy seeds

1. Sprinkle the yeast over the warm water. Stir to combine well, and allow the mixture to sit for 10 minutes.

2. In a large bowl combine the potatoes, potato water, butter, salt, and sugar and mix well.

3. Stir in the yeast mixture. Slowly stir in the flour, 1 cup at a time, and continue stirring until the dough forms a ball, about 5 minutes.

4. Place the dough on a lightly floured surface and knead until the dough is soft, about 10 minutes.

5. Brush a bowl with olive oil. Place the dough in the bowl and rotate the dough to coat it with oil. Cover the bowl with plastic wrap and leave the dough to rise in a warm place until it has doubled in volume, about 1½ hours.

6. Line a baking sheet with parchment paper and dust its surface with cornmeal.

7. Remove the plastic wrap from the bowl of dough, punch the dough down, re-cover, and allow the dough to rest for 10 minutes.

8. Divide the dough into 8 equal pieces and form into balls. Pat each ball into a circle 3 to 4" in diameter. Arrange the dough circles on the baking sheet, cover with plastic wrap, and leave to rise in a warm place for 45 minutes.

9. Preheat the oven to 350 degrees.

10. Remove the plastic wrap from the baking sheet, and use the heel of your hand to compress the buns gently. Brush the buns lightly with the beaten egg, sprinkle with poppy seeds, and bake until golden brown, about 20 minutes.

11. Remove from the oven, allow to cool slightly, and cut the buns in half horizontally.

Makes 8 buns.

BARNEY'S BRIOCHES

Wonderful for breakfast or brunch with butter and jam, these fancy little breads can also come to dinner with Scalloped Oysters (see index).

1 pkg. dry yeast
¼ cup warm water (about 115 degrees)
½ cup (1 stick) unsalted butter, plus more for greasing, room temperature
¼ cup granulated sugar

¼ tsp. salt
5 large eggs
3½ cups all-purpose flour, plus more for kneading, divided
1 large egg yolk
1 tbsp. water

1. Early in the day, dissolve the yeast in the warm water for 5 minutes.

2. Combine the butter, sugar, and salt in a large bowl. With an electric mixer set at medium speed, beat until well blended. Beat in the yeast, 5 eggs, and 1 cup of the flour and continue beating for 3 minutes. Slowly beat in the remaining flour until there is a smooth dough. Cover the bowl and refrigerate for 8 hours.

3. Lightly grease 36 brioche molds or muffin cups (½-cup capacity each). Remove the bowl from the refrigerator. Turn out the dough on a lightly floured surface. Punch down the dough and divide it into 4 equal sections. Set one section aside and divide the remaining three into 12 equal parts each, making 36. Roll each small piece into a ball, roughly the size of a golf ball. Place each ball in a brioche mold or muffin cup.

4. Divide the section of dough you set aside into 36 marble-sized balls. Dip your finger lightly in flour, and use it to make a small dent in the center of each of the larger dough balls. Place a smaller ball into each of these indentations. Cover with dish towels and place in a warm spot to rise until double in size, about 45 minutes. About 15 minutes before the end of the rising time, preheat the oven to 375 degrees.

5. Beat the egg yolk with the water to make an egg wash. Remove the dish towels, brush the brioches with the egg wash, and bake until golden brown, about 12 minutes. Remove from the oven and cool slightly.

Makes 36 brioches.

PUFF PASTRY TWISTS

These twists are so pretty on the table, standing in a vase or jar. Serve any variation with almost any dip, especially Crabby Cheese Dunk (see index), or just put them out to munch with cocktails.

BASIC RECIPE

One 16-oz. pkg. frozen puff pastry, thawed according to pkg. directions

Parchment paper

1. Preheat the oven to 400 degrees.
2. Lay a piece of parchment paper the size of the pastry sheets flat on a work surface. Unroll the pastry sheets on top of the parchment. Using a pastry cutter, cut the sheets lengthwise into ½" strips, then cut them in half horizontally.
3. Twist the strips into loose corkscrews and arrange them 1" apart on ungreased baking sheets. Bake until puffy and golden brown, about 15 minutes. Serve immediately, or cool and store in an airtight container.

Makes 60 twists.

Variations:

2 large egg whites, lightly beaten

¼ cup sesame, caraway, or poppy seeds

1. Before cutting the pastry sheets, brush them with beaten egg whites and sprinkle with seeds. Cut, twist, and bake as above.

1 tbsp. cayenne pepper, OR
¼ cup freshly grated Parmesan cheese, OR

2 tbsp. dried herbs, OR
¼ cup minced fresh herbs, OR
Your own brilliant creation

1. Sprinkle whatever you're adding before cutting the pastry sheets. Gently press what you're adding into the pastry, but don't press hard or the twists won't puff up.

MRS. O'HARA'S FOCACCIA

Delicious spread with butter, this crispy treat is wonderful as a savory accompaniment for many dishes, such as Baked Trout with Mushrooms and Almonds (see index).

3 cups all-purpose flour, plus more
    for kneading
2 tbsp. minced fresh parsley
1 tsp. dried rosemary
1 tsp. dried thyme
½ tsp. dry rubbed sage

1 cup warm water (about 115 degrees)
4 tbsp. olive oil, plus more for bowl,
    divided
1 tsp. salt
1 tsp. granulated sugar
1 pkg. dry yeast

1. In a large bowl combine the flour with the parsley, rosemary, thyme, and sage.

2. In a separate large bowl combine the water, 2 tbsp. of the oil, the salt, and sugar. Sprinkle the yeast on top and stir to dissolve. Gradually stir in the herbed flour and blend with your hands until the mixture forms a smooth dough.

3. Lightly flour a work surface and turn out the dough. Knead the dough with a push-and-fold motion (see index) for 5 minutes. Grease a large, deep bowl, place the dough in the bowl, and cover with a towel. Set the bowl in a warm place until the dough has doubled in volume, about 1 hour.

4. Punch down the dough and turn it out on a large baking sheet. Use your fingers to push the dough into a free-form circle about 12" in diameter. With your fingertips, press indentations in the dough. Brush with the remaining 2 tbsp. oil, cover loosely, and allow to rise again until the dough has doubled in size, about 30 minutes.

5. While the dough is rising, preheat the oven to 450 degrees. Remove the towel and bake the focaccia until golden brown, about 20 minutes. Cool slightly and cut into wedges to serve.

Makes 1 focaccia loaf.

BASIC PIZZA CRUST

This and Whole-Wheat Pizza Crust (see variation below) are perfect conduits for Vegetable Cheese Pizza Pie (see index). Or be creative and design your own toppings.

½ tbsp. (1½ tsp.) granulated sugar
½ tsp. salt
¾ cup warm water (115 to 130 degrees)
2½ tbsp. olive oil, divided

One ¼-oz. pkg. (2 tsp.) active dry yeast
2¼ cups all-purpose flour, plus more for kneading

1. In a large bowl combine the sugar, salt, water, and 1½ tbsp. of the oil. Sprinkle the yeast over the mixture and stir to dissolve. Gradually stir in the flour, until the mixture comes away from the sides of the bowl and becomes a cohesive dough ball.

2. Turn the dough out onto a lightly floured work surface and knead with a push-and-fold motion (see index) until the dough is smooth and satiny, about 5 minutes.

3. Grease a very large, deep bowl* with the remaining 1 tbsp. oil and place the dough in the bowl. Cover the bowl with plastic wrap and place it in a warm spot until it has doubled in volume, about 1 hour.

4. Punch down the dough. Use your hands to pat the dough either into a 12" pizza pan or into a free-form circle on a baking sheet or pizza stone, pinching up the sides slightly to form an edge. Cover with plastic wrap and allow the dough to rise again in a warm place, until double in size, about 45 minutes.

5. Meanwhile, preheat the oven to 450 degrees. Bake for 5 minutes before topping and baking according to recipe directions.

Makes one 12" crust.

Variation: To make a whole-wheat crust, substitute whole-wheat flour for all-purpose and proceed as above.

*It is important to let the dough rise in a bowl or container large and deep enough so that the dough doesn't rise over the sides.

BLACKBERRY MUFFINS WITH LEMON GLAZE

The Irish like fruit in their cakes, pies, and muffins, and so do Americans. The combined taste on the tongue of blackberries and lemon makes these sweet-tart muffins a great way to wake up.

1½ cups all-purpose flour
2 tsp. baking powder
½ tsp. baking soda
⅛ tsp. salt
¾ cup granulated sugar
½ cup (1 stick) unsalted butter, softened

2 large eggs
⅔ cup milk
1 tsp. pure vanilla extract
1 cup fresh blackberries
1 cup confectioners' sugar
1½ tbsp. freshly squeezed lemon juice

1. Preheat the oven to 350 degrees. Grease and flour a 12-cup muffin pan, or line the cups with paper liners.

2. In a bowl, sift together the flour, baking powder, baking soda, and salt.

3. In another bowl, using an electric mixer, cream together the granulated sugar and butter until light yellow and fluffy, about 4 minutes. Beat in the eggs one at a time, beating well after each. Stir in the milk and vanilla. Slowly add the dry ingredients, blending well. Gently fold in the blackberries.

4. Spoon the batter into the muffin cups, until they are about two-thirds full. Bake until a toothpick inserted in a muffin comes out clean, about 20 minutes. Lay a sheet of wax paper under a wire rack and place the muffin pan on the rack to cool for 20 minutes.

5. While the muffins are baking, combine the confectioners' sugar and lemon juice in a small bowl, and blend well. Drizzle half of this glaze over the hot muffins. When the muffins have cooled for 20 minutes, drizzle the remaining glaze over them. Serve warm or at room temperature.

Makes 12 muffins.

GINGERBREAD WAFFLES WITH
IRISH COFFEE SYRUP AND GINGER SUGAR

For the best brunch you've ever served, look no further. The syrup has a robust flavor, somewhat like Irish coffee. If you prefer a milder taste, use less coffee.

SYRUP
1½ cups water
1 cup granulated sugar
1 tbsp. powdered instant coffee, or
    to taste

¼ cup Irish whiskey

GINGER SUGAR
2 tbsp. granulated sugar

1 tsp. ground ginger

WAFFLES
3 large eggs, separated
½ tsp. salt
1½ cups all-purpose flour
1½ tbsp. baking powder
½ tsp. ground cloves
½ tsp. ground cinnamon
¼ cup plus 2 tbsp. granulated sugar,
    divided

2 tsp. ground ginger, divided
3 tbsp. molasses
1½ cups milk
2½ tbsp. vegetable oil, plus more for
    greasing
½ cup heavy cream

1. To make the syrup, combine the water and sugar in a small saucepan over medium-high heat. Bring to a boil, stirring occasionally, and cook until syrupy, 8 to 10 minutes. Remove from the heat, stir in the coffee, and allow the mixture to sit for about 3 minutes. Return the saucepan to medium-high heat, stir in the whiskey, and cook until the alcohol cooks out and the mixture is thick and syrupy, about 10 minutes. Remove from the heat and set aside (the syrup will thicken more as it stands). Makes about 1 cup.

2. To make the Ginger Sugar, combine the sugar and ginger and mix thoroughly.

3. To make the waffles, in a small bowl beat the egg whites until soft. Add the salt and continue to beat until stiff peaks form, about 6 minutes in all.

4. In a large bowl combine the flour, baking powder, cloves, cinnamon, ¼ cup

sugar, and 1 tsp. ginger. Make a well in the center and add the egg yolks, molasses, milk, and 2½ tbsp. oil. Gently work the wet ingredients into the dry until all are incorporated. Fold in the egg whites.

5. Heat the waffle iron and brush the top and bottom lightly with oil. Pour ⅓ cup of the waffle mixture into the iron, cover, and bake until the waffle is golden brown, about 4 minutes. Keep waffles warm as you prepare the rest.

6. While the waffles are baking, whip the cream with the remaining 2 tbsp. sugar and 1 tsp. ginger until soft peaks form, about 5 minutes.

7. Serve the waffles with the Irish Coffee Syrup, Ginger Sugar, and a blob of whipped cream.

Serves 6.

ORANGE IRISH WHISKEY MARMALADE

Just a few easy additions bring everyday orange marmalade into the realm of the special.

¼ cup plus 2 tbsp. water
¼ cup granulated sugar

1 cup good-quality orange marmalade
2 tbsp. Irish whiskey

1. Combine the water and sugar in a saucepan over medium-high heat. Bring to a boil and cook until a candy thermometer reads 200 degrees. Stir in the marmalade and cook until the thermometer reads 240 degrees. Stir in the whiskey and cook, stirring, until thoroughly incorporated, about 1 minute.

2. Remove from the heat and allow the mixture to come to room temperature. Spoon the marmalade into a clean jar, cover, and store in the refrigerator for up to 1 month.

3. Serve with Irish Soda Bread or Bacon Bread.

Makes about 1 cup.

BACON BREAD IRISH TOAST
WITH "HAIR O' THE DOG" SYRUP

You've heard of French toast—this is Irish toast, made with hearty Bacon Bread and smothered in a rum and coffee syrup for an unforgettable breakfast or brunch. Top o' the mornin'!

SYRUP
1½ cups water

1 cup granulated sugar

2 tsp. powdered instant coffee

¼ cup rum

IRISH TOAST
3 large eggs

1 cup milk

¼ tsp. salt

6 turns freshly ground black pepper

¼ cup unsalted butter

1 loaf Bacon Bread, cut into twelve
 ¾" slices

1. To make the syrup, combine the water and sugar in a small saucepan over medium-high heat. Bring to a boil, stirring occasionally, and cook until syrupy, 8 to 10 minutes. Remove from the heat, stir in the coffee, and allow the mixture to sit for about 3 minutes. Return the saucepan to medium-high heat, stir in the rum, and cook until the alcohol cooks out and the mixture is thick and syrupy, about 10 minutes. Remove from the heat and set aside (the syrup will thicken more as it stands). Makes about 1 cup.

2. To prepare the Irish Toast, combine the eggs, milk, salt, and pepper, and beat well until frothy.

3. Heat the butter in a large skillet. Dip the bread slices in the egg mixture and fry in batches until crisp and golden brown on both sides, about 3 minutes each side. Serve with the warm syrup.

Serves 6 for brunch.

Variation: Dublin Eggs Bacondict

1. Prepare the Irish Toast as above, without the syrup.

2. Fry 6 slices of bacon until crisp; drain on paper towels.

3. Prepare White Wine Cream Sauce (see below).

4. Poach 12 eggs.

5. Arrange 2 slices of Irish Toast on each of 6 plates. Top each with a poached egg and some of the sauce, using only a total of 1 cup of the sauce. Crumble the cooked bacon over the sauce and serve.

WHITE WINE CREAM SAUCE

2 cups milk
1 tsp. salt, or to taste, divided
4 tbsp. butter, room temperature,
   divided
2 tbsp. all-purpose flour
½ tsp. ground white pepper
1 cup dry white wine or ⅔ cup dry
   vermouth

4 tbsp. mixed chopped fresh herbs,
   such as parsley, tarragon, chervil,
   and dill
2 tbsp. minced shallots or scallions
4 tbsp. minced fresh curly parsley

1. Heat the milk and ¼ tsp. of the salt in a small saucepan over medium heat until it reaches the boiling point. Turn off the heat.

2. Melt 2 tbsp. of the butter in a medium, heavy-bottomed saucepan over low heat. Stir in the flour and cook, stirring constantly, until you have a thick white roux, about 2 minutes. Remove from the heat and allow the roux to stop bubbling.

3. Stir in the hot milk and whisk vigorously. Set the saucepan over medium-high heat and stir with the whisk until the sauce begins to boil. Cook, stirring constantly, until the sauce has thickened and there are no lumps, about 1 minute. Reduce the heat to low and stir in the remaining salt and the white pepper.

4. Heat the wine, herbs, and shallots in a small saucepan over medium-high heat and bring to a boil. Cook until the wine has reduced to about ¼ cup. Strain the wine into the white sauce, pressing the herbs with a wooden spoon to extract all of the liquid. Cook over low heat, stirring constantly, until everything is well blended, 2 to 3 minutes. Remove from the heat.

5. Cut the remaining butter into bits and stir them, one bit at a time, into the sauce. Stir in the parsley and serve immediately.*

Makes about 2 cups.

*If you don't want to use the sauce immediately, don't add the remaining butter or chopped parsley (step 5). Pour the sauce into an airtight container and allow it to cool to room temperature. Then refrigerate for up to 2 days or freeze for up to 1 month. Thaw and reheat, stirring constantly. Proceed with step 5, adding the last measure of butter and parsley.

BEER-BATTERED OYSTERS
WITH MUENSTER CHEESE GRITS

Oysters are a favorite at many pubs, but fry them up crisp and plump, add cheesy grits, and you've got a wow of a brunch. What a way to start a Sunday!

GRITS

6⅔ cups water
1 tsp. salt, divided
1½ cups grits (not instant)
¼ cup (½ stick) unsalted butter, room temperature

½ cup heavy cream
6 turns freshly ground black pepper
⅛ tsp. cayenne pepper
2 tsp. grated Muenster cheese

OYSTERS

1 cup self-rising cornmeal
1 cup self-rising flour
¼ tsp. cayenne pepper
2 large eggs
½ cup beer
¼ cup milk

1½ tbsp. minced watercress, plus more for garnish
4 cups vegetable oil
20 oz. freshly shucked oysters or two 10-oz. containers oysters, drained
Whole watercress sprigs for garnish

1. To make the grits, combine the water and ½ tsp. salt in a large saucepan over medium-high heat. Bring the water to a boil and stir in the grits. Reduce the heat to low, cover, and cook, stirring occasionally, until the water is absorbed, about 10 minutes. Remove from the heat and stir in the butter, cream, black pepper, cayenne, and remaining salt. Fold in the cheese and stir until the cheese is melted. Cover and set aside.

2. To make the oysters, in a small bowl combine the cornmeal, flour, cayenne, eggs, beer, and milk. Stir well until the mixture resembles pancake batter. Stir in 1½ tbsp. minced watercress.

3. Heat the oil in a large, deep skillet until a bit of water dropped into it sizzles. Meanwhile coat the oysters with the batter. Drop the oysters one by one into the sizzling oil and fry them, turning once, until golden brown, 2 to 3 minutes. (This should be done in batches; don't coat oysters until they're ready to be fried or the batter will turn gummy.) Remove from the oil and drain on paper towels.

4. To serve, mound grits in 6 flat soup bowls and arrange 6 to 8 oysters around the sides of each bowl. Garnish each portion with minced watercress and several whole watercress sprigs.

Serves 6 for lunch or brunch.

TOADS IN A HOLE

Succulent sausage hiding beneath a puffy soufflé of eggs, this aptly named dish is fun to eat and great for lunch or brunch.

1 lb. bratwurst sausage, in 2" slices
2 cups sliced onions
2 cups sliced green bell peppers
2 cups sliced mushrooms
1 tsp. salt, divided
4 turns freshly ground black pepper

1½ cups amber ale
1 cup all-purpose flour
1 cup grated sharp Cheddar cheese
½ cup milk
½ cup water
2 large eggs, slightly beaten

1. Preheat the oven to 425 degrees.

2. Brown the sausage on all sides in a large, deep skillet over medium heat. Add the onions, bell peppers, mushrooms, ½ tsp. salt, and the black pepper. Stir in the ale and bring to a boil. Lower the heat, cover the skillet, and simmer 15 minutes. Remove the cover, turn up the heat to medium-high, and cook, stirring often and scraping the bottom of the skillet, until all of the liquid has evaporated and the sausage and vegetables are caramelized, 20 to 25 minutes.

3. Remove from the heat and turn the mixture into a shallow 1½-qt. baking pan. Use tongs to arrange the sausage pieces over the vegetables. Place in the oven while you prepare the batter.

4. In a large bowl combine the flour, cheese, milk, water, eggs, and the remaining ½ tsp. salt. Blend well, remove the baking pan from the oven, and pour the batter over the sausage and vegetables. Return to the oven and bake for 15 minutes. Reduce the heat to 350 degrees and bake until golden brown and puffy, 15 to 20 minutes longer.

5. To serve, spoon up into serving plates or shallow bowls.
Serves 8.

Finger
Foods:

Appetizers and
Party Picks

It's the treat before we eat—and sometimes it's everything we eat. It's an appetizer, a dip, a tidbit, a bite. It's eaten sitting at a table set with silver and china; it's eaten standing up, juggling a drink and a napkin.

What makes these "small plates" so attractive to so many of us? What prompts the patron reach for the bowl of goodies at the bar? Well, we love to nosh, which in chic circles is known as "grazing." We like little things on little dishes, and we enjoy eating with our fingers. At least most of us do.

Try some of the tempting appetizers in this chapter on your family and friends: Potato Goat-Cheese Napoleons with Olive Pesto, Pickled Beer-Boiled Shrimp, Davey Byrnes' Fondue, or Crab and Asparagus Cheesecake with Roasted Red Pepper Puree. Or wow 'em at your next cocktail party by serving Baby Reuben Turnovers with Honey-Beer Mustard, Crabby Cheese Dunk with Puff Pastry Twists, Garlicky Roasted Mushrooms, or Dilly Carrots and Parsnips.

Whether you're teasing appetites into enthusiasm for more food to come or providing the nibbles to spice up the drinks, serve these dishes without rules, because they're meant to be fun.

CRABBY CHEESE DUNK

This dip can be served with crackers or raw vegetables, but for a special treat serve it with Puff Pastry Twists (see index).

½ cup unsalted butter
½ cup all-purpose flour
2 cups heavy cream
2 cups grated Emmenthaler cheese
½ cup cream sherry
1 lb. lump crab meat, picked over for cartilage and shells (see index)

¾ tsp. salt
6 turns freshly ground black pepper
⅛ tsp. cayenne pepper
½ cup chopped scallions (green onions)
½ cup minced fresh parsley

1. Melt the butter in the top half of a double boiler directly over medium heat. Stir the flour into the butter and cook, stirring constantly, until you have a light-golden roux. Slowly whisk in the cream and cook, stirring often with the whisk, until the mixture begins to bubble and thicken, 5 to 7 minutes.

2. Meanwhile, fill the bottom of the double boiler with about 2" water and bring it to a simmer over medium heat.

3. Stir the cheese into the cream sauce and place the pot over the simmering water. Allow the cheese to melt, stirring occasionally, about 20 minutes. Stir in the sherry, crab meat, salt, black pepper, and cayenne. Cook, stirring occasionally, until the mixture is thick and bubbly, about 5 minutes.

4. Stir in the scallions and parsley and serve in a bowl, accompanied by Puff Pastry Twists.

Serves 16 for a party.

PADDY'S ARTICHOKE AND SPINACH DIP

This party dip started out as a special on McGuire's catering list, but it was so popular it wound up on the restaurant menu. Put it on the table and watch your guests practically lick the bowl clean. A big plus: Paddy's Dip makes a great St. Patrick's Day party item because not only is it delicious—it's green!

1½ cups heavy cream
½ lb. Monterey jack cheese, grated
10 oz. cream cheese
½ tsp. Worcestershire sauce
¼ tsp. garlic powder
¼ tsp. salt
4 turns freshly ground black pepper
¾ lb. fresh (rinsed, stemmed, and coarsely chopped) or frozen chopped spinach (thawed and thoroughly drained)

1 cup frozen artichoke hearts, thawed, drained, and coarsley chopped
2 scallions (green onions), chopped
¼ cup freshly grated Parmesan cheese
Tortilla chips or fresh vegetables for dipping

1. Bring the cream to a simmer in a large saucepan over medium heat. Stir in the Monterey jack, cream cheese, Worcestershire, garlic powder, salt, and pepper. Bring to a bubble and cook over medium heat, stirring often to keep the mixture from sticking to the pot, until the cheeses have melted and the mixture is blended.

2. Fold in the spinach, artichoke hearts, and scallions. Continue folding until the vegetables are incorporated and the mixture is thoroughly heated.

3. Pour into a chafing dish, sprinkle with Parmesan, and provide tortilla chips or raw vegetables for dipping.

Serves 10-12 for a party.

CHEESE AND ALE CROCK

Cheese making has become a restored art in Ireland, with a number of serious entrepreneurs raising it to the ranks of fine wine making. It wouldn't be unusual to find a crock such as this one set up on the bar of a local tavern, filled with a creamy cheese spread to be slathered on hard bread or crackers and consumed with an after-work pint.

16 oz. cream cheese, softened
8 oz. Gorgonzola or other blue cheese, softened
½ cup (1 stick) unsalted butter, softened
2 tbsp. brown ale

2 tbsp. honey
½ tsp. cracked black pepper
¼ tsp. cayenne pepper
1 cup coarsely chopped walnuts, toasted (see index) and completely cooled

1. A day ahead, combine the cream cheese, Gorgonzola, and butter in a large bowl. Use an electric mixer at medium-high speed to blend until smooth and creamy.

2. Stir in the ale, honey, and black and cayenne peppers and blend with the mixer. Fold in the walnuts.

3. Spoon the mixture into a 4-cup crock or decorative serving bowl, cover, and refrigerate overnight. Serve with assorted crackers and crisp breads.

Serves about 16 for a party.

SHEEP DIP

Cheeses made from sheep's milk are quite popular in Ireland and this tasty party dip uses two—feta and ricotta. Whether your feta and ricotta come from sheep's, cow's, or goat's milk, the mixture will be delicious.

1⅓ cups (8 oz.) feta cheese
1 cup whole-milk ricotta cheese
2 tbsp. brandy

¼ cup minced scallions (green onions)
¼ cup pine nuts, toasted (see index)
3 tbsp. snipped fresh dill

1. In the bowl of a food processor combine the cheeses and process until smooth. Add the brandy and puree. Turn the mixture into a bowl.

2. Fold in the scallions, pine nuts, and dill and continue to fold until the mixture is well blended. Spoon into a 2-cup crock or serving bowl. Cover and chill at least 2 hours.

3. Serve with French bread, crackers, or crisp breads.
Serves 10-12 for a party.

SUN-DRIED TOMATO GOAT-CHEESE SPREAD

This tangy spread is smooth on the tongue and will disappear quickly every time you serve it. Better make copies of the recipe because you're sure to be besieged by requests for it. Better yet, tell 'em to buy the book!

3 oz. sun-dried tomatoes (not
    packed in oil)
4 oz. chèvre (goat cheese)
½ cup cottage cheese, drained of liquid
¼ tsp. dried or 1 tsp. fresh thyme
    leaves

¼ cup minced fresh basil
½ cup chopped black Calamata or
    Niçoise olives
Crackers, toast points
Celery sticks, fennel bulb slices,
    jicama slices
Genoa salami slices

1. Place the sun-dried tomatoes in a small bowl. Cover with boiling water and allow the tomatoes to plump for 10 minutes. Drain off all of the liquid.

2. In the bowl of a food processor, combine the chèvre, cottage cheese, and thyme, and process until smooth. Add the tomatoes and process until thoroughly pureed, pulsing 5 to 6 times, about 5 seconds each time. Stir in the basil.

3. Turn the mixture into a serving bowl and garnish with chopped olives. Serve with baskets of crackers and toast points and dishes of celery sticks, fennel bulb and jicama slices, and rolled-up salami slices.

Serves about 15-25 for a party.

DAVEY BYRNES' FONDUE

Davey Byrnes is an Irish pub immortalized in James Joyce's %iUlysses.%r Every Bloomsday (June 16) the pub serves red wine and Gorgonzola cheese just as Joyce described it in his legendary novel.

1½ cups milk
1 tsp. minced fresh garlic
1 cup heavy cream
1 lb. Gorgonzola cheese, crumbled
1 lb. mozzarella cheese, shredded

1 cup freshly grated Parmesan cheese (about 6 oz.)
⅓ cup dry red wine
Irish Soda Bread (see index), toasted
Chopped fresh chives for garnish

1. Combine the milk and garlic in a saucepan over medium-high heat and bring just to a boil. Immediately reduce the heat to low. Stir in the cream, Gorgonzola, mozzarella, and Parmesan and cook, stirring often, until all of the cheese has melted and the mixture is bubbly, about 30 minutes.

2. Push the mixture through a strainer to remove any unmelted cheese curds. Return the strained mixture to the saucepan and stir in the wine. Cook, stirring constantly, until the wine is blended through and the fondue is hot and thick, 3 to 4 minutes.

3. Break the soda bread into pieces or cut into large cubes and arrange in a basket with long forks.

4. Transfer the fondue to a heated chafing dish and garnish with chives. Encourage guests to spear soda bread and swirl it in the fondue. Provide lots of wine or cold beer.

Serves 8-12 for a party.

GARLICKY ROASTED MUSHROOMS

Irish people enjoy mushroom ketchup as a flavoring. Here in America, it would probably be impossible to wean the average eater from tomato ketchup. But we are a nation of mushroom lovers, and this dish—which would be known as a "mushroom frigacy" in an Irish pub—is a spicy treat you might want to include on your next party menu.

½ cup olive oil
1 tbsp. minced fresh garlic
½ tsp. salt
½ tsp. paprika

¼ tsp. dried red pepper flakes
2 lb. small white mushrooms
3 tbsp. chopped fresh parsley, divided

1. Preheat the oven to 400 degrees.

2. Heat the oil in a medium saucepan over medium heat. Add the garlic and cook, stirring once or twice, until soft, 1 to 2 minutes. Stir in the salt, paprika, and red pepper flakes and reduce the heat to medium-low. Cook, stirring occasionally, until the mixture is blended, 2 to 3 minutes. Remove from the heat.

3. Rinse and pat dry the mushrooms. Arrange them in a single layer on a baking sheet and brush them all over with the garlicky oil. Roast for 15 minutes. Turn the mushrooms over and continue baking until they are golden brown, about 10 minutes.

4. During the last 10 minutes, return the saucepan to the stove over low heat. When the mushrooms are ready, turn them into the saucepan along with any juices that have accumulated on the baking sheet. Stir well to coat the mushrooms. Add 1 tbsp. of the parsley and stir again.

5. Pour into a chafing dish to keep warm. Garnish with the remaining parsley and serve with toothpicks.

Makes about 90 mushrooms; serves 20-30 for a party.

PICKLED BEER-BOILED SHRIMP

This is one of those blessedly convenient party foods you can prepare a day ahead of the event.

3 cups beer
2 tbsp. pickling spice
1 lb. large shrimp, shelled and
   deveined, tails intact
1 tbsp. Dijon mustard
1 tsp. freshly grated or prepared
   horseradish

1 tsp. celery salt
8 turns freshly ground black pepper
2 scallions (green onions), chopped
¼ cup vegetable oil

1. Combine the beer and pickling spice in a large pot over medium-high heat, and bring to a boil. Add the shrimp and cook just until pink, 2 to 3 minutes—no longer. Remove the shrimp and pickling spice with a slotted spoon and set aside. Reserve ½ c. of the beer.

2. In a medium bowl combine the mustard, horseradish, celery salt, pepper, scallions, and reserved beer. Slowly whisk in the oil until the mixture is emulsified.

3. Fold in the shrimp and pickling spice. Cover and refrigerate overnight. Serve cold or at room temperature.

Serves 10 for a first course.

PICKLED PEARLS

According to pub lore, pickled onions, eggs, mushrooms, and mussels were the forerunners of the chips, nuts, and pretzels ubiquitous in bars today. The former items are much more interesting and also make good condiments for other foods. Try to find both white and purple pearl onions for visual interest. Polish up these pearls at least 3 weeks before serving them.

3 qt. plus 1 cup water, divided
3 lb. pearl onions, preferably half
   white, half purple, unpeeled
2½ cups distilled white vinegar
1 cup granulated sugar
6 bay leaves
12 whole cloves

2½ tsp. celery salt
1 tsp. whole black peppercorns
1 tsp. whole mustard seed
1 tsp. whole coriander
1 tsp. whole allspice
½ tsp. red pepper flakes

1. Bring 3 qt. water to a boil in a large pot over high heat. Add the onions, bring back to a boil, and cook 1 minute. Remove the onions and drain. When the onions are cool enough to handle, slice off the end of each, and peel. Drop the onions into three 1-qt. or six 1-pt. Mason jars, leaving 1" at the top of each.

2. To make the pickling juice, combine the remaining cup of water with the remaining ingredients in a large saucepan over low heat. Cook, stirring, just until the sugar has dissolved. Increase the heat to medium-high and bring the mixture to a boil. Continue to cook until the flavors have blended, about 5 minutes.

3. Ladle the pickling juice over the onions to ½" of the top of each jar. Use a wooden spoon handle or a rubber spatula to push the onions gently together under the juice to make sure there is no air trapped in the jar. Seal the jars with their caps and screw on the lids tightly.

4. Place the jars in a large stockpot and add enough water to come up to the lids on the jars. Bring to a boil over high heat, reduce the heat to a bare simmer, and leave the jars for 20 minutes. Remove the jars from the pot and allow them to sit at room temperature until the caps "pop," about 2 hours. (If a cap doesn't pop, press down on the center of the lid. If the lid moves, it wasn't sealed properly. You can return the jar to the pot and heat for another 10 minutes or refrigerate once the jar is cool.)

5. Allow the onions to pickle for 3 weeks before eating. Refrigerate any opened jar; the onions will keep for months in the refrigerator.

Makes 3 qt.

DILLY CARROTS AND PARSNIPS

Nutritious but homely root vegetables acquire new sophistication in this sweet, tangy, dilly marinade.

1 lb. fresh carrots	2 tbsp. snipped fresh dill
1 lb. fresh parsnips	1 tsp. mixed pickling spices
2 cups distilled white vinegar	1 tsp. minced fresh garlic
½ cup water	1 tbsp. salt
¼ cup honey	6 turns freshly ground black pepper

1. Peel the carrots and parsnips and cut them into 3" sticks.

2. Combine the remaining ingredients in a large saucepan over medium-high heat. Bring to a boil, add the carrot sticks, and reduce the heat to medium-low. Cover and cook for 5 minutes. Add the parsnip sticks and continue cooking until the vegetables are tender-crisp, about 5 minutes longer. Remove from the heat.

3. Transfer the vegetables and liquid to a bowl; cover and refrigerate 4 hours or overnight.

4. To serve, remove the carrots and parsnips from the marinade and stand them up in glasses or cups for a healthy party snack.

Serves 10-12 for a party.

CRAB AND ASPARAGUS CHEESECAKE WITH ROASTED RED PEPPER PUREE

This is a great icebreaker at a cocktail party, but it could also be a dazzling first course at a sit-down dinner.

CRUST

2½ cups fresh whole-wheat bread crumbs (see index)

½ cup freshly grated Parmesan cheese

½ cup (1 stick) melted unsalted butter

FILLING

1 cup chopped fresh asparagus (in ¾" pieces)

4 tbsp. unsalted butter, divided

½ cup chopped leeks, tops and bottoms (mostly white)

3 tbsp. all-purpose flour

1 cup milk

½ cup chicken stock (see index)

½ cup grated Swiss cheese

1 tsp. Worcestershire sauce

1½ tsp. salt, divided

4 turns freshly ground black pepper

1 lb. lump crab meat, picked over (see index)

1¾ lb. cream cheese, softened

4 large eggs

ROASTED RED PEPPER PUREE

2 large red bell peppers, roasted, peeled, and seeded (see index)

½ cup sour cream

1½ tsp. chopped fresh or ½ tsp. dried thyme

¼ tsp. salt

3 turns freshly ground black pepper

1. To make the crust, line the bottom and sides (about halfway up) of a 9½" springform pan with aluminum foil.

2. Combine the bread crumbs and cheese in a small bowl. Add the butter and mix well until blended. Pat the mixture into the bottom of the foil-lined springform pan. Set aside.

3. To make the filling, bring a teakettle full of water to a boil, and prepare a medium-size bowl of ice water. Place the asparagus in a strainer or colander and pour the boiling water over it. Immediately immerse the strainer in the ice water.

Drain, and leave the blanched asparagus in the strainer until you're ready for it. Preheat the oven to 350 degrees.

4. Melt 1 tbs. of the butter in a small skillet over medium heat. Add the leeks and cook, stirring or shaking the skillet occasionally, until the leeks are just barely tender, about 3 minutes. Remove from the heat and set aside.

5. Melt the remaining 3 tbs. butter in a medium-large saucepan over medium heat. Stir in the flour and cook, whisking, until you have a light-brown roux, about 4 minutes. Slowly whisk in the milk and the stock and bring to a bubble, whisking. Cook, whisking occasionally, until the mixture is thick and creamy, 4 to 5 minutes.

6. Fold in the cheese, reduce the heat to low, and cook, stirring, until the cheese has melted. Stir in the Worcestershire, 1 tsp. of the salt, and the pepper and remove from the heat. Fold in the asparagus, leeks, and crab meat, blending thoroughly but taking care not to break up the lumps of crab meat. Set aside to cool slightly.

7. In a large bowl with an electric mixer, beat the cream cheese with the remaining ½ tsp. salt until fluffy, about 5 minutes. Beat in the eggs one at a time, beating well after each. Fold the asparagus mixture into the cream cheese and blend thoroughly. Pour the mixture into the crust in the springform pan.

8. Prepare a water bath, or bain-marie: Fill a deep pan several inches larger around than the springform pan with about 1" of water, and place the pan carefully on the center rack of your oven. Place the springform pan in the larger pan and carefully add enough water to the larger pan until it comes halfway up the side of the springform.

9. Bake until a deep, golden brown, about 1½ hours. Check at 45 minutes, and if the cheesecake is browning too quickly, cover it loosely with foil and continue baking. Remove from the oven and cool on a wire rack for 20 minutes. Remove the sides and place the cake on a serving platter. Refrigerate at least 6 hours or overnight.

10. To make the puree, coarsely chop the peppers and combine them with the remaining ingredients in the bowl of a food processor. Pulse 10 times, 2 seconds each pulse. Scrape down the sides of the food processor and pulse 5 to 6 times more, or until the mixture is completely pureed. Transfer to a container, cover, and chill.

11. To serve, cut the cheesecake into wedges. Spoon a puddle of puree in the center of each plate, and place a wedge of the cheesecake on top.

Serves 12-15 for a party; serves 8 for a first course.

COUSIN NATHAN'S IRISH LOBSTER ROLLS WITH TOMATO-GINGER VINAIGRETTE

McGuire's cousin Nathan has a fabulous food repertoire that seems endless. Now he's at it again, coming up with irresistible, crunchy rolls of fillo stuffed with lobster and vegetables and served with a tangy vinaigrette for dipping.

ROLLS

1 cup plus 6 tbsp. unsalted butter, divided

2 cups julienned carrots

1 cup minced scallions (green onions)

1 cup julienned turnips

1 tsp. salt

8 turns freshly ground black pepper, divided

1 cup julienned fresh beets

4 cup rinsed, chopped fresh spinach

½ cup chopped fresh parsley

3 tsp. crushed fennel seeds

1½ lb. cooked lobster meat, chopped into ¼" pieces

24 sheets fillo dough, thawed according to pkg. directions

VINAIGRETTE

2 cloves garlic

1 tsp. salt

2 large ripe tomatoes, peeled (see index), seeded, and chopped

3½ tsp. chopped fresh gingerroot

2 tbsp. tomato paste

8 turns freshly ground black pepper

6 tbsp. balsamic vinegar

1 cup olive oil

1. To prepare the filling for the rolls, melt 4 tbsp. of the butter in a skillet over medium heat. Add the carrots, scallions, turnips, salt, and pepper. Cook, shaking the skillet occasionally, until the vegetables are tender but crunchy, 6 to 7 minutes. Transfer the vegetables to a large bowl.

2. Melt 2 tbs. of the butter in the same skillet over medium heat. Add the beets and cook until firm-tender, 3 to 4 minutes. Remove the beets with a slotted spoon and drain on several layers of paper towels. Cover the beets with more paper towels and blot them to remove excess moisture.

3. Add the spinach, parsley, and fennel seeds to the vegetables in the bowl, and toss. Add the lobster meat and toss again. Carefully fold in the beets (don't over-mix or the beets will turn the other vegetables red).

4. Melt the remaining 1 cup butter over lowest heat. Lay the stack of fillo sheets

on a clean work surface and cut the stack into three 6" x 4⅔" sections. Cover with a sheet of plastic wrap and top it with a damp dish towel.

5. Preheat the oven to 400 degrees.

6. Set up your work station so that everything you need is close: the warm, melted butter and a pastry brush, the bowl of filling and a spoon, and the stack of fillo sheets. To make each roll, place one 6" x 4⅔" sheet of fillo in front of you and brush it with some of the butter. Place another sheet on top and brush that with butter. Repeat twice until you have four buttered sheets. Place 2 to 3 tbsp. of the filling at one end, about 1" from the edge. Roll up, tucking in the ends, and brush the edges with butter. Place on a buttered baking dish and cover with plastic wrap while you repeat the process to make the remaining rolls.

7. Bake until crisp and golden brown, 12 to 15 minutes. Serve warm or at room temperature with Tomato-Ginger Vinaigrette.

8. To make the vinaigrette, mash together the garlic and salt and place the mixture in the bowl of a food processor. Add the tomatoes, ginger, tomato paste, pepper, and vinegar and process until smooth. Keeping the processor running, slowly stream in the oil. Continue to process until the vinaigrette is emulsified, about 30 seconds longer. Serve at room temperature with Cousin Nathan's Irish Lobster Rolls.

Makes 18; serves 12-18 for a party; serves 6-9 for a first course.

POTATO GOAT-CHEESE NAPOLEONS
WITH OLIVE PESTO

Everyone sits up and pays attention when these gorgeous savory pastries appear. Make sure you follow them with an equally exciting main course. You'll need parchment paper and 3 baking or cookie sheets to prepare the napoleons.

1 lb. small red new potatoes
1½ tbsp. salt, divided
6 turns freshly ground black pepper
1½ tsp. chopped fresh or ½ tsp. dried thyme
1½ tsp. chopped fresh or ½ tsp. dried marjoram
1¼ cups pitted black olives, divided
1 cup fresh basil leaves
1 tsp. minced fresh garlic
3 tbsp. olive oil, divided

2½ cup chopped leeks, tops and bottoms (mostly white)
10 oz. Montrachet goat cheese, softened
6 oz. cream cheese, softened
2 tbsp. chopped parsley, plus more for garnish
2 sheets frozen puff pastry, thawed
4 water-packed sun-dried tomatoes, drained and minced

1. Combine the potatoes, 1 tbsp. salt, and water to cover in a saucepan over high heat. Bring to a boil, reduce the heat to medium, and cook until the potatoes are firm-tender, about 15 minutes. Drain and allow the potatoes to cool. When cool enough to handle, cut the potatoes in ¼" slices, and spread them on paper towels to dry. Sprinkle the potatoes with the pepper, thyme, marjoram, and remaining salt.

2. In a food processor combine 1 cup olives, the basil, garlic, and 1 tbsp. oil. Pulse until the mixture is minced but not pureed. Set aside.

3. Heat the remaining oil in a large, deep skillet over medium heat. Add the leeks and cook until they are tender and translucent, about 6 minutes. Remove the leeks with a slotted spoon and drain them on paper towels, patting off the excess oil.

4. In a medium bowl combine the Montrachet with the cream cheese and 2 tbsp. parsley, and beat until the mixture is thoroughly blended and fluffy. Transfer the cheese mixture to a pastry bag with a star tip.

5. To prepare the pastry, roll each sheet of puff pastry on a lightly floured surface into a rectangle 14" x 18". Cover 2 baking sheets with parchment paper. Cut

a piece of cardboard into a rectangle measuring 4" x 3". Using the cardboard as a guide, cut 24 rectangles of dough with a pastry cutter or serrated knife. As you cut the dough, place the rectangles on the parchment-covered baking sheets. Prick each piece of dough about 4 times with the tines of a fork. Cover with another sheet of parchment and refrigerate for 30 minutes.

6. Preheat the oven to 400 degrees.

7. Remove 1 baking sheet from the refrigerator. Cover with an unused baking sheet (for weight) and bake for 15 minutes. Prick the pastry again, re-cover with parchment and baking sheet, and bake another 5 minutes. Remove the top baking sheet, discard the top parchment, and continue to bake until the pastry is a light golden color, 5 to 7 minutes. Transfer to a wire rack to cool. Repeat the process with the second baking sheet.

8. To assemble, set aside the 12 best-looking pastry rectangles for the tops of the napoleons. Place the remaining 12 pieces on a work surface and pipe some of the cheese mixture around the edges of each. Pipe a dot in the center of each and set aside the remaining cheese mixture. Arrange 2 to 3 potato slices over the cheese, and spoon on approximately 2½ tbsp. of the olive mixture. Top with some of the leeks. Pipe cheese on the pastry pieces designated for the tops in the same way as you did the bottom pastry. Invert the tops and press them gently, being careful not to crush the pastry.

9. Slice the remaining olives and decorate the top of each napoleon with olives, sun-dried tomatoes, and chopped parsley.

Serves 12 for a first course.

BABY REUBEN EGG ROLLS
WITH HONEY-BEER MUSTARD

A tribute to Saint Rube (just kidding), the Reuben sandwich is a great alternative to its heavier cousin, corned beef and cabbage. McGuire's Reuben egg rolls are an even better alternative, especially if you're wondering what kind of finger food to serve at your next party or tailgate picnic. These can be made well ahead because they freeze well and can be served hot or at room temperature. If you make several egg rolls, they're perfect for lunch or as a hearty appetizer.

FILLING
¾ lb. cooked corned beef, coarsely
   chopped
1 cup coarsely grated Swiss cheese
1 cup sauerkraut, drained and
   coarsely chopped
½ cup mayonnaise

¼ cup commercial chili sauce
2 tbsp. chopped green pimiento-
   stuffed olives
1 tbsp. capers
¼ cup caraway seeds

EGG ROLLS
6" egg-roll wrappers
Egg wash (1 large egg beaten with 1
   tbsp. water)

Caraway seeds

HONEY-BEER MUSTARD
1 cup dark beer
2 tbsp. cornstarch

½ cup yellow mustard
⅓ cup honey

   1. To make the filling, in a large bowl combine the corned beef, cheese, and sauerkraut.

   2. In another bowl, combine the mayonnaise, chili sauce, olives, capers, and caraway seeds, and mix thoroughly.

   3. Turn the contents of the second bowl into the corned-beef mixture and blend well.

   4. Preheat the oven to 400 degrees (unless you are frying; see below).

5. Place 1 tbsp. of the filling mixture in the center of each egg-roll wrapper. Fold in the corners and roll each into a 3" egg roll. Place the egg rolls on an ungreased baking sheet.

6. Brush each egg roll lightly with the egg wash and sprinkle with caraway seeds. Bake until the egg rolls are golden brown, about 8 to 10 minutes, or fry at 350 degrees for 3 minutes. Serve warm or at room temperature with Honey-Beer Mustard.

7. To make the mustard, in a saucepan over medium heat combine the beer and cornstarch. Bring to a bubble and simmer, stirring, until slightly thickened. Remove from the heat and stir in the mustard and honey. Serve warm or at room temperature with the egg rolls.

Makes 6-8 egg rolls.

Between the Bread:

Creative Sandwiches

Take two pieces of bread, stuff them with canned tuna or American cheese slices, and you have what passes for a sandwich with many people who haven't yet explored the wonderful world of the Creative Sandwich.

Here, in this almost untrod territory, you may find kielbasa sausage smothered under a wine-infused sauce of tomatoes and mixed peppers on a French baguette, as in Dublin Dogs; spicy corned beef hash on soft, homemade buns in Beery Hash Burgers on Potato Buns; and paper-thin rye bread rolled around corned beef, Swiss cheese, sauerkraut, and a devil of a sauce in Reuben Rolls with Devil Sauce.

Or try an interesting twist on grilled cheese sandwiches—Finnegan's Cheese Bake on Mrs. O'Hara's Focaccia; a vegetarian delight—Leeky Brie and Cherry Tomatoes on Bloody Mary Bread; or a new way to serve hamburgers—Roquefort Potato Beefburgers.

You might not find these creations at your local pub, but with not much effort they can be available at your own home eatery. Use these recipes to come up with some creative sandwich ideas of your own; all you need is a little ingenuity and a good appetite.

CORNED BEEF WITH HORSERADISH CABBAGE CONFIT ON ONION RYE ROLLS

These open-face delights are so satisfying you could easily serve them for dinner. The cabbage confit truly makes it an Irish feel-good dish.

2 tbsp. unsalted butter

2 tbsp. all-purpose flour

1 cup milk

2 tbsp. prepared white horseradish

1 tsp. salt

8 turns freshly ground black pepper

2 tbsp. olive oil

1 cup chopped onions

¾ cup chopped green bell peppers

3 cups torn cabbage leaves

½ cup heavy cream

12 paper-thin slices lean corned beef

6 Onion Rye Rolls (see index)

2 tbsp. snipped fresh dill

1. Melt the butter in a saucepan over medium heat and stir in the flour. Cook, stirring constantly, 3 to 4 minutes.

2. Slowly whisk in the milk until the consistency is smooth, then whisk in the horseradish, salt, and pepper. Bring to a bubble, stirring constantly. Reduce the heat and simmer, stirring often, until the sauce has thickened, 3 to 5 minutes. Turn off the heat and keep warm.

3. Heat the oil in a large skillet over medium-high heat. Add the onions and bell peppers and cook, stirring occasionally, until they are tender, about 4 minutes. Add the cabbage and cook, stirring or shaking the skillet occasionally, until the cabbage is lightly browned and just tender, 4 to 5 minutes.

4. Stir in the warm sauce and the cream. Bring to a bubble, reduce the heat to medium-low, and simmer, stirring occasionally, 3 to 5 minutes. Adjust seasoning if necessary.

5. Heat the corned beef on a covered plate over simmering water.

6. To assemble, split the rolls in half and arrange on 6 individual serving plates. Place 2 slices of corned beef over each roll half and top with the cabbage confit. Garnish with snipped dill.

Serves 6 for a main course.

REUBEN ROLLS WITH DEVIL SAUCE

The Reuben sandwich is a big favorite in this country, especially in New York City. Here, the corned beef, sauerkraut, and Swiss cheese are wrapped in a spicy sauce, rolled up in rye, and baked for a fun, delicious melt. Perfect pub food!

DEVIL SAUCE

½ cup mayonnaise
1/4 cup ketchup
1 tbsp. honey
1 tsp. prepared horseradish
½ tsp. lemon juice

1½ tbsp. chopped green pimiento-stuffed olives
1 tbsp. capers
1 tbsp. minced fresh parsley

ROLLS

12 slices rye bread, trimmed of crusts
60 paper-thin slices corned beef (about ½ lb.)
Devil Sauce

12 thin slices (about 4 oz.) Swiss cheese (each slice ⅓ the size of a bread slice)
1½ cups well-drained sauerkraut
¼ cup (½ stick) melted unsalted butter

1. Combine all of the sauce ingredients in a small bowl and mix well until blended. Cover and refrigerate for at least 1 hour.

2. When the sauce is chilled, remove it from the refrigerator. Preheat the oven to 400 degrees.

3. To make the rolls, using a rolling pin, flatten the bread on a work surface, rolling 2 to 3 times over each slice to make it thin. Arrange 5 slices of corned beef on each piece of bread, and brush the meat with 2 to 3 tsp. of the sauce. At one end of the bread place 1 slice of cheese, top it with 1 tbsp. of the sauerkraut, and roll up from the cheese end first, to form a "roulade," or roll. Secure with a toothpick and place the roll seam side down on an ungreased baking sheet. Repeat with the remaining rolls.

4. Brush the rolls with the melted butter, and bake until the bread is toasty-brown and firm to the touch, about 12 minutes.

5. To serve, arrange 2 rolls on each of 6 plates, and top with some of the remaining sauce.

Serves 6.

BEERY HASH BURGERS ON POTATO BUNS

McGuire's is known for its fabulous burgers—some outrageous, others more traditional. In fact, the burger hunger can be assuaged at McGuire's with anything from a Jamaican Jerk Burger or a Creole Blackened Burger to a Gourmet Burger—smothered in mushrooms and a rich wine gravy—or just an old-fashioned Cheddar Cheeseburger. This burger deliciously incorporates the corned beef, cabbage, and potatoes so often associated with Irish cuisine.

4 tbsp. vegetable oil, divided
6 peeled, medium-sized potatoes, cubed (¼")
1½ cups chopped onions (about 1 large onion)
½ tsp. crushed red pepper flakes
½ cup beer
½ tsp. salt
1½ lb. cooked corned beef, chopped
8 Potato Buns (see index)
Three-Cabbage Slaw (see index)

1. Heat 2 tbsp. oil in a large, deep skillet over medium-high heat. Add the potatoes, onions, and red pepper flakes and cook, stirring and shaking the skillet occasionally, until the vegetables begin to soften, 3 to 4 minutes.

2. Stir in the beer and salt, cover the skillet, and steam until the vegetables are tender, 10 to 15 minutes. Stir in the corned beef and remove from the heat. When the mixture is cool enough to handle, form into 8 patties.

3. In a large clean skillet heat the remaining 2 tbs. oil over medium heat. Add the burgers and fry until brown and crispy, 3 to 4 minutes each side.

4. To serve, place a potato bun on each plate, top with a burger, and add a mound of the cabbage slaw beside each. Serve with spicy mustard.

Serves 8.

ROQUEFORT POTATO BEEFBURGERS

These are for great big appetites—don't serve them to sissies. They're best on Potato Buns or Onion Rye Rolls (see index), but if you don't feel like baking, serve them on extralarge kaiser rolls.

2 cups small red-skinned potatoes,
   unpeeled
2 tbsp. plus 1 tsp. salt, divided
2 tbsp. olive oil
1 tbsp. unsalted butter
18 turns freshly ground black
   pepper, divided

3 lb. ground round
1 tbsp. garlic powder
¼ cup crumbled Roquefort cheese
6 Potato Buns, Onion Rye Rolls, or
   large kaiser rolls, split

1. Preheat oven broiler or charcoal grill.

2. Scrub the potatoes and place them in a large saucepan. Cover with water, add 1 tbsp. of the salt, and bring to a boil over high heat. Reduce the heat to medium-low and simmer the potatoes until they are firm-tender, 6 to 8 minutes. Drain the potatoes and allow them to cool slightly. When they are cool enough to handle, pat them dry, and cut them into ¼" slices.

3. Heat the oil and butter in a large skillet over medium-high heat. Add the potato slices and cook, turning them once or twice, until they are a light golden color, 6 to 7 minutes. Remove the potatoes with a slotted spoon and drain them on paper towels. Sprinkle with 1 tsp. of the salt and 6 turns of the pepper.

4. In a bowl, combine the ground meat with the garlic powder, the remaining 1 tbsp. salt, and 12 turns pepper. Blend the seasonings into the meat with your hands, and divide the mixture into twelve ½"-thick patties.

5. Top 6 of the patties with a layer of 3 or 4 potato slices, and top the potatoes with 2 tsp. of the cheese. Add another layer of potatoes. Top each with another patty, and use your fingers to seal the edges of the meat together, forming a package around the filling.

6. For medium-rare burgers, broil 4 to 5 minutes on each side. If you're grilling them, it's 3 to 4 minutes per side.

7. Meanwhile, toast the rolls. Place one burger on each roll and serve.
Serves 6.

SPINACH-STUFFED BURGERS

Here's a whole meal-in-a-burger, covering your basic food groups. These are so delicious, condiments aren't really needed, but have some handy in case there's a ketchup diehard in the crowd. Serve the burgers on Onion Rye Rolls (see index) for a hearty, satisfying lunch or dinner.

¼ cup unsalted butter
2 cups sliced white mushrooms
1 cup sliced fresh onion rings
½ cup white zinfandel wine
10 oz. fresh spinach, rinsed and
    stemmed

1 tbsp. plus 1 tsp. salt, divided
22 turns freshly ground black
    pepper, divided
3 lb. ground round
1 tbsp. garlic powder
6 Onion Rye Rolls, split

1. Preheat oven broiler or charcoal grill.

2. Melt the butter in a large skillet over medium heat. Add the mushrooms and onions and cook, stirring occasionally, until tender, about 15 minutes. Stir in the wine and deglaze the bottom of the skillet. Fold in the spinach, 1 tsp. of the salt, and 8 turns of the pepper. Cover the skillet and cook until the spinach is wilted, about 3 minutes. Remove the cover and cook, stirring occasionally, just until all of the liquid has been absorbed, 6 to 8 minutes. Remove from the heat and set aside.

3. In a bowl, combine the ground meat with the garlic powder, the remaining 1 tbsp. salt, and 14 turns pepper. Blend the seasonings into the meat with your hands, and divide the mixture into twelve ½"-thick patties. Divide the spinach mixture equally among 6 of the patties, mounding it in the center of each, and leaving a 1" border all the way around. Top each with another patty, and use your fingers to seal the edges of the meat together, forming a package around the filling.

4. For medium-rare burgers, broil 4 to 5 minutes on each side, or charcoal-grill them 3 to 4 minutes per side.

5. Meanwhile, toast the rolls. Place one burger on each roll and serve.
Serves 6.

DUBLIN DOGS

Who says the hot dog is just an American obsession? This one may yet catch on in Dublin—or even Kansas City.

1 lb. kielbasa sausage*
2 tbsp. olive oil
1½ cups sliced green bell peppers
   (¼" strips)
1½ cups sliced red bell peppers
   (¼" strips)
1 cup sliced fresh onion rings
   (¼" thick)

1 cup sliced scallions (green onions)
1½ tsp. salt
8 turns freshly ground black pepper
1 cup dry red wine
1 cup slivered, seeded fresh
   tomatoes
4 individual French baguettes, about
   6 to 7" long
2 tbsp. plus 2 tsp. Dijon mustard

1. Cut the sausage into 4 equal lengths, each about 6" long. Split each piece in half.

2. Heat the oil in a large skillet over medium heat. Add the sausage and cook, turning once, until brown, about 5 minutes on each side. Remove the sausage to a dish and set aside.

3. To the skillet add the green and red peppers, onions, scallions, salt, and pepper. Cook, stirring often until the vegetables are brown, 5 to 6 minutes.

4. Add the wine and scrape to deglaze the skillet. Return the sausage to the skillet, arranging the pieces on top of the peppers, and add the tomatoes and the accumulated juices from the sausage dish. Cover, reduce the heat to medium-low, and cook 20 minutes. Remove the cover and continue to cook until the liquid has been absorbed, about 30 minutes.

5. Meanwhile, preheat the oven to 425 degrees.

6. While the meat and peppers are cooking, split the baguettes lengthwise, without slicing all the way through, and spread them cut side down on a baking sheet. Bake until the bread is heated through and slightly crispy, 3 to 4 minutes. Remove from the oven.

7. Place a baguette cut side up on each of 4 plates, and spread the bread with 2 tsp. of the mustard. Arrange 2 sausage halves on the bread. Using a slotted spoon, add one-quarter of the pepper mixture over the top of the sausage, and serve the sandwiches hot.

Serves 4.

*Kielbasa is a Polish sausage that can be bought at most supermarkets.

FINNEGAN'S CHEESE BAKE
ON MRS. O'HARA'S FOCACCIA

Sure, focaccia is an Italian delicacy—a crusty, pizzalike bread, fit for topping with almost anything. But don't tell Mrs. O'Hara, since she's certain it's an Irish bread with a misguided name.

½ cup sun-dried tomatoes (not packed in oil)
2 cups boiling water
4 wedges (about 4" at widest end) Mrs. O'Hara's Focaccia (see index)
½ lb. Havarti cheese, in ¼" slices

8 slices crisp-cooked bacon, drained
¼ cup coarsely chopped fresh basil leaves
12 turns freshly ground black pepper
Whole fresh basil sprigs for garnish

1. Place the sun-dried tomatoes in a small bowl and cover with boiling water. Allow the tomatoes to sit until enough water is absorbed to make them plump, 15 to 20 minutes. Remove the tomatoes and drain on paper towels.

2. Preheat the oven to 400 degrees. Split the focaccia wedges in half horizontally to make 2 sandwich halves, holding your free hand lightly on top of each wedge as you slice through.

3. Place the 4 bottom halves of focaccia on a baking sheet, and arrange one-eighth of the cheese slices on each. Place 2 slices of bacon over the cheese, one-fourth of the tomatoes, and one-fourth of the chopped basil. Sprinkle with 3 turns of the pepper, and top with the remaining cheese. Place the focaccia tops over all and cover lightly with a sheet of foil.

4. Bake until the cheese is melted, 10 to 12 minutes. Garnish the sandwiches with basil sprigs and serve hot.

Serves 4.

WINEY EGG SALAD ON BACON BREAD

Egg salad never tasted so good. Served on Bacon Bread, this would make a terrific brunch or even a breakfast sandwich.

6 large hard-boiled eggs
¼ cup mayonnaise
3 tbsp. Dijon mustard
2 tbsp. dry white wine
1½ tsp. salt
26 turns freshly ground black
   pepper, divided

½ cup sliced black olives
2 tbsp. capers
12 slices Bacon Bread (see index)
1 medium red onion, in ½" rings

1. Peel the eggs and place them in a bowl. Mash them fine with the back of a fork. Using a wooden spoon, mash in the mayonnaise, mustard, wine, salt, and 8 turns of the pepper. Stir in the olives and capers.

2. Spread 6 slices of the bread with the egg mixture, add some onion rings, and sprinkle each with 3 turns of the remaining pepper. Top with the remaining bread slices, cut each sandwich into thirds, and serve.

Serves 6.

LEEKY BRIE AND CHERRY TOMATOES
ON BLOODY MARY BREAD

This sandwich partners intense flavors that make it an out-of-the-ordinary, snap-to-make lunch.

¼ cup (½ stick) unsalted butter
2 cups minced leeks, tops and
  bottoms, mostly white
8 oz. brie, softened to room
  temperature

12 slices Bloody Mary Bread (see
  index)
6 oz. alfalfa sprouts
12 cherry tomatoes, quartered

1. Melt the butter in a small skillet over medium heat. Add the leeks and cook, stirring often, until tender, 8 to 10 minutes. Remove from the heat and allow to cool to room temperature.

2. Remove the rind from the brie. Place the cheese in a medium bowl and mash with a fork. Mash in the leeks and continue to work until they are incorporated into the brie.

3. Spread the mixture on 6 slices of Bloody Mary Bread. Spread sprouts over the cheese and arrange tomatoes on top of the sprouts. Top each sandwich with another slice of bread, cut each in half, and serve.

Serves 6.

The
Kettle:

Soups
and Stews

In Ireland, the earliest soups that poor people ate were made of boiled oatmeal with vegetables. Meat was added to the pot only on special occasions. Rich Protestant landowners sometimes ran soup kitchens on their estates for starving peasants, who were often Catholics. The landowners used these opportunities to evangelize, and whenever a Catholic peasant converted to Protestantism, he was called a "souper."

Today, Irish soups tend to have fewer religious overtones and are enjoyed for what they are. Big pots of bubbling soups and stews are almost always found in Irish pub kitchens and in Irish-American pubs as well. The coziness of the tavern and the strength of the drink seem to go well with the substantial fare of a pot dinner. Just imagine a chilly winter night, warming up beside one of McGuire's roaring hearths with a mug of ale and a thick crock of rich Oyster Chowder, hot and spicy Black Beer Chili, or Three-Cheese Beer Soup with Sausage.

When the heat of the summer fades and the air begins to nip at your nose and fingers, plan a bone-warming one-bowl dinner of lamb-laden Rosemary-Scented Irish Stew with Roasted Vegetables or gingery Red-Wine Beef Stew with Parsley Dumplings. Just add a crisp green salad and a loaf of dense bread. Or start a lighter meal with a steaming bowl of soup: tangy Mean Gene's Mulligatawny, hearty Pig 'n Pea Soup, stick-to-the-ribs Red Cabbage and Bacon Chowder, or creamy Smoked Salmon Bisque. Whatever comes from the kettle seems to bring love and good feelings with it, so do it often.

CROCKED ONION SOUP

The onion is one of Ireland's staple vegetables, and its history as a flavoring in many traditional dishes goes back for centuries. Here's a version of an Irish onion soup that gets crocked—two ways.

¼ cup all-purpose flour
2 tsp. salt, divided
16 turns freshly ground black
  pepper, divided
7 cups sliced onions (about 3 to 4
  large onions)
¼ cup olive oil
4 cups beef stock (see index)

3 cups lager ale
1 tbsp. Worcestershire sauce
½ tsp. dried thyme
⅛ tsp. ground allspice
2 bay leaves
One 1-lb. pkg. puff pastry sheets
½ lb. grated fontina cheese
8 individual oven-proof soup crocks

1. In a large bowl, combine the flour with 1 tsp. of the salt and 8 turns of the pepper. Separate the onion slices into rings, add the rings to the seasoned flour, and toss to coat them.

2. Heat the oil in a large pot over medium heat. Add the floured onions and reduce the heat to medium-low. Cook, stirring occasionally, until the onions are golden brown and tender, about 30 minutes.

3. Increase the heat to medium-high and stir in the stock, ale, Worcestershire, thyme, allspice, bay leaves, and the remaining salt and pepper. Bring to a bubble, reduce the heat to low, and cover. Cook, uncovering occasionally to stir, until the flavors are rich and have blended, about 1 hour. Remove the bay leaves. About 15 minutes before the soup is finished cooking, preheat the oven to 400 degrees.

4. Meanwhile, thaw the puff pastry according to package directions. Using a dish about ½" wider than the top diameter of the soup crocks, cut 8 circles from the puff pastry.

5. Place the crocks on a baking sheet, and ladle in the hot soup. Divide the cheese and sprinkle it evenly over the soup. Place a round of puff pastry over the top of each serving, sealing the edges to the crocks. Use extra pastry to create a decoration (a shamrock for St. Patrick's Day?) for the top of each, brushing it with a little water to affix it to the top of the puff pastry.

6. Slide the baking sheet into the oven and bake until the top of the pastry is puffed and golden brown, 10 to 12 minutes. Serve immediately or the puff will deflate.

Serves 8 for a generous first course.

ONION, LEEK, AND MUSHROOM SOUP
WITH BRIE CROUTONS

Earthy flavors combine in this soup. Serve it as a first course or as a light meal accompanied by a green salad and a hearty peasant loaf of Irish Buttermilk Bread (see index).

½ cup (1 stick) unsalted butter
3 cups thin-sliced fresh onion rings
1 cup thin-sliced leeks*
1 lb. thin-sliced fresh mushrooms, preferably a mixture of wild and white mushrooms
6 cups beef stock (see index)

¼ cup dry white wine
½ tsp. Worcestershire sauce
8 turns freshly ground black pepper
¼ cup olive oil
1 tbsp. chopped fresh tarragon
8 slices French bread
8 oz. brie, cut into 8 pieces

1. Melt the butter in a heavy soup pot over medium heat. Add the onions and leeks and sauté over medium heat until they are caramel colored, about 6 minutes. Stir in the mushrooms and cook until lightly browned, 2 to 3 minutes.

2. Stir in the stock, wine, Worcestershire, and pepper. Bring to a bubble, reduce the heat to low, and simmer, stirring occasionally, until the flavors have infused, about 45 minutes.

3. Meanwhile, preheat the oven to 200 degrees.

4. In a small skillet, heat the olive oil with the tarragon. Place the bread slices on a baking sheet and spread them lightly with the tarragon oil. Bake until crisp, turning once and brushing with more oil, 30 to 45 minutes. Remove the croutons and turn the oven up to 350 degrees.

5. Ladle the soup into oven-proof bowls set on the baking sheet. Top each with a crouton and 1 oz. of the brie, and bake until the cheese is melted, 3 to 5 minutes.

Serves 8 for a first course.

*Leeks should be carefully cleaned before use: Remove dirty outer layers, then split the leeks vertically. Hold leeks under cool, running water to rinse any dirt from between the layers. Drain and chop crosswise in thin slices.

ONION BISQUE

Everyone seems to love onion soup. This easy-to-make version has a rich, creamy twist because it's thickened by pureeing.

¼ cup (½ stick) unsalted butter
6 cups thinly sliced white onions
2 cups chicken stock (see index),
    room temperature
1 cup heavy cream

1 tsp. salt
4 turns freshly ground black pepper
4 turns freshly ground nutmeg, plus
    more for garnish

1. Melt the butter in a large saucepan over medium heat. Stir the onions into the butter and cover the pot. Reduce the heat to low and cook, stirring occasionally, until the onions are tender, about 30 minutes.

2. Transfer the onions to a food processor. Add the stock and puree until smooth (you may need to do this in batches).

3. Return the mixture to the saucepan over medium heat and bring to a bubble. Stir in the cream and reduce the heat to medium-low. Cook at a slow bubble, stirring occasionally, until the soup is thick and creamy and the flavors have blended, about 15 minutes. Stir in the salt, pepper, and 4 turns nutmeg.

4. To serve, ladle the soup into 4 bowls or 6 mugs, and top each with a turn of fresh nutmeg.

Serves 4-6 for a first course.

BRANDIED CREAM OF PORTABELLO SOUP

Portabellos are very dear mushrooms—both in flavor and price. If you're feeling thrifty, you can make this rich soup using less costly mushrooms; try a mixture of any fresh, wild mushrooms you like.

4 tbsp. (½ stick) unsalted butter

¼ cup chopped onions

4½ cups coarsely chopped portabello mushrooms (about 1 lb.)

3 cups beef stock (see index), divided

2 tbsp. chopped fresh parsley, plus more for garnish

1 tbsp. ground paprika

1 tsp. salt

4 turns freshly ground black pepper

2 large egg yolks

1 cup sour cream, plus more for garnish

3 tbsp. cognac

1. Melt the butter in a large pot over medium heat. Add the onions and cook, stirring often, until the onions are translucent, about 5 minutes. Add the mushrooms and cook until the mushrooms are limp and most of their liquid has cooked out, 8 to 10 minutes. Transfer the contents of the pot to the bowl of a food processor. Add ½ cup of the stock and process until the mixture is fairly smooth.

2. Return the mixture to the pot over medium-high heat. Stir in the parsley, paprika, salt, pepper, and the remaining 2½ cups stock. Bring to a bubble, cover the pot, and reduce the heat to low. Cook, uncovering the pot to stir occasionally, until the flavors are thoroughly blended, about 45 minutes.

3. In a small bowl, beat the egg yolks until frothy and lemon colored. Stir a bit of the hot soup into the egg yolks to temper the mixture. Stir a little more into the yolks, then turn the mixture into the soup, stirring well. Increase the heat to medium and cook, stirring often, until the mixture has thickened to a thick buttermilk consistency.

4. Stir a little of the soup into the sour cream, tempering it as you did the egg yolks. Stir the sour-cream mixture into the soup. Reduce the heat to low and cook, stirring often, until the mixture is thoroughly incorporated, about 5 minutes. Stir in the cognac and cook until the alcohol has cooked off, 2 to 3 minutes.

5. To serve, ladle the soup into 6 shallow bowls. Streak sour cream through the soup, forming a decorative pattern, or just add a dollop of the sour cream. Sprinkle with chopped parsley and serve.

Serves 6 for a generous first course.

IRISH POTATO SOUP

The best-known and most widely used vegetable in Ireland is, of course, the humble potato. When coaxed into a lovely soup such as this, however, the spud loses a lot of its humility.

½ cup (1 stick) unsalted butter
1 cup thinly sliced onions
1 cup thinly sliced leeks
4 cups peeled, sliced potatoes
6 cups chicken stock (see index)
1 tsp. salt

20 turns freshly ground black pepper
½ cup freshly grated Cheddar cheese
4 slices crisp-cooked bacon, drained
    and crumbled
½ cup chopped fresh chives

1. Melt the butter in a large heavy pot over low heat. Add the onions and leeks and stir to cover them with butter. Cover the pot and cook slowly to allow the vegetables to "sweat," about 20 minutes.

2. Add the potatoes, stir them into the butter, cover the pot, and cook over low heat another 15 minutes.

3. Stir in the stock, salt, and pepper. Increase the heat to medium-high and bring the soup to a bubble. Reduce the heat and simmer until the potatoes are tender, 20 to 30 minutes.

4. In a food processor or blender, puree the soup in batches and return it to the pot. Heat thoroughly.

5. Serve garnished with Cheddar cheese, bacon, and chives.

Serves 8 for a first course.

POTATO, ARTICHOKE, AND ROASTED GARLIC CHOWDER

A fine combination of tasty vegetables makes this rich, creamy chowder flavorful and delicious.

3 cups peeled, cubed potatoes
1 tbsp. salt, divided
3½ cups chicken stock (see index)
2 heads peeled, roasted garlic (see index)

1 pkg. frozen artichoke hearts, thawed
6 turns freshly ground black pepper
1½ cups heavy cream
6 tbsp. snipped fresh dill

1. Combine the potatoes with 1½ tsp. salt and cold water to cover in a large saucepan over high heat. Bring to a boil, reduce the heat to medium, and cook until the potatoes are firm-tender, about 10 minutes. Remove from the heat and drain the potatoes.

2. Combine the potatoes, stock, and roasted garlic in a large saucepan over medium-high heat and bring to a bubble. Reduce the heat to medium-low and cook, stirring occasionally, until the potatoes are tender and the flavors infused, 20 to 25 minutes. Turn the mixture into the bowl of a food processor or blender and puree until thick and smooth, 20 to 30 seconds.

3. Return the mixture to the saucepan over low heat. Fold in the artichoke hearts, the remaining 1½ tsp. salt, and the pepper and cook, stirring occasionally, 10 minutes. Stir in the cream and heat through, about 3 minutes.

4. Serve in shallow soup bowls, garnishing each portion with 1 tbsp. dill.
Serves 6 for a first course.

MEAN GENE'S MULLIGATAWNY

"Mean Gene" is really Gene Lang, also known as the "tenor chef" around McGuire's Irish Pub because he sings tenor with the Pensacola Opera Company. The kitchen staff fondly calls him "Mean Gene" because he has the audacity to insist that everything be done just right. Here's Gene's recipe for a traditional sweet and pungent soup.

¼ cup vegetable oil
1 cup chopped onions
1 cup chopped carrots
2 cups chopped cooking apples
    (Granny Smith or Rome Beauty
    are best)
¼ cup all-purpose flour
2 tbsp. curry powder

5 cups beef stock (see index)
½ cup raisins
2 tbsp. chutney*
½ tsp. granulated sugar
½ tsp. freshly squeezed lemon juice
1 apple, any type, grated (do this at
    the end so it won't turn brown)

1. In a medium soup pot, heat the oil and sauté the onions, carrots, and chopped apples over medium heat for 1 minute.

2. Combine the flour with the curry powder and stir the mixture into the pot, thoroughly coating the onions, carrots, and apples. Cook, stirring and shaking the pot, until the flour is golden, about 2 minutes. Remove from the heat.

3. Slowly add the stock, a little at a time, stirring constantly. Return the pot to medium heat and bring to a boil, stirring often. Reduce the heat to low and cook, stirring occasionally, until the soup is thickened and rich in color, 15 to 20 minutes.

4. Stir in the raisins, chutney, sugar, and lemon juice and simmer over low heat, stirring occasionally, until all of the flavors have thoroughly blended, about 1 hour.

5. Strain the soup, return the liquid to the pot, and heat thoroughly. Meanwhile, grate the remaining apple. Ladle the soup into bowls and top with the grated apple.

Serves 4-6 for a first course.

*Chutney is a spicy Indian relish usually made of fruits, vegetables, and spices. The type most readily available in American supermarkets is a mango chutney bearing the "Major Grey's" label.

CREAM OF SWISS CHARD SOUP
WITH PINE NUT CREAM

Chard is grown in the gardens of cottages and farmhouses all over Ireland, along with the ubiquitous potatoes, cabbages, carrots, and onions, but it was usually boiled and served simply. This soup, however, is rather elegant. For a really dazzling presentation, pull the pine nut cream through the finished soup (see step 7).

5 tbsp. unsalted butter, divided
½ cup pine nuts, divided
¼ cup chopped onions
¼ cup grated carrots
1 lb. Swiss chard, rinsed, patted dry, and chopped
2 tsp. salt, divided
¼ cup plus 1 tbsp. dry sherry, divided

2 cups chicken stock (see index)
¼ tsp. plus 1 pinch ground nutmeg, divided
6 turns freshly ground black pepper
2 cups heavy cream
2 egg yolks
1 cup half-and-half
⅛ tsp. white pepper

1. Melt 1 tbsp. of the butter in a small skillet over medium heat. Add 1 tbsp. of the pine nuts and cook, shaking the skillet constantly, until the nuts are lightly toasted on all sides, about 3 minutes. Remove the nuts to drain and cool on paper towels. Reserve the skillet.

2. Melt 3 tbsp. of the butter in a large saucepan or pot over medium heat. Add the onions and carrots and cook, stirring occasionally, until the vegetables are tender, about 5 minutes. Add the chard and 1 tsp. of the salt and cook, stirring often, until the chard has wilted, 2 to 3 minutes. Transfer the vegetables to the bowl of a food processor. Add the 1 tbs. toasted pine nuts and ¼ c. of the sherry. Process until smooth (you may have to do this in batches). Turn the mixture back into the pot over medium-high heat.

3. Stir in the stock, ¼ tsp. of the nutmeg, the black pepper, and ½ tsp. of the salt. Bring to a bubble, reduce the heat to low, and cook, stirring occasionally, until the soup is slightly reduced and the flavors blended, about 30 minutes.

4. Increase the heat to medium-high and slowly stir in the cream. Bring to a bubble, reduce the heat to medium-low, and cook, stirring occasionally, until the soup has a thick, creamy consistency, 10 to 12 minutes.

5. While the soup is cooking, prepare the Pine Nut Cream: In a small bowl, beat the egg yolks lightly with a whisk. Whisk in the half-and-half, the white pepper,

the remaining ½ tsp. salt, and the remaining pinch nutmeg and continue to beat until well blended.

6. Melt the remaining 1 tbsp. butter in the small skillet over medium heat. Add the remaining pine nuts and cook, shaking the skillet constantly, until the nuts are lightly toasted all over. Stir in the remaining 1 tbsp. sherry and bring to a bubble. Reduce the heat to medium-low and slowly stir in the egg mixture. Cook, stirring constantly, until the cream is the consistency of a light custard. Transfer to a clean food processor and puree.

7. To serve, ladle the hot soup into 4 shallow soup bowls. Drizzle or draw the cream in a decorative pattern through the soup—or use a squeeze bottle (you can purchase one at almost any supermarket).

Serves 4 for a first course.

THREE-CHEESE BEER SOUP WITH SAUSAGE

Creamy and hearty, this soup can come to the table as a one-dish meal. Just add a green salad and Bacon Bread or Onion Rye Bread (see index). You won't find any added salt in this recipe because the sausage and cheese contribute all that's needed.

2 cups milk
1½ cups (12 oz.) beer
1½ cups grated sharp Cheddar
   cheese
½ cup cubed Gruyère cheese
¼ cup crumbled Stilton cheese

¼ lb. pork sausage meat
1 cup heavy cream
¼ cup chopped fresh parsley
¼ tsp. crushed red pepper flakes
1 cup chicken stock (see index)

1. Combine the milk and beer in a large saucepan over medium-low heat. Add the Cheddar, Gruyère, and Stilton cheeses and cook, stirring occasionally, until the cheese has melted and the mixture looks grainy, about 30 minutes. Remove from the heat and refrigerate for at least 1 hour.

2. Meanwhile, brown the sausage in a skillet, breaking up the meat with a wooden spoon to crumble and brown evenly. Remove from the heat; pour off and discard the fat. Blot the sausage meat with paper towels.

3. When the fat has hardened on top of the cheese mixture, remove it from the refrigerator and skim off the fat. Heat the mixture slowly over low heat until it has melted again, about 20 minutes. Press the cheese mixture from the first pot into a clean pot through a strainer, using a wooden spoon or spatula to press all of the liquids through. Discard the solids remaining in the strainer.

4. Place the new pot on the stove over low heat. Stir in the cream, parsley, and red pepper flakes and simmer, stirring often, to keep the mixture from sticking to the bottom of the pan, about 10 minutes.

5. Meanwhile, heat the stock in a small saucepan over medium heat. Slowly whisk the stock into the simmering cheese soup. Cook, stirring often until the soup thickens, 6 to 10 minutes.

6. To serve, ladle the soup into bowls and top with crumbled sausage.

Serves 8 for a first course or 6 for a main course.

SENATE BEAN SOUP

A soup very much like this was first served in the U.S. Senate for just 18 cents. Today, you can have the same tasty bean soup at McGuire's for the same low price. Or you can make it yourself. It might cost more, but if you live in San Francisco or Chicago and factor in the airfare to Pensacola, accommodations . . .

1 lb. dried navy beans	½ cup chopped onions
4 qt. water	2 stalks celery, roughly chopped,
1 bay leaf	including leaves
3 whole cloves	2 large carrots, peeled and sliced
One large ham bone, preferably with	1½ tsp. salt
bits of meat on it*	16 turns freshly ground black pepper

1. The day before, rinse the beans and place them in a large bowl. Add the water and allow the beans to soak, covered, overnight.

2. The next day, make a cheesecloth pouch containing the bay leaf and cloves. Drain the beans and place them in a large stockpot with the ham bone. Add cold water to cover plus 2", and bring to a boil over high heat.

3. Add the spice pouch, onions, celery, carrots, salt, and pepper. Reduce the heat to medium and cook, stirring occasionally, until the beans are tender and the meat is falling off the bone, about 3 hours. Add hot water if the level gets too low.

4. Remove the spice pouch and the bone. Shred the meat from the bone and add it to the soup before serving.

Serves 6-8 for a first course.

*If you haven't made ham recently (to give you a leftover bone), ask your butcher to save one for you. In the future, freeze ham and beef bones for soups and stocks.

PIG 'N PEA SOUP

Throughout the centuries in Ireland the pig was known as the "gentleman" who provided dinner. Beef was affordable only to the wealthy, but almost everyone could have pork at least once in awhile. Consequently, pigs were treated well and sometimes brought into the family house if the weather was inclement, which gave rise to the expression referring to the Irish "keeping pigs in the parlor." Next time you serve ham, freeze the bone and leftover meat, and you'll be all set to make this soup.

2 tbsp. vegetable oil
1½ cups chopped onions
1½ cups chopped celery
1 tsp. dried thyme
2 cups dried split peas, picked over
    for stones
1 cup chopped carrots
½ cup dry white wine

4 cups chicken stock (see index)
2 cups peeled, cubed potatoes (1")
1 large ham bone
4 cups cubed leftover ham
2 bay leaves
¼ cup chopped fresh parsley
1 tbsp. salt
8 turns freshly ground black pepper

1. Heat the oil in a large soup pot over medium heat. Add the onions, celery, and thyme and cook, stirring occasionally, until the vegetables are translucent, 8 to 10 minutes.

2. Add the split peas and carrots, and stir in the wine until it sizzles. Increase the heat to medium-high and add the stock, potatoes, ham bone, ham, and bay leaves. Bring to a fast bubble and reduce the heat to low. Cover and cook until the peas and potatoes are tender, about 1 1/2 hours.

3. Stir in the parsley, salt, and pepper and simmer for 10 minutes before serving.

Serves 8-10 for a first course.

RED CABBAGE AND BACON CHOWDER

Green cabbage stewed with bacon is a favorite Irish dish and can be found in many pubs. Red cabbage in Ireland is most often pickled, but it works perfectly to flavor this tasty soup.

½ lb. bacon
3 cups coarsely chopped red cabbage
½ cup coarsely chopped onions
2 tbsp. all-purpose flour

1 cup chicken stock (see index)
½ tsp. salt
4 turns freshly ground black pepper
4 cups (1 qt.) milk

1. Fry the bacon in a skillet over medium heat until crispy. Crumble the bacon and set aside.

2. Pour the bacon drippings into a stockpot over medium heat. Add the cabbage and onions and cook, stirring occasionally, until the onions start becoming translucent, about 2 minutes. Sprinkle with the flour and cook, stirring, until the flour is golden, about 3 minutes.

3. Slowly stir in the stock, a little at a time, stirring constantly until smooth and bubbling. Stir in the salt and pepper, reduce the heat to medium-low, and simmer to infuse the flavors, stirring often, 6 minutes.

4. Increase the heat to medium and gradually stir in the milk. Bring to a bubble and simmer until the flavors have blended, 5 to 6 minutes. Stir in the crumbled bacon, reserving about 2 tbsp. for garnish.

5. Serve the soup in shallow bowls with reserved bacon sprinkled on top.
Serves 6 for a first course.

OYSTER CHOWDER

Sea creatures are the treasures of Ireland, and one of the dearest is the oyster. Native Irish oysters are harvested from hundreds of acres of natural oyster beds. The Irish like their oysters raw and briny, with mugs of stout and thick brown bread. But they wouldn't mind them at all in a pot of rich, creamy chowder. You can still add the brown bread and stout.

4 slices bacon
½ cup (1 stick) unsalted butter, divided
1 cup chopped onions
½ cup chopped celery
1 tsp. minced fresh garlic
1½ tbsp. salt
14 turns freshly ground black pepper
1 bay leaf
¾ tsp. dried thyme
5 tbsp. all-purpose flour

4 cups shucked oysters in their liquor
1½ to 2 cups fish stock (see index)
½ cup dry white wine
2 cups chopped carrots
4 cups peeled, cubed potatoes (½")
4 cups heavy cream
¼ cup chopped fresh parsley, plus more for garnish
⅛ tsp. cayenne pepper

1. Combine the bacon with 2 tbsp. of the butter in a large stockpot over medium heat, and cook until the fat is rendered and the bacon crispy, 6 to 7 minutes. Remove the bacon pieces with a slotted spoon and discard.

2. Add the onions, celery, and garlic to the fat in the pot and cook over medium heat, stirring occasionally, until the vegetables are tender, about 5 minutes. Stir in the salt, pepper, bay leaf, thyme, and flour and cook, stirring often, until the flour is golden, 4 to 5 minutes.

3. Increase the heat under the stockpot to medium-high. Drain the oyster liquor into a large measuring cup and set the oysters aside. Add enough fish stock to the oyster liquor to make 3 cups, and slowly stir the stock into the pot. Stir in the wine and bring to a bubble. Reduce the heat to medium-low, cover, and cook, stirring occasionally, until the flavors have infused and the mixture has thickened, about 20 minutes.

4. Uncover the pot and increase the heat to medium. Fold in the carrots and cook 15 minutes. Fold in the potatoes and continue to cook, stirring occasionally, until the carrots and potatoes are tender, about 20 minutes.

5. Stir in the cream. Cook, stirring often, until the soup is thick and creamy, 12 to 15 minutes. Fold in the parsley, cayenne, and oysters and cook just until the edges of the oysters curl, 2 to 3 minutes.

6. To serve, ladle the chowder into shallow bowls, and float a pat of butter and a sprinkling of chopped parsley on the surface of each.

Serves 8 for a generous first course or 6 for a main course.

SMOKED SALMON BISQUE

Aside from the potato, nothing defines the Irish diet more than salmon. Irish folklore has it that the salmon is the life force, the soul, and is endowed with wisdom and healing powers. An Irish saying—"Bradán Beatha"—means "the Salmon of Life." The king of fish in Ireland, salmon is prepared in many delightful ways, smoked being one of the most popular. It appears in an infinite variety of sumptuous dishes, like this silky bisque.

3 tbsp. unsalted butter
2 tbsp. chopped onions
2 tbsp. chopped celery
2 tbsp. chopped carrots
¼ cup chopped fresh mushrooms
1½ cups fish stock (see index)
⅛ tsp. salt (depending on the saltiness of your smoked salmon; you might not want to add any salt at all)

½ tsp. crushed red pepper flakes
½ lb. smoked salmon, store bought or home smoked (see below), chopped into small pieces, divided
1½ cups heavy cream
½ cup dry white wine
2 tbsp. chopped fresh dill

1. Melt the butter in a heavy saucepan over medium heat. Add the onions, celery, carrots, and mushrooms, and cook until tender, 2 to 3 minutes.

2. Add the stock, salt, and red pepper flakes, and bring to a bubble over medium-high heat. Reduce the heat to low and simmer, stirring once or twice, 10 to 15 minutes. Remove from the heat.

3. Pour the mixture into a food processor or blender, add half the smoked salmon, and process until smooth. Return the mixture to the saucepan over medium heat.

4. Stir in the cream, wine, and the remaining smoked salmon and simmer until the alcohol has cooked off, about 5 minutes.

5. Ladle the bisque into shallow soup bowls, garnish with the dill, and serve. Serves 4 for a first course.

HOME-SMOKED SALMON

2 cups sugar
2 cups coarse salt

2 lb. salmon fillets
1½ cups hardwood chips

1. Combine the sugar and salt.
2. Rub the mixture into both sides of the salmon fillets.
3. Allow the salmon to marinate for up to 1 hour.
4. Soak the hardwood chips in water.
5. Place the chips into a small fire in a covered grill or smoker.
6. Wrap the salmon loosely in foil, and poke holes in the foil to vent. Cover and smoke until firm, 15 to 20 minutes.

IRISH FISHERMAN'S BOUILLABAISSE

In Brazil it's called mariscada; in California, cioppino; in France, bouillabaisse. Since the Celtic name for the Irish version of tomato-base seafood stew is something of a mystery, McGuire's Irish Pub has adopted the French nomenclature. This rich stewy-soup is a hot item at McGuire's and is always on the menu.

¼ cup olive oil
2 cups chopped onions
½ cup chopped green bell peppers
3 tbsp. minced fresh garlic
1 cup chopped fennel bulbs and tops
3 cups tomato sauce
2 cups peeled, seeded, chopped fresh or canned tomatoes
1 cup dry white wine
1½ cups fish stock (see index)
2 bay leaves

1 tsp. salt
½ tsp. freshly ground black pepper
12 littleneck clams, scrubbed
12 mussels, scrubbed and debearded
12 large fresh shrimp, shelled and deveined, tails left on
1 lb. cod or other firm-fleshed fish, cut into bite-size pieces
12 shucked oysters in their liquor
Sliced green onions and chopped fennel leaves for garnish

1. Heat the olive oil in a large heavy pot over medium heat. Add the onions, bell peppers, garlic, and fennel bulbs and tops and cook, stirring occasionally until the onions are translucent, about 10 minutes.

2. Stir in the tomato sauce, tomatoes, wine, and stock and bring to a bubble over medium-high heat. Stir in the bay leaves, salt, and pepper. Reduce the heat to medium-low and simmer, stirring occasionally, until the liquid has reduced and the flavors have married, about 45 minutes.

3. Add the clams, cover the pot, and simmer 1 minute. Add the mussels, re-cover the pot, and simmer 1 minute. Add the shrimp and fish, gently pushing the seafood into the soup. Cover and simmer 2 minutes. Stir in the oysters and their liquor and simmer just until the edges of the oysters begin to curl, about 1 minute.

4. Ladle the soup, fish, oysters, and shrimp into 6 shallow soup plates. Arrange 2 clams and 2 mussels around the edge of each bowl, and garnish with green onions and chopped fennel leaves.

Serves 6.

Note: Pay attention to step 3 of this recipe because timing is crucial. Seafood can get overcooked in a heartbeat, and the actual cooking time of each piece of seafood will depend on its size. The shrimp and fish should just lose their translucence. The clams and mussels are finished cooking as soon as they have completely opened—any longer and they will overcook. The oysters just need to be heated through, and when their edges curl they must be removed from the heat.

TRADITIONAL IRISH STEW
WITH ROASTED ROOT VEGETABLES

A much-maligned dish, Irish stew can mean anything from leftover beef swimming in a heavy gravy to whatever the "perpetrator" would like it to mean. In this version, lamb is lovingly seasoned and simmered in beer with vegetables. The result is a dish of tender, garlicky lamb and vegetables.*

2 lb. lamb shanks
2 cloves garlic, slivered
1 tsp. salt
¾ tsp. freshly ground black pepper
3 tbsp. bleached all-purpose flour
2 tbsp. olive oil
2 medium yellow onions, quartered
3 ribs celery, cut into ½"-thick slices
4 carrots, cut into ½"-thick slices
2 sprigs fresh thyme
4 bay leaves

2 tbsp. tomato paste
10 cups beef broth
1 cup Irish stout
10 small red potatoes (about 1 lb.), peeled and halved
2 large turnips (about 8 oz.), peeled and cubed
4 parsnips (about 4 oz.), peeled and cubed
¼ cup water

1. Trim all visible fat from the lamb. Cut slits in the meat and insert garlic slivers.

2. Season the lamb with ½ tsp. salt and ¼ tsp. pepper and dust with 1 tbsp. flour.

3. Heat the olive oil in a large, heavy, deep pot or Dutch oven over medium-high heat. Add the shanks to the pot and cook, turning to brown evenly, for about 10 minutes.

4. Add the onions, celery, carrots, and remaining salt and pepper and cook for about 2 minutes. Add the thyme, bay leaves, and tomato paste, stirring to mix. Cook for 2 minutes.

5. Add the broth and stout and stir to mix. Bring to a boil, reduce the heat to medium, and cover. Cook until the meat is very tender, about 1½ hours.

6. When the lamb is tender, remove it from its cooking liquid and reserve the liquid or stock. Remove the meat from the bone, cutting it into 1" cubes. Some of the meat will probably fall off the bones, and that's okay. Set aside.

7. Add the potatoes, turnips, and parsnips to the stock and cook, uncovered, until the vegetables are fork-tender, about 30 minutes. Dissolve the remaining flour in the water and add to the stew, stirring to blend.

8. Add the meat back to the stew. Simmer for 30 minutes. Remove from the heat. Remove the bay leaves.

9. Serve the stew in deep bowls and accompany with Irish Soda Bread.

Serves 8.

*Many believe that Irish stew is made with beef, but lamb stew is actually the national dish of Ireland.

RED-WINE BEEF STEW
WITH PARSLEY DUMPLINGS

A cozy booth in your favorite pub, a pint of beer or a glass of red, and a hearty, marrow-warming stew—what could be better? Well, you could reproduce the same in your own home and not have to go out and brave the elements.

STEW

1 cup dry red wine, preferably
    Cabernet Sauvignon

1 tsp. minced fresh garlic

1 bay leaf

2½ tsp. salt, divided

8 turns freshly ground black pepper

2 lb. lean stew beef, in 1" cubes

Cheesecloth

½ cup chopped onions

½ cup chopped celery, including
    leaves

2 tbsp. chopped fresh parsley

2 tbsp. dried or 1 tbsp. chopped
    fresh thyme

8 cloves

8 black peppercorns

One 1" piece fresh gingerroot, peeled
    and sliced

2 tbsp. vegetable oil

2 cups beef stock (see index), room
    temperature

1 cup sliced carrots

½ cup sliced parsnips

DUMPLINGS

2 cups all-purpose flour
1 tbsp. baking powder
1½ tsp. salt
4 turns freshly ground black pepper
½ tsp. granulated sugar
¼ tsp. dried thyme
¼ tsp. ground nutmeg

¼ tsp. ground cloves
2 tbsp. unsalted butter, room temperature
½ cup minced fresh parsley, plus more for garnish
1 cup milk

1. To make the stew, in a container with an airtight lid, combine the wine, garlic, bay leaf, 1½ tsp. salt, and 8 turns pepper. Add the beef and stir to coat the meat with the wine mixture. Cover tightly and marinate, refrigerated, at least 6 hours or overnight. Shake the container or turn it over several times during the marinating.

2. About 5 hours before serving, remove the meat from the refrigerator, pour the marinade into a cup or bowl, and reserve.

3. Cut a piece of cheesecloth about the size of a paper towel. In its center mound the onions, celery, parsley, thyme, cloves, peppercorns, and gingerroot. Tie the cheesecloth bundle with another strip of cheesecloth.

4. Heat the oil in a large heavy pot or Dutch oven over medium-high heat. Add the meat and cook, stirring occasionally, until the meat is brown on all sides, 5 to 8 minutes total. Stir in the stock, reserved marinade, and the remaining 1 tsp. salt. Add the cheesecloth bag, submerging it in the stock. Bring to a bubble, reduce the heat to medium-low, and cover the pot. Cook, opening occasionally to stir and scrape the bottom of the pot, until the meat is very tender and falling apart, about 2½ hours.

5. Stir the carrots and parsnips into the stew, cover, and cook until the vegetables are tender, about 20 minutes.

6. While the stew is cooking, prepare the dumplings. Combine the flour, baking powder, salt, pepper, sugar, thyme, nutmeg, and cloves in a bowl. Cut in the butter with a fork until the mixture has a cornmeal consistency. Blend in the parsley and add the milk, a little at a time, stirring as you go, to incorporate all into a stiff batter. Try not to overhandle, or the dumplings will be heavy. Cover and refrigerate until the stew is almost ready.

7. Remove the dumpling batter from the refrigerator. Remove and discard the cheesecloth bag from the stew. Increase the heat under the stew to medium-high, and drop in the dumpling batter by large spoonfuls. Cover, reduce the heat to medium, and cook until the dumplings are light and fluffy, about 15 minutes—no peeking.

Serves 6-8.

BLACK BEER CHILI

This is not Texas chili, but Irish pub chili, with a big, deep flavor that comes from the beer. Save this dish for a cold or rainy night when you really need to warm up.

1 lb. dried black beans
4½ cups dark beer or stout, divided
¼ cup (4 tbsp.) olive oil, divided
2 lb. top round of beef, in 2" cubes
1 cup chopped onions
1½ tbsp. minced fresh garlic
2 tbsp. chopped fresh jalapeño peppers
¼ cup chili powder
¼ cup ground cumin

1 tsp. cayenne pepper
2 cups beef stock (see index)
2 tbsp. balsamic vinegar
1 tbsp. salt
6 turns freshly ground black pepper
½ cup grated Monterey jack cheese
½ cup sour cream
¼ cup minced fresh leeks or onions

1. Rinse and sort the beans, place them in a large bowl, and add hot water to 1" above the beans. Cover with a large plate and soak overnight.

2. The next day, drain the beans and place them in a stockpot with 3 cups of the beer. Bring to a boil over high heat and reduce the heat to medium-low. Cook at a slow bubble until the beans are tender, stirring occasionally and adding water to keep up the level of liquid if necessary, 1 to 1½ hours.

3. Meanwhile, heat 2 tbsp. of the oil in another large pot over medium-high heat. Add the beef and cook, stirring occasionally, until the meat is brown on all sides, 3 to 4 minutes. Remove the meat from the pot and set aside.

4. Add the remaining 2 tbsp. oil to the same pot over medium heat. Stir in the onions, garlic, jalapeño peppers, chili powder, cumin, and cayenne and cook, stirring constantly, until the onions are tender, 4 to 6 minutes.

5. Into the onions stir the stock, vinegar, and the remaining 1½ cups beer. Fold in the meat, bring to a bubble, and reduce the heat to low. Cover and simmer, stirring occasionally to keep the meat from sticking to the bottom of the pot, until the meat is very tender and shreds easily with a fork, about 1½ hours.

6. Transfer 1½ cups of the beans with their cooking juices to the bowl of a food processor and puree until smooth. Drain the remaining beans and stir them, with the pureed beans, into the meat pot. Stir in the salt and pepper and continue to simmer, stirring occasionally, until all of the flavors have blended and the chili is heated through, about 15 minutes.

7. Serve the chili in bowls, garnished with cheese, sour cream, and minced leeks or onions.

Serves 8-10.

Creature
Comforts:

Fish, Fowl,
and Meat

There's nothing dainty about pub food, nor Irish food, for that matter. In fact, the whole concept of an Irish pub signifies coziness and warm feelings. So naturally, much of what a pub serves is comfort food. The recipes in this chapter will help you cook some of the most comforting, robust food you've ever tasted, like Honey Beer-Braised Ribs, Baked Trout with Mushrooms and Almonds, Lamb Shanks and Lentils Baked in Wine, and Chicken Dumplings in Madeira Gravy—to name just a few.

In good pubs around the world, no self-respecting proprietor would be caught without a steak or chop on his menu. The same is true of McGuire's, where there are always a number of steaks to choose from, as well as prime rib, lamb, corned beef, and "Kosher" pork ribs. Check out Irish Whiskey Steak, Beer-Braised Honey-Mustard Pork Chops with White Bean Puree, and Crusted Rack of Lamb with Port-Wine Cherry Sauce.

Poultry has always been an important part of the Irish household economy—hens were used for barter; treasured for their eggs, which could be sold; and even eaten on special occasions. Included in this chapter are tender McGuire's Panéed Turkey Cutlets, Cornish Game Hens (stuffed with a mixture of corn bread, dates, figs, and walnuts) with Applejack Gravy, and sausage-Stuffed Quail with Pilsner Sauce.

The bounty of seafood in Ireland is legendary. Lobster (a favorite of Saint Patrick), oysters, scallops, periwinkles, cockles, and mussels; salmon, pike, trout, mackerel, snapper, and herring—all are abundant in the seas and rivers of Ireland, and all find their way to the Irish table. The pub, whether in Ireland or America, is a good place to indulge in a seafood dinner. Give it a go at home, with Oatmeal-Battered Snapper with Apricot Horseradish Sauce, Scallops in Saffron Cream over Polenta, or Giddy Lobster Cake with Champagne Tarragon Sauce and Salmon Caviar.

Whichever creature comfort intrigues you, make a meal of it to please family and friends.

CHARDONNAY POACHED SALMON
WITH WATERCRESS BUTTER

There is almost nothing more elegant than poached salmon, and this one is worthy of your most important guests.

SALMON

2 tbsp. unsalted butter, room temperature, divided

One 5- to 6-lb. fresh whole salmon, gutted and scaled

6 to 8 thin slices lemon (about 1 large lemon), divided

8 sprigs watercress, plus more for garnish, divided

1½ tsp. salt

4 turns freshly ground black pepper

2½ cups Chardonnay wine

BUTTER

1½ cups fish stock (see index)

½ cup reserved poaching liquid

2 tbsp. freshly squeezed lemon juice

½ tsp. salt

½ cup firmly packed watercress leaves

6 tbsp. unsalted butter, room temperature

1. To poach the salmon, preheat the oven to 400 degrees.

2. Use 1 tbsp. of the butter to grease a 9" x 13" shallow baking dish or fish poacher. Spread open the cavity of the salmon and fill it with half the lemon slices and 4 sprigs of the watercress. Sprinkle the cavity with the salt and pepper.

3. Place the salmon in the buttered dish. Pour the wine over the salmon and dot the top with the remaining 1 tbsp. butter. Arrange the remaining lemon slices and watercress sprigs over the salmon and cover tightly with a double layer of foil or the poacher lid. Bake until the salmon flakes easily when touched lightly with a fork, about 30 minutes.

4. Remove the salmon to a heated serving platter and cover to keep warm. Discard the lemon slices and watercress. Pour the poaching liquid through a strainer, discarding the solids and reserving 1/2 cup of the liquid (the remaining liquid may be frozen and used as stock in another dish).

5. To make the watercress butter, combine the stock and reserved poaching liquid in a small saucepan over medium-high heat. Bring to a boil, reduce the heat to medium-low, and simmer until reduced by about half, 20 to 30 minutes. Stir in the lemon juice and salt.

6. When the stock is almost ready, combine the watercress and butter in a food processor and pulse until well blended, 6 to 8 pulses. Whisk the watercress-butter mixture into the stock, still over medium-low heat, 1 tbsp. at a time, until thoroughly melted and blended in.

7. To finish the dish, nap the salmon with the sauce, garnish with chopped watercress, and serve immediately.

Serves 4-6.

Variation:

Poached salmon (see above),   Watercress sprigs for garnish
    through step 3   Lemon slices for garnish
2 very thinly sliced cucumbers   Mayonnaise

1. For cold poached salmon, allow the salmon to cool to room temperature in its poaching liquid, then transfer the salmon to a serving platter.

2. Cover the salmon with the cucumber, overlapping the edges of the slices to resemble fish scales.

3. Garnish with watercress sprigs and lemon slices and serve with mayonnaise.

BAKED TROUT WITH MUSHROOMS AND ALMONDS

This flavorful dish features one of the most popular fish in both Ireland and America. Serve it with a green salad, Onion Pudding, and Mrs. O'Hara's Focaccia (see index).

¾ cup fresh onion rings
1 cup sliced carrots (⅛" thick)
2 bay leaves
1 tsp. dried thyme
½ tsp. ground cinnamon
2 tsp. minced fresh garlic, divided
1 tbsp. salt, divided
12 turns freshly ground black
    pepper, divided
1½ cups dry white wine, divided

3 lb. rainbow trout fillets
¾ cup all-purpose flour
¼ cup olive oil, divided
½ cup fish stock (see index)
2 cups thinly sliced white mush-
    rooms
1 cup coarsely chopped peeled,
    seeded tomatoes
2 tbsp. minced fresh parsley
¾ cup sliced almonds

1. In a large bowl, combine the onions, carrots, bay leaves, thyme, cinnamon, 1 tsp. of the garlic, 1 tsp. of the salt, 4 turns of the pepper, and 1 c. of the wine. Mix this marinade well.

2. Arrange the trout fillets in a large baking dish and pour the marinade over them. Cover with plastic wrap and refrigerate for 1 hour.

3. Preheat the oven to 350 degrees. Remove the dish from the refrigerator. Lift the fillets carefully out of the marinade to a plate, and reserve the marinade with its vegetables.

4. In a dish, combine the flour with the remaining salt and pepper. Heat 2 tbsp. of the oil in a large skillet over medium heat. Dust half the fillets lightly with the seasoned flour, place them in the skillet, and cook until brown, 3 to 4 minutes on each side. Remove and place in a large baking dish while you heat the remaining oil and repeat the process with the remaining trout fillets. Transfer these to the baking dish.

5. Stir the remaining 1 tsp. garlic into the skillet over low heat until golden, about 2 minutes. Stir in the remaining ½ cup wine over medium-high heat and scrape the skillet to deglaze it. Stir in the reserved marinade and its vegetables and the fish stock. Cook, stirring often, until the mixture is heated through and the vegetables are tender, 3 to 4 minutes. Fold in the mushrooms, tomatoes, and parsley and cook until the vegetables just start to get tender, 2 to 3 minutes. Remove from the heat.

6. Pour the contents of the skillet over the trout and sprinkle with the almonds. Bake until the almonds are golden brown, 15 to 20 minutes. Serve immediately.

Serves 8.

OATMEAL-BATTERED SNAPPER
WITH APRICOT HORSERADISH SAUCE

A pint of frosty ale goes perfectly with the unusual combination of flavors in this surprisingly simple dish. Add a crisp green salad, and you've got dinner.

⅔ cup apricot jam
3 tbsp. prepared horseradish
1 tsp. freshly squeezed lime juice
1 cup uncooked oatmeal (rolled oats)
⅓ cup all-purpose flour

2 tsp. salt
6 turns freshly ground black pepper
3 large eggs
2 cups vegetable oil
2 lb. snapper fillets, cut into 3" x 3" medallions

1. To make the sauce, melt the jam in a small saucepan over low heat. Stir in the horseradish and lime juice and heat through, stirring well. Remove from the heat and set aside.

2. To make the batter, combine the oatmeal, flour, salt, and pepper in a food processor and pulse until the mixture looks like coarse cornmeal, about 20 seconds. Transfer the mixture to a shallow bowl. Beat the eggs in another shallow bowl until they are frothy.

3. Heat the oil in a large skillet over medium-high heat. Pat the fish dry with a paper towel. When the oil is hot, dip each piece of fish into the oatmeal mixture, then into the eggs, then back into the oatmeal. Slip each piece into the sizzling oil and fry, turning once, until golden brown, 3 to 4 minutes. Top each serving with a dollop of sauce.

Serves 6-8.

CHEESY SEAFOOD CUPS

These individual ramekins of fish and oysters in a velvety blue cheese sauce are fun to eat. Serve them with Three-Cabbage Slaw and a warm loaf of Dill Bread (see index).

¼ cup (½ stick) unsalted butter
3/4 cup minced onions
½ cup minced celery
½ cup (4 oz.) crumbled blue cheese
¼ cup half-and-half
1 tbsp. Worcestershire sauce
½ tsp. freshly squeezed lemon juice
1 tsp. salt

5 turns freshly ground black pepper
½ lb. cod fillets, cut into 1" chunks
½ pt. shucked oysters, thoroughly
   drained
1 cup bread crumbs, preferably fresh
   (see index)
½ cup sour cream
2 tbsp. chopped fresh parsley

1. Preheat the oven to 375 degrees.

2. Melt the butter in a large saucepan over medium heat. Add the onions and celery and cook until tender, stirring occasionally, about 6 minutes.

3. Reduce the heat to low and add the blue cheese, half-and-half, Worcestershire, lemon juice, salt, and pepper. Cook until the mixture is thick and the cheese has melted, about 8 minutes. Remove from the heat.

4. Fold in the fish, oysters, and bread crumbs. Temper in the sour cream, stirring a little of the hot mixture into the sour cream before slowly stirring all the sour cream into the pan. Fold in the parsley and remove immediately from the heat.

5. Divide the mixture among four 3/4-cup ramekins on a baking sheet. Bake until brown and bubbly, about 15 minutes. Serve immediately.

Serves 4.

SCALLOPED OYSTERS

Oysters are a hot ticket in Ireland and in American pubs as well, probably because they carry the natural briny taste of the sea. These luscious oysters make a dramatic presentation served over Barney's Brioches.

20 oz. (1¼ pt.) freshly shucked oysters, or two 10-oz. containers oysters, in their own liquor
½ cup (approx.) milk
¼ cup (½ stick) unsalted butter
¼ cup minced onions
¼ cup minced green bell peppers
½ tsp. minced fresh garlic
¼ cup all-purpose flour

½ cup heavy cream
¾ tsp. salt
8 turns freshly ground black pepper
⅛ tsp. cayenne pepper, plus more for garnish
1 bay leaf
½ tsp. Worcestershire sauce
2 tbsp. dry sherry
12 Barney's Brioches (see index)

1. Drain the oysters, reserving the liquor in a 3-cup measure. Add enough milk to make 2½ cups of liquid.

2. Melt the butter in a large skillet over medium heat. Add the onions, bell peppers and garlic, and cook, stirring occasionally, until the vegetables are soft, 4 to 5 minutes. Stir in the flour and cook, stirring constantly, until the flour turns a light golden color, about 5 minutes.

3. Stir the oyster liquor-milk mixture slowly into the mixture in the skillet, still over medium heat, stirring constantly. Stir in the cream, salt, black pepper, cayenne, bay leaf, and Worcestershire. Cook, stirring constantly, until the sauce has thickened to the consistency of a cream gravy, 8 to 10 minutes.

4. Stir in the sherry and fold in the drained oysters. Heat through just until edges of the oysters curl, 2 to 3 minutes. Remove the bay leaf.

5. Meanwhile, remove the topknot from each brioche. Gently scoop out some of the bread from the center of each brioche with a grapefruit spoon or small serrated knife, to create a shell. Place 2 brioches on each plate and fill them with some of the scalloped oysters, allowing the sauce to run over the sides. When all of the brioches are filled, spoon more of the scalloped oysters around them on the plate. Add the topknots and sprinkle with a bit of the cayenne pepper.

Serves 6.

SHRIMP FONDUE CUPS

This recipe is a staple for the "versatile" file. You can spoon it into puff pastry and serve it at dinner as either a main or first course, or it can be presented in a chafing dish at a party, with French bread for dunking—like a fondue.

2 qt. water
2 lb. small to medium shelled
    shrimp
2 cups shrimp stock (see index),
    divided
¼ cup Roasted-Garlic Butter (see
    index)
¼ cup all-purpose flour
1 tsp. salt

6 turns freshly ground black pepper
½ tsp. paprika
1¼ cups heavy cream
1 cup coarsely grated Swiss cheese
¼ cup dry sherry
¼ cup chopped fresh parsley
6 packaged puff pastry shells, baked
    according to pkg. directions

1. Bring the water to a boil in a large pot over high heat. Add the shrimp and cook just until they turn pink, about 2 minutes. Drain the shrimp, set aside about 12 shrimp, and transfer the remaining shrimp to the bowl of a food processor. Add ½ cup of the stock and puree until the mixture is pasty.

2. Melt the Roasted Garlic Butter in a large saucepan over medium heat. Stir in the flour, salt, pepper, and paprika and cook, stirring often, until the flour is light brown, about 5 minutes. Whisk in the remaining 1½ cups stock and cook, stirring constantly, until the sauce has thickened, about 5 minutes.

3. Stir in the cream and when it comes to a bubble, fold in the cheese. Fold in the pureed shrimp, reduce the heat to low, and cook, stirring occasionally, until the cheese is thoroughly melted and the sauce thick, about 7 minutes.

4. Stir in the sherry. Fold in the parsley and the reserved 12 shrimp and cook, stirring occasionally, 3 to 4 minutes.

5. To serve, place 1 or 2 baked pastry shells on each plate. Place 2 of the whole shrimp into each shell. Spoon in enough of the shrimp fondue so that it runs over the sides of the shell, and top loosely with the lid.

Serves 6 for a first course or 3 for a main course.

WINEY BAKED MUSSELS

"She wheels her wheelbarrow. . . . " Mollusks have always been very popular in Ireland—mussels, oysters, and cockles are all considered treasures of the sea, guaranteed to lure the pickiest of eaters to the table. Mussels were once regarded in Ireland as the poor man's oysters, but they have gained a respectability of their own and have become very popular in the best of pubs.

2 lb. mussels, cleaned and debearded (see index)
¾ cup dry white wine
2 stalks celery, cut into thirds
¼ cup (½ stick) unsalted butter
½ cup minced onions
3 cloves garlic, minced

¼ cup chopped fresh parsley
½ tsp. chopped fresh thyme
1 cup fresh bread crumbs (see index)
¼ cup freshly grated Parmesan cheese

1. Preheat the oven to 350 degrees.

2. Combine the mussels, wine, and celery in a large saucepan or deep skillet over medium heat. Cover the pot and steam just until the mussels have opened, 5 to 7 minutes. Remove the pot from the heat. Using a slotted spoon lift the mussels from the liquid and discard the celery.

3. Shell the mussels, discard the shells, and return the mussels to the cooking liquid off the heat.

4. Melt the butter in a medium skillet over medium heat. Add the onions, garlic, parsley, and thyme and cook, stirring occasionally, until the onions are tender, 3 to 4 minutes. Remove the skillet from the heat and stir in the bread crumbs, moistening the crumbs and blending thoroughly.

5. Drain the mussels, reserving ¼ cup of the cooking liquid. Place the mussels in a shallow 1-qt. casserole. Sprinkle the reserved cooking liquid over the mussels. Spread the bread-crumb mixture evenly over the top, sprinkle with Parmesan, and bake until golden brown, about 10 minutes.

Serves 4 for a first course or 2 for a main course.

SCALLOPS ST. McGUIRE
IN DUCHESSE POTATO CRUST

You've heard of Coquilles Saint-Jacques, that rich classical French dish of scallops served in individual shells; Scallops St. McGuire is the Irish-pub version, baked like a pie under a luscious crust of creamy potatoes. This can be prepared in individual shells or dishes or in a single casserole dish.

2 lb. baking potatoes
¾ cup plus 1 tbsp. unsalted butter, divided
1¼ tsp. salt, divided
½ tsp. white pepper
¼ tsp. ground nutmeg
2 large whole eggs
4 large egg yolks, divided
¾ cup sliced white mushrooms
3 tbsp. chopped scallions (green onions), white part only

1 lb. bay scallops (if you can only get sea scallops, cut them in quarters)
½ cup dry white wine
2 tbsp. chopped fresh parsley, plus more for garnish
1 tbsp. freshly squeezed lemon juice
⅛ tsp. cayenne pepper
¼ cup all-purpose flour
1 cup milk

1. Preheat the oven to 400 degrees.

2. Bake the potatoes until tender, 45-60 minutes. Remove the potatoes and allow them to cool slightly. Meanwhile, reduce the oven temperature to 350 degrees.

3. Spoon the potatoes out of their skins and discard the skins. Using a ricer, food mill, or food processor, mash the potatoes in batches until they are very smooth.

4. Turn the potatoes into a bowl and stir in 3 tbsp. of the butter, ½ tsp. of the salt, the white pepper, nutmeg, 2 whole eggs, and 2 of the egg yolks. Whip until the potatoes are light and fluffy and all of the ingredients are incorporated. Spoon the potato mixture into a pastry bag with a large decorative tip, and set aside.

5. Melt ¼ cup of the butter in a large, heavy skillet over medium-high heat. Add the mushrooms and scallions and cook until soft, 4 to 5 minutes. Add the scallops, then stir in the wine, 2 tbsp. of the parsley, the lemon juice, ¾ tsp. of the salt, and the cayenne. Reduce the heat to medium, cover the skillet, and cook until the scallops are tender, 2 to 3 minutes. Remove from the heat and pour off all of the cooking liquid, reserving 1 cup.

6. Melt ¼ cup of the butter in another skillet over medium heat. Slowly stir in

the flour, stirring constantly until the mixture is smooth. Cook for 1 minute, stirring constantly. Add the milk in gradual increments and cook, stirring constantly, until the mixture has thickened and coats the back of a spoon, 5 to 7 minutes.

7. In a small bowl, beat the remaining 2 egg yolks until thick and frothy, about 3 minutes. Gradually stir ¼ c. of the hot sauce into the egg yolks until incorporated. Pour this mixture slowly into the sauce in the skillet, stirring constantly. Stir in the reserved scallop cooking liquid. Cook, stirring, until this sauce has thickened, about 3 to 4 minutes. Fold in the scallops and vegetables from the first skillet. Remove from the heat.

8. Melt the remaining 2 tbs. butter.

9. Spoon the scallop and sauce mixture into individual baking shells or a 9½" deep-dish pie pan. Pipe the potato mixture over the top of the scallops to form a crust. Drizzle all over with the remaining butter and bake until the top of the potato crust is lightly browned, about 10 to 15 minutes. Garnish with the remaining parsley before serving.

Serves 6-8.

SCALLOPS IN SAFFRON CREAM OVER POLENTA

The Irish and Americans alike love the slightly sweet, delicate flavor of scallops. This recipe calls for sea scallops, but the smaller bay scallops would do just as well.

1 cup chicken stock (see index)
2 tsp. saffron threads
¼ cup unsalted butter, divided
1 tbsp. minced fresh garlic
¾ cup heavy cream
¼ cup olive oil

Six ¾" slices McGuire's Polenta
   (see index)
2 lb. sea scallops*
½ tsp. salt
4 turns freshly ground black pepper
2 tbsp. chopped fresh parsley

1. Bring the stock to a light bubble in a small saucepan over medium heat. Stir in the saffron, remove from the heat, and allow to cool for 15 minutes.

2. Melt 2 tbsp. of the butter in a large skillet over medium heat. Add the garlic and cook, shaking the skillet a couple of times, until the garlic soft, 1 to 2 minutes. Stir in the saffroned chicken stock and the cream, increase the heat to high, and bring to a boil. Reduce the heat to medium and cook, stirring often, until the sauce has reduced by half and is thick enough to coat the back of a spoon, about 10 minutes. There should be about ¾ cup sauce. Remove from the heat, cover, and keep warm.

3. Heat the oil in a large skillet over medium-high heat. Add the polenta slices and cook until golden brown, turning once, about 4 minutes on each side. Remove the polenta from the skillet and drain on paper towels.

4. Spread the scallops on paper towels and sprinkle them with the salt and pepper. Melt the remaining butter in a large, clean skillet over medium-high heat. When the butter sizzles, add the scallops and cook, shaking the skillet occasionally, just until the scallops are tender and light golden brown in color, 1 to 2 minutes per side, depending on the size of the scallops. Remove from the heat and fold the scallops into the warm cream sauce.

5. To serve, place 1 slice of polenta on each plate, spoon some of the scallops and cream over the polenta, and sprinkle with 1 tsp. chopped parsley.

Serves 6.

*Scallops are usually marketed in this country out of the shell. Look for scallops that are firm and white. Be sure you see a little notch where the scallop was attached to its shell, so you know you're getting scallops, not stamped-out pieces of fish.

GIDDY LOBSTER CAKE WITH CHAMPAGNE TARRAGON SAUCE AND SALMON CAVIAR

The vodka makes the lobster giddy and the lovely champagne sauce with its luxurious caviar topping brings this deliciously whimsical dish into the realm of the elegant. The "roll" is really a savory sponge cake covered with lobster mousse and rolled up jelly-roll style.

Softened butter or vegetable oil spray
6 tbsp. all-purpose flour
1½ cups milk
4 large eggs, separated
⅛ tsp. ground nutmeg
¾ tsp. plus ⅛ tsp. salt, divided
6 tsp. chopped fresh tarragon, divided
1 cup cream cheese, softened
2 tbsp. sour cream
½ tbsp. vodka

2 tbsp. chopped fresh parsley
1½ cups minced steamed lobster
   meat, from one 1½-lb. lobster*
1⅓ cups dry champagne
Reserved lobster shells
¼ cup (½ stick) unsalted butter
1 tbsp. minced shallots
¼ cup heavy cream
4 tbsp. red salmon caviar

1. To prepare the roll, use the softened butter or oil spray to lightly grease a baking sheet 15" x 11" x 1" deep. Line the pan with a sheet of parchment paper. Lightly grease the parchment. Preheat the oven to 350 degrees.

2. Place the flour in a small saucepan and slowly stir in the milk over medium heat. Continue to stir until the mixture has thickened to a gravylike consistency. Turn off the heat.

3. In a small bowl beat the egg yolks with an electric mixer at high speed until thick and lemon colored, about 4 to 5 minutes.

4. Measure ½ cup of the milk mixture and whisk this slowly into the egg yolks until thoroughly blended. Whisk in the remaining milk mixture. Stir in the nutmeg, ¾ tsp. of the salt, and 1½ tsp. of the tarragon.

5. In another bowl beat the egg whites until stiff peaks form, 4 to 5 minutes. Fold the egg whites into the egg yolk mixture and continue to fold and blend until completely incorporated.

6. Pour the batter out evenly into the greased baking pan and bake until the cake is spongy to the touch and toothpick-clean, 15 to 20 minutes. Remove from the oven and with a small sharp knife loosen the cake from the sides of the pan. Place a linen towel over the cake and invert it onto the towel. Place a clean sheet

of parchment or waxed paper on top of the cake and roll it up into a long roll. Place the roll on a wire rack to cool completely.

7. While the cake is baking, make the lobster mousse: Combine the cream cheese, sour cream, vodka, and the remaining ⅛ tsp. salt. Cream the mixture until very soft and fluffy. Fold in the parsley and lobster meat.

8. Unroll the cooled cake and remove the parchment. Spread the lobster mousse evenly over the entire sponge cake, leaving a 1" border all the way around. Reroll and place seam side down on a serving platter. Cover tightly with plastic wrap and refrigerate for 2 to 3 hours.

9. To prepare the sauce, heat the champagne with the reserved lobster shells in a medium saucepan over medium-high heat. Bring to a boil, reduce the heat to medium-low, and simmer 10 minutes. Strain the liquid through cheesecloth or a strainer into a small container.

10. Melt the butter in a small saucepan over medium heat. Add the shallots and cook, stirring often, until the shallots are soft and translucent, about 3 minutes. Stir in the champagne, the heavy cream, and the remaining 4½ tsp. tarragon. Bring to a bubble, reduce the heat to low, and simmer, stirring occasionally, until the sauce has reduced by half, 10 to 15 minutes.

11. To serve, cut the lobster roll in diagonal slices with a serrated knife. Place 1 slice on each plate and spoon or squirt the sauce around it. Top each lobster-roll slice with a dollop of the caviar.

Serves 6-8.

*To steam a 1½-lb. lobster, bring a large pot of salted water (1 tbsp. salt per qt. of water) to a rapid boil over high heat. Place the lobster in the freezer for 1 or 2 minutes; this will immobilize him and make the meat more tender. Plunge the lobster head first into the water and allow the water to return to a rapid boil. Cover the pot, reduce the heat to medium, and cook until the shell is bright red and the meat has lost its translucence, about 7 minutes. Remove the lobster from the water. When the lobster is cool enough to handle, place it on its back on a clean work surface. Using a large, sharp knife, slit the lobster in half from its head to its tail. Remove the intestinal vein, the sac behind the head, and the green and coral (the latter are edible; you may want to save them for a treat on toast points). Twist off the head and claws. Crack the claws with a mallet and remove the meat. Use a sharp knife to separate the tail meat from the shell.

BRAISED CHICKEN BREASTS
IN ROSEMARY-PEAR CREAM

This dish is similar to a chicken fricassee, but updated for contemporary palates with fresh pears and rosemary in the cream sauce.

4 boneless, skinless chicken breasts
½ tsp. salt
8 turns freshly ground black pepper
½ cup (1 stick) unsalted butter, divided
4 small Bosc, Comice, or Anjou pears

⅓ cup minced shallots
1 tbsp. crushed fresh or 1 tsp. dried rosemary
½ cup apple juice
¼ cup freshly squeezed lemon juice
1 cup chicken stock (see index)
½ cup heavy cream

1. Sprinkle the chicken evenly with the salt and pepper. Place the chicken breasts between two sheets of parchment or wax paper and use a meat mallet or heavy pan to flatten them to ½" thickness.

2. Melt 2 tbsp. of the butter in a large skillet over medium-high heat. Add the chicken and cook until the juices run clear, 4 to 5 minutes on each side. Remove the chicken to a plate, cover, and keep warm.

3. Peel, core, and cut each pear into 6-8 slices. Melt the remaining 6 tbsp. butter in the skillet over medium heat. Add the pears and cook, stirring and shaking the pan from time to time, until the pears turn a light brown color, 2 to 3 minutes. Remove the pears from the skillet and add them to the chicken breasts. Cover and keep warm.

4. Add the shallots to the skillet and cook over medium heat until soft, 2 to 3 minutes. Stir in the rosemary, apple juice, and lemon juice and stir to deglaze the bottom of the skillet, scraping up any brown matter sticking to it and stirring it into the liquid in the pan. Bring to a boil and cook until the liquid has reduced to about ¼ cup, about 5 minutes.

5. Stir in the stock, bring to a boil, and cook until the mixture has reduced by about half (approximately ¾ cup liquid remaining). Stir in the cream, pears, and any juices that have accumulated from the chicken and pears. Bring to a bubble and cook until the sauce has thickened slightly, about 2 minutes. Add the chicken breasts and toss with the cream sauce just to heat through.

6. To serve, place one chicken breast on each plate and top with some of the rosemary-pear cream.

Serves 4.

CHICKEN DUMPLINGS IN MADEIRA GRAVY

Just saying "chicken dumplings" makes you feel good, so imagine how you'll feel eating them—especially on a cold, wintry day.

½ cup milk
1½ sticks (¾ cup) unsalted butter, room temperature, divided
1¼ cups all-purpose flour, divided
¾ tsp. salt, divided
1 large egg
3 large egg yolks
1 lb. ground chicken breast

¼ cup heavy cream
¼ tsp. ground nutmeg
8 turns freshly ground black pepper, divided
4 cups chicken stock (see index)
2 cups beef stock (see index)
½ cup Madeira
½ cup chopped fresh parsley

1. Combine the milk with 3 tbsp. of the butter in a 2-qt. saucepan over medium-high heat. Bring to a boil, stirring once or twice. Add 1 cup of the flour and ¼ tsp. of the salt all at once. Stir with a large wooden spoon until the mixture forms a ball of dough. Remove from the heat, turn into a large bowl, and let cool for a few minutes.

2. Using the spoon, beat in the egg and egg yolks, and continue beating until the eggs are thoroughly incorporated.

3. Fold in the ground chicken and blend with the wooden spoon. Blend in 5 tbsp. butter, the cream, nutmeg, and 4 turns of the pepper. Cover and refrigerate for at least 2 hours.

4. About an hour before serving, bring the chicken stock to a boil in a large pot over high heat, about 10 minutes. Reduce the heat to medium and allow the stock to bubble until you're ready for it.

5. Meanwhile, remove the chicken mixture from the refrigerator and form about 20 round dumplings, placing them in a large, deep skillet or pot.

6. Pour the bubbling chicken stock over the dumplings, place over low heat, and cook until the dumplings float to the surface of the stock, 15 to 20 minutes. Remove from the heat.

7. Melt the remaining ¼ cup butter in a medium saucepan over medium heat. Stir in the remaining ¼ cup flour, ½ tsp. salt, and 4 turns pepper. Cook, stirring constantly, until the mixture is golden brown, about 5 minutes. Whisk in the beef stock and cook, whisking constantly, until the sauce thickens, 8 to 10 minutes. Stir in the wine and cook, stirring, until the alcohol has cooked off and the sauce has a smooth, gravylike consistency, about 5 minutes.

8. Use a slotted spoon to transfer the chicken dumplings to serving plates. Spoon the sauce over them and serve, allowing 3 to 5 dumplings per portion. Garnish each serving with chopped parsley.

Serves 4-6.

CHICKEN TIMBALES
WITH ORANGE TARRAGON CREAM

This pretty dish of individual unmolded timbales will be the centerpiece of your party table. You may want to double the recipe in the event of extra guests—or in the event of a request for a second helping.

TIMBALES
2 large chicken breasts, with skin
   and bones
1 large carrot, chopped
2 sprigs fresh parsley
1 tbsp. plus 1 tsp. salt, divided
12 turns freshly ground black
   pepper, divided
¾ cup milk
3 tbsp. unsalted butter, plus more
   for greasing

1 cup minced onions
½ cup minced green bell peppers
½ cup sliced white mushrooms
2 large eggs plus 2 large egg yolks
1 dash hot sauce
1 tbsp. chopped fresh tarragon
Four 8-oz. custard cups or individual
   molds
Whole fresh tarragon sprigs for
   garnish

CREAM
¾ cup chicken stock (see index)
⅓ cup dry white wine
1 tbsp. dry vermouth
¼ cup minced shallots
½ cup heavy cream

1 tbsp. freshly squeezed orange juice
1 tbsp. chopped fresh tarragon
½ tsp. salt
4 turns freshly ground black pepper

1. To make the timbales, place the chicken in a large saucepan and cover with water. Add the carrots, parsley, 1 tbsp. of the salt, and 6 turns of the pepper. Bring to a boil over high heat, reduce the heat to medium, and cook just until the chicken meat loses its pink color all the way through, 10 to 12 minutes.

2. Remove the chicken from the cooking stock and allow it to cool slightly. Remove and discard the skin and bones from the chicken. Chop the meat into small pieces, approximately ¼" square. Set aside.

3. Strain the stock and reserve ¾ cup. Stir the milk into this reserved stock and set aside.

4. Melt 3 tbsp. butter in a medium skillet over medium heat. Add the onions, bell peppers, and mushrooms and cook, stirring occasionally, until the vegetables are soft, about 5 minutes. Set aside.

5. Preheat the oven to 350 degrees.

6. In a small bowl, beat the eggs with the egg yolks until well blended. Pour the stock-milk mixture into a small saucepan over medium heat. Cook just until the mixture begins to bubble, about 3 minutes. Whisk some of this mixture into the egg yolks to temper them. Whisk in some more, then turn it all back into the saucepan. Stir in the hot sauce, chopped tarragon, and the remaining salt and pepper, and heat through.

7. Grease the custard cups or molds with butter. Divide the chicken evenly among the cups. Top each with an equal amount of the sautéed vegetables, and pour the sauce over all.

8. Place the custard cups in a deep baking pan and pour water around the cups to reach about halfway up their sides. Bake until brown and a knife inserted comes out clean, about 45 minutes. Remove from the oven and remove the cups from the pan.

9. Make the cream while the timbales are baking. Combine the stock, wine, vermouth, and shallots in a small saucepan over medium-high heat. Bring to a boil and cook at a rapid bubble until the liquid has reduced to ⅓ cup, about 10 minutes. Stir in the cream and bring back to a bubble. Cook, stirring, until the sauce coats the back of a spoon, about 2 minutes.

10. Stir in the orange juice, tarragon, salt, and pepper and heat through, stirring occasionally, about 2 minutes. Keep warm.

11. To serve, run a sharp knife around the edge of each custard cup and invert on a serving plate. Spoon some of the sauce over each timbale and garnish with tarragon sprigs.

Serves 4.

McGUIRE'S PANEED TURKEY CUTLETS

Cutlets and chops have always been popular pub fare. A "chop and a pint" is a common request at taverns throughout Dublin, Belfast, Carrickmacross, Kalamazoo, and Boston. Less common is a turkey cutlet, since the turkey is usually reserved for special occasions. Sometimes we forget that we actually like the taste of turkey.

Four 6-oz. boneless, skinless turkey-breast cutlets
⅔ cup olive oil
¼ cup plus 2 tbsp. freshly squeezed lemon juice, divided
1 tbsp. Dijon mustard
1 pinch cayenne pepper

2 tsp. dried sage, divided
1½ tsp. salt, divided
8 turns freshly ground black pepper
¾ cup bread crumbs
1 stick unsalted butter
½ cup chopped parsley
2 tbsp. capers

1. Place the turkey cutlets between sheets of wax paper and flatten them with a heavy meat mallet. Place the fillets in a glass baking dish large enough to hold them in a single layer.

2. In a small bowl combine the oil, ¼ cup of the lemon juice, the mustard, cayenne, 1½ tsp. of the sage, 1 tsp. of the salt, and the black pepper. Mix well and pour over the turkey. Cover and marinate in the refrigerator for 1 hour, turning the cutlets after 30 minutes.

3. Combine the bread crumbs with the remaining ½ tsp. salt and ½ tsp. sage in a shallow bowl. Remove the cutlets from the marinade and dredge them in the seasoned bread crumbs, shaking off any excess.

4. Melt the butter in a large, heavy skillet over medium-high heat. Add the turkey cutlets and cook until brown, about 3 minutes each side. Transfer the cutlets to a platter and keep warm.

5. With the skillet still over medium-high heat, add the remaining 2 tbsp. lemon juice, and scrape up the browned bits to deglaze. Stir in the parsley and capers and pour the sauce over the turkey cutlets. Serve immediately.

Serves 4.

STUFFED CORNISH GAME HENS
WITH APPLEJACK GRAVY

You might want to reconsider the main dish you'll be serving on Thanksgiving this year and surprise your family with these delectable stuffed hens swimming in a pool of tipsy gravy.

Four 1- to 1½-lb. Cornish hens
1 tbsp. plus ½ tsp. salt, divided
16 turns freshly ground black pepper
6 tbsp. unsalted butter, divided
1 cup applejack brandy, divided
2 cups crumbled corn bread

¼ cup chopped dates
¼ cup chopped figs
¼ cup chopped walnuts
1 large egg, beaten
¼ cup apple jelly, melted
1 cup heavy cream

1. Preheat the oven to 350 degrees. Clean and rinse the hens and remove the giblets. Combine 1 tbsp. of the salt with the pepper, and sprinkle and rub one-fourth of the mixture on both the inside and outside of each hen.

2. Melt 4 tbs. of the butter in a small saucepan over low heat. Remove from the heat and stir in ¼ cup of the brandy. Set aside.

3. To prepare the stuffing: In a large bowl, combine the crumbled corn bread with the dates, figs, walnuts, and the remaining ½ tsp. salt. Toss the mixture with your hands. Add the beaten egg, and toss again.

4. In a small bowl, combine ¼ cup of the brandy with the melted jelly. Stir this mixture into the corn-bread mixture and blend thoroughly.

5. Divide the stuffing evenly among the hens, filling the cavities loosely. Secure with toothpicks.

6. Place the hens on a rack in a large roasting pan. Brush the hens lavishly with some of the cooled butter-brandy mixture. Roast, basting with the butter-brandy sauce every 20 minutes, until the hens are brown and crisp on the outside, and the legs move easily when jiggled, 1 to 1½ hours.

7. When the hens are done, remove them to a platter, cover loosely with foil, and keep warm. Place the roasting pan on the stove over medium-high heat. Stir the remaining ½ cup brandy into the pan drippings, and deglaze the pan, scraping with a wooden spoon or spatula. Bring to a boil, reduce the heat to medium, and simmer until the alcohol has cooked off, 2 to 3 minutes.

8. Stir in the cream and bring to a bubble, stirring. Cook, stirring constantly,

until the sauce has thickened and reduced by half, about 10 minutes. Remove the pan from the heat and whisk in the remaining 2 tbsp. butter.

9. To serve, pour a puddle of the sauce on each of 4 plates, and top with a hen. Serves 4.

STUFFED QUAIL WITH PILSNER SAUCE

For sweet, flavorful meat you can't do better than the tiny quail. Filled with savory sausage stuffing and floating on a cloud of sauce flavored with pilsner beer and fresh thyme, this dish makes a memorable meal.

QUAIL
Eight 14- to 16-oz. quail
1 tbsp. plus ½ tsp. salt, divided
14 turns freshly ground black pepper, divided
½ lb. whole-wheat bread (about 9 slices)
2 cups peeled, cubed turnips (¼")
1 cup chicken stock (see index)
1 cup milk

¼ lb. sweet Italian sausage
¾ cup chopped onions
¼ cup chopped leeks, white part only
3 tbsp. applejack brandy
2 tbsp. minced fresh parsley
½ tsp. fennel seeds
1 large egg, beaten
Vegetable oil for greasing

SAUCE
3 tbsp. unsalted butter, divided
¾ cup chopped onions
1 tbsp. minced fresh garlic
2 tbsp. all-purpose flour
3 tbsp. pilsner
2 cups chicken stock
1 tbsp. soy sauce

1 tbsp. Dijon mustard
1 tbsp. chopped fresh thyme
1 dash hot sauce
¼ tsp. salt
6 turns freshly ground black pepper
Whole thyme sprigs for garnish

1. Preheat the oven to 250 degrees.

2. Rinse the quail and pat dry with towels. Use a total of 2 tsp. of the salt and 8 turns of the black pepper to sprinkle the insides of the birds, rubbing the seasonings in with your fingers. Set aside.

3. Arrange the bread slices in a single layer on an ungreased baking sheet and

bake, turning the slices once, until toasted through, about 30 minutes. Remove from the oven and increase the oven heat to 350 degree.

4. While the bread is toasting, combine the turnips with the stock and ½ tsp. salt in a medium saucepan over high heat. Bring to a boil and reduce the heat to low. Cover and simmer until the turnips are tender, about 12 minutes. Remove from the heat.

5. Allow the toasted bread to cool slightly, then cut into ½" cubes. Place the cubes in a large bowl, add the milk, and toss to moisten. Allow to stand until the milk is absorbed, stirring once or twice, about 10 minutes.

6. Squeeze the sausage meat out of its casing into a skillet over medium heat. Cook, breaking the meat apart with a fork, until the sausage is brown, about 7 minutes. Remove the sausage with a slotted spoon, reserving the drippings in the skillet, and drain the meat on paper towels.

7. To the drippings in the skillet add the onions and leeks and cook over medium heat, stirring occasionally, until the onions are tender and translucent, about 5 minutes. Stir in the brandy and cook for 2 minutes. Remove from the heat.

8. Turn the onion mixture from the skillet into the bowl of bread. Add the sausage meat, parsley, fennel seeds, egg, and the remaining 1 tsp. salt and 6 turns pepper. Drain the turnips, reserving the stock for another recipe, and fold the turnips into the stuffing mixture. Blend well with a wooden spoon.

9. Grease a large baking sheet with the oil. Divide the stuffing equally among the 8 quail and stuff the cavities. Place the quail breast side up on the baking sheet and roast until golden brown and the juices run clear when pierced with a fork, 35 to 40 minutes.

10. While the quail are roasting, prepare the sauce: Melt 2 tbsp. of the butter in a small saucepan over medium heat. Add the onions and garlic and cook, stirring occasionally, until tender, 4 to 5 minutes. Stir in the flour and cook, stirring often, until it turns a light golden brown, about 4 minutes.

11. Increase the heat to medium-high. Stir in the pilsner and cook for 30 seconds. Stir in the stock, soy sauce, mustard, thyme, and hot sauce and bring to a bubble. Reduce the heat to low and cook, stirring occasionally, until the sauce is thick enough to coat the back of a spoon, about 10 minutes. Remove from the heat.

12. Strain the sauce, discarding the solids. Return the sauce to the saucepan over low heat. Add the salt and pepper, whisk in the remaining tbsp. butter, and heat through.

13. To serve, spoon a puddle of sauce onto each of 4 plates and top with 2 quail. Garnish with sprigs of thyme.

Serves 4.

DUCK BREASTS WITH RASPBERRY PORT-WINE SAUCE

Ducks and geese are often saved for festive times, such as Christmas, but this dish can be enjoyed any time you like.

1½ cups fresh raspberries, divided*
2 tbsp. freshly squeezed lemon juice
¼ cup water
1 tbsp. cornstarch

¼ cup port
4 boneless duck breasts, with skin
½ tsp. salt
8 turns freshly ground black pepper

1. Preheat the broiler.

2. To prepare the sauce, combine 1¼ cups of the raspberries with the lemon juice and water in a small saucepan over medium-high heat. Bring to a boil, reduce the heat to medium-low, and cook until syrupy, stirring occasionally, 10 minutes.

3. Strain the mixture. Discard the seeds and return the syrup to a clean saucepan. Stir in the cornstarch and simmer over low heat until the sauce thickens, about 6 minutes. Stir in the port and cook, stirring occasionally, until the alcohol cooks off, 3 to 4 minutes. Fold in the remaining ¼ cup raspberries and heat through.

4. Place the duck breasts on a broiler pan and season evenly with the salt and pepper. Turn skin side down and place under the broiler until brown, about 6 minutes. Turn the breasts over and broil about 2 minutes longer. Remove the duck to a cutting board, remove and discard the skin, and cut the meat into thin diagonal slices.

5. To serve, place one sliced duck breast on each plate and spoon some of the sauce over it.

Serves 4.

*If raspberries are out of season, thaw and drain an equal quantity of frozen raspberries.

IRISH WHISKEY STEAK

The Irish believe that a person can't have too much Irish whiskey, so eating food made with it, as well as drinking it, must be a real blessing. It flavors meat beautifully and makes this Celtic dish a delicious treat.

¾ cup olive oil
¼ cup balsamic vinegar
2 tbsp. freshly squeezed lemon juice
2 tbsp. Irish whiskey
2 tbsp. soy sauce
1 tbsp. Worcestershire sauce

2 tbsp. chopped fresh parsley
1 tbsp. dry mustard
1 tsp. minced fresh garlic
12 turns freshly ground black pepper
2 lb. flank steak

1. A day ahead: In a small bowl combine the oil, vinegar, lemon juice, whiskey, soy sauce, Worcestershire, parsley, mustard, garlic, and pepper. Place the meat in a large glass baking dish and pour the marinade over it. Turn the meat to coat it evenly, cover the dish, and refrigerate overnight, turning the meat once or twice.

2. Before serving: Preheat a broiler or charcoal grill. Broil or grill the meat, brushing with marinade, about 5 minutes each side for medium-rare.

3. Heat the remaining marinade in a small saucepan over medium heat.

4. Slice the meat against the grain in thin slices and spoon some of the marinade over the slices. Serve with Potatoes and Wild Mushrooms au Gratin (see index).

Serves 6-8.

STAGGERING SKILLET STEAKS
WITH WINEY WILD MUSHROOMS

This is a royal dish for a special occasion. Serve it with Wild Rice Pancakes (see index).

Four 4- to 6-oz. filets mignons, 1¼" thick
3½ tsp. salt, divided
8 turns freshly ground black pepper
½ cup (1 stick) unsalted butter, divided
2 cups sliced fresh wild mushrooms (a mix of chanterelles, shiitakes, creminis, cepes, or your favorites)

¼ cup dry red wine
¼ cup chopped fresh parsley, plus more for garnish, divided
¼ cup olive oil
1 cup chopped onions
⅔ cup Irish whiskey
¾ cup heavy cream

1. Season the steaks with 2 tsp. of the salt and the pepper, and allow them sit out until they are room temperature.

2. Meanwhile, melt ½ stick of the butter in a large skillet over medium heat. Add the mushrooms and 1½ tsp. of the salt and cook, stirring occasionally, until the mushrooms have wilted, about 7 minutes. Stir in the wine, reduce the heat to low, and cover the skillet. Cook, opening to stir occasionally, until the wine has been absorbed by the mushrooms, 10 to 15 minutes. Stir in 2 tbsp. of the parsley, remove from the heat, and set aside to keep warm.

3. Heat the oil with the remaining ½ stick butter in a large, heavy skillet over medium heat. Add the onions and cook until they are tender and translucent, about 5 minutes. Push the onions to one side of the skillet.

4. Increase the heat to medium-high and when the fat sizzles, add the steaks. Cook until rare, 3 minutes on each side, or medium-rare, 5 minutes per side. Just before they are cooked on the second side, add the whiskey, ignite it with a long match, and allow the whiskey to burn off. Remove the steaks to a platter and cover to keep warm.

5. Increase the heat under the skillet to high and stir in the cream and 2 tbsp. parsley. Cook, stirring often, until the sauce has reduced by half, about 5 minutes.

6. To serve, spoon a puddle of the cream sauce on each plate, place a fillet on the sauce, and top with the mushrooms and parsley.

Serves 4.

BURGUNDY-SOUSED ROAST
WITH LEEKS AND WILD MUSHROOMS

Beef is a traditional Sunday lunch in Ireland. But any time you serve this savory roast it's going to get wows. The meat's long soak in a Burgundy marinade makes it tender and delicious.

One 3- to 4-lb. eye of round roast, trimmed
1 tsp. salt, divided
12 turns freshly ground black pepper, divided
¼ tsp. garlic powder
1½ cups red Burgundy

3 lb. fresh wild mushrooms, any kind
2 tbsp. olive oil
3 cloves garlic, minced
2 large leeks, cleaned thoroughly, in ¼" rings
1 cup chicken stock
1 tbsp. unsalted butter

1. A day ahead: Rub the roast all over with ½ tsp. of the salt, 8 turns of the pepper, and the garlic powder. Place the roast in a bowl and pour the wine over. Cover the bowl and marinate in your refrigerator for 24 hours, turning the meat every 3 to 8 hours (don't wake yourself up during the night to turn the meat; it can wait until morning).

2. About an hour and a half before serving, preheat the oven to 325 degrees.

3. Remove the roast from the bowl and place it in a shallow baking dish. Pour the marinade over the meat and roast until a meat thermometer inserted into the thickest part registers 140 degrees, about 50 to 60 minutes. Allow the meat to cool slightly before slicing.

4. While the meat is roasting, prepare the mushrooms and leeks: Slice the mushrooms into quarters. Heat the oil in a large heavy skillet over high heat. Add the mushrooms and cook, shaking the pan from time to time, until they begin to caramelize—turning brown and sticky—5 to 7 minutes. Stir in the garlic and ¼ tsp. of the salt. Cook until the garlic is soft, about 3 minutes. Remove from the heat and set aside.

5. In a medium saucepan over medium heat, cook the leeks in the stock with the remaining ¼ tsp. salt and the remaining 4 turns black pepper. Simmer until the leeks are soft and the stock cooked off almost completely, about 20 minutes. Stir the leeks into the mushrooms, and fold in the butter.

6. Spoon the mixture over the sliced meat and serve with Horseradish Potato Mash or Potato Dumplings with Wild Mushroom Cream.

Serves 6.

GUINNESS-STOUT POT ROAST

Porter, which is a weaker beer although darker in color than Guinness, was originally used for stewing meat. But the Irish discovered that one of their national drinks—Guinness stout—gives meat a richer flavor. Make this the day before serving it to allow the flavors to marry and to make it easy to remove as much fat as possible.

½ cup all-purpose flour
1½ tbsp. salt, divided
8 turns freshly ground black pepper, divided
2 tbsp. vegetable oil
One 3-lb. chuck or blade roast
1½ cups peeled, sliced onions (½" thick)

3 cups Guinness stout
1 cup beef stock (see index)
1 bay leaf
2 lb. new potatoes (about 12), in their skins
2 cups sliced carrots
1 cup pitted prunes
2 tbsp. chopped fresh parsley

1. Combine the flour with 1 tbs. of the salt and 4 turns of the pepper in a large bowl. Start heating the oil in a large, heavy pot over medium-high heat.

2. Place the roast in the bowl and coat it with the seasoned flour. Reserve the remaining flour mixture. When the oil is spitting hot, add the roast and cook until it is brown all over, 3 to 4 minutes on each side. Add the onions and cook 1 minute. Reduce the heat to medium and stir in the reserved flour. Cook, stirring often, until the mixture is golden, 3 to 5 minutes.

3. Stir in the Guinness, stock, bay leaf, and the remaining ½ tbsp. salt and 4 turns pepper. Cover the pot, reduce the heat to medium-low, and cook until the meat is tender and falling off the bone, about 3 hours. Remove the meat to a bowl and pour the gravy into a container. Allow both to cool to room temperature, and refrigerate overnight.

4. The next day, remove the meat and gravy from the refrigerator. Skim the congealed fat from the gravy, and return both meat and gravy to the pot over medium-high heat. When the gravy bubbles, add the potatoes, carrots, and prunes. Cover the pot and reduce the heat to medium-low. Cook until the vegetables are firm-tender, 25 to 30 minutes. Remove the bay leaf.

5. Remove the roast and slice thin. To serve, arrange several slices of meat on each plate, spoon some of the gravy over the meat, and sprinkle with chopped parsley. Serve with icy mugs of stout.

Serves 6.

BEEFCAKE WITH BURGUNDY MUSHROOM CREAM

A meat loaf by any other name would taste just as good, and in this case, bet-ter. This one is a juicy loaf topped with a sauce that resembles a Stroganoff reduction laced with Burgundy.

BEEFCAKE

1 tbsp. vegetable oil
⅔ cup minced onions
2 lb. ground sirloin or other lean ground beef
1½ cups fresh bread crumbs (see index)
2 large eggs, beaten

2 tbsp. ketchup
1 tsp. Worcestershire sauce
2 tbsp. chopped fresh parsley
½ tsp. dried or 2 tsp. chopped fresh thyme
1½ tsp. salt
6 turns freshly ground black pepper

BURGUNDY MUSHROOM CREAM

6 tbsp. unsalted butter, divided
½ cup chopped onions
1 tsp. minced fresh garlic
3 cups sliced fresh white mush-rooms, divided
1½ cups beef stock (see index)

½ cup Burgundy or other dry red wine
1 tsp. paprika
½ tsp. salt
8 turns freshly ground black pepper
1 cup sour cream
2 tbsp. minced fresh parsley

1. Preheat the oven to 350 degrees.

2. Heat the oil in a small skillet over medium heat. Add the onions and cook, stirring occasionally, until the onions are tender, about 5 minutes. Remove from the heat.

3. In a large bowl combine the beef, onions, bread crumbs, eggs, ketchup, Worcestershire, parsley, thyme, salt, and pepper, and mix thoroughly with your hands. Gently shape the mixture into a loaf (don't pack it or it will be heavy) on a broiler pan or the perforated grid of a baking pan and bake until golden brown on the outside and medium inside, about 1 hour.

4. While the beefcake is baking, prepare the sauce. Melt 4 tbsp. of the butter in a large, deep skillet over medium heat. Add the onions, garlic, and 2 cups of the mushrooms. Cook, stirring occasionally, until the vegetables are tender and most of the mushroom liquid has evaporated, 6 to 8 minutes. Transfer the mixture to the bowl of a food processor and puree until smooth. Return the mixture to the skillet.

5. Melt the remaining 2 tbsp. butter in a medium skillet over medium heat. Add the remaining 1 cup mushrooms and cook, shaking the skillet often, until tender, 4 to 5 minutes.

6. Fold the sautéed mushrooms into the puree in the large skillet. Stir in the rich (reduced) stock, wine, paprika, salt, and pepper and bring to a bubble. Reduce the heat to low and simmer, stirring occasionally, until the wine is incorporated and the alcohol cooked off, about 5 minutes.

7. Temper some of the hot sauce—a little at a time—into the sour cream, then fold the sour cream into the sauce. Stir in the parsley and heat through, 3 to 4 minutes.

8. To serve, spoon some of the sauce onto each plate and top with 1 or 2 slices of the beef loaf. Complete the meal with buttered egg noodles.

Serves 6-8.

SOUSED CORNED BEEF IN HORSERADISH SAUCE

Corned beef and cabbage is probably the best-known traditional Irish meal in America, but it usually holds no surprises. So chef Sharan Sheppard coaxed this standby into something even more flavorful and inventive. In her version, the tender corned beef, which has simmered for hours in ale, comes served up in horseradish sauce. You can dazzle the crowd on St. Patrick's—or any other day—with this feast, especially if you serve it with Cabbage Bread Pudding.

CORNED BEEF

2 tbsp. vegetable oil

One 4- to 5-lb. corned beef brisket

12 oz. pale ale

1 bay leaf

¼ tsp. ground cloves

1 tsp. salt

8 turns freshly ground black pepper

1 recipe Cabbage Bread Pudding (see index)

HORSERADISH SAUCE

¼ cup unsalted butter

¼ cup all-purpose flour

8 turns freshly ground black pepper

1 cup strained, defatted drippings from corned beef

2 cups milk

2 tbsp. prepared white horseradish

½ cup chopped fresh parsley

1. To cook the beef, heat the oil in a large, heavy pot over medium-high heat. Add the corned beef and sear lightly on all sides. Add the ale, bay leaf, cloves, salt, and pepper. Add enough water to cover the beef, tip the lid halfway over the pot, and bring to a boil. Reduce the heat to medium-low, and simmer until the meat is tender, adding hot water as necessary, 3½ to 4 hours.

2. Remove the corned beef, reserving the drippings. Shred the meat, removing and discarding as much visible fat as possible. Set aside, covered, in a warm place.

3. To prepare a roux for the sauce, melt the butter in a saucepan over medium heat. Stir in the flour and cook, stirring constantly, 3 to 4 minutes. Stir in the pepper.

4. Slowly whisk in the beef drippings and milk. Bring to a bubble, reduce the heat to low, and simmer, stirring often, until the sauce has thickened, 9 to 10 minutes. Stir in the horseradish and the corned beef and heat thoroughly.

5. To serve, cut the bread pudding into squares, top with the sauced corned beef, and garnish with the parsley.

Serves 8.

Note: Every St. Patrick's Day, chef Gene Lang and the kitchen crew at McGuire's cook up 1,500 lb. of corned beef and cabbage for about 2,000 celebrants!

VEAL SCALLOPS AND ARTICHOKES

For a marriage made in heaven, serve this with Lemon Rice Bundt.

2 lb. veal scallops
½ cup all-purpose flour
1 tsp. salt
5 turns freshly ground black pepper
2 tbsp. olive oil
1 tbsp. unsalted butter, room temperature
1 tsp. minced fresh garlic

2 cups chicken stock (see index)
⅔ cup dry vermouth
½ tsp. dried marjoram
2 bay leaves
3 cups frozen artichoke hearts, thawed and quartered
4 lemon slices (¼" thick)
Chopped fresh parsley

1. Place the veal scallops between sheets of plastic wrap and pound them with a meat mallet until they are thin and tender. Combine the flour, salt, and pepper in a shallow bowl or pan.

2. Start heating the oil and butter in a large skillet over medium heat. Dredge

the veal in the flour mixture and shake off any excess. When the fat in the skillet is hot and sizzling, add the veal scallops in batches, dredging immediately before putting them in the fat. Cook until the veal is light brown, turning once, 2 to 3 minutes on each side. Remove the scallops as they cook and keep warm.

3. To the skillet over medium-high heat, add the garlic and cook, stirring occasionally, until soft, 1 to 2 minutes. Add the stock, vermouth, marjoram, and bay leaves. Bring to a rapid bubble, stirring constantly.

4. Return the veal and any accumulated juices to the skillet. Add the artichoke hearts and lemon slices, folding them into the liquid. Cover the skillet, reduce the heat to low, and cook at a simmer for 10 minutes. Remove the bay leaves and lemon slices and transfer the meat and artichokes to a platter. Garnish with chopped parsley and serve with Lemon Rice Bundt (see index).

Serves 8.

CRUSTED RACK OF LAMB
WITH PORT-WINE CHERRY SAUCE

At one time in Ireland, the meat of sheep, or mutton, was frequently served in households that could afford to eat meat. Today mutton is rarely served, since the younger, more tender cuts of lamb are preferred. For special effect, present the uncut rack at the table before slicing it into individual chops.

LAMB

One 2½- to 3-lb., 8-rib rack of lamb,
   trimmed of excess fat (have a
   good butcher prepare this for you)
¼ cup Dijon mustard
¼ cup bread crumbs
¼ cup minced hazelnuts (filberts)
¼ cup minced walnuts

1 tbsp. crushed whole juniper
   berries*
1 tsp. dried thyme
½ tsp. salt
8 turns freshly ground black pepper

SAUCE

1⅓ cups port
⅔ cup beef stock (see index)
6 tbs. honey
1 tsp. dried or 1 tbsp. chopped fresh
    thyme
½ tsp. dry mustard

½ tsp. salt
1½ tbsp. cornstarch
¼ cup balsamic vinegar
One 16-oz. can pitted dark cherries
    (not sweet), drained

1. Preheat the oven to 375 degrees.

2. Place the lamb, standing up in a crown shape, in a roasting pan. Smear the entire surface of the roast with mustard. In a small bowl, combine the bread crumbs, hazelnuts, walnuts, juniper berries, thyme, salt, and pepper. Using your hands, carefully pat the mixture over the lamb, forming a crust.

3. Insert a meat thermometer into the thickest part of the meat. Roast for 15 minutes, then cover with foil. Continue roasting until the meat thermometer reaches 145 degrees and the meat is brown and crusty and pink inside, about 45 minutes in all. While the meat is roasting, prepare the sauce. Remove the meat from the oven and allow it to stand for 10 minutes before slicing.

4. In a saucepan over medium-high heat, combine the port, stock, honey, thyme, mustard, and salt. Bring to a boil and cook, stirring, 1 minute.

5. Combine the cornstarch with the vinegar in a cup and stir until the cornstarch is completely dissolved. Stir this into the port mixture and cook, stirring, until the sauce thickens, about 6 minutes. Stir in the cherries, and heat through.

6. To serve, separate the lamb chops, arrange 2 on each plate, and cover with some of the sauce.

Serves 4.

*Juniper berries are available at specialty food markets and many grocery stores.

LAMB SHANKS AND LENTILS BAKED IN WINE

With the meat fairly melting off the lamb bones into a bed of winey vegetables, this peasant-style dinner embodies quintessential feel-good-ness.

1 tbsp. olive oil
¼ cup chopped onions
1 tsp. minced fresh garlic
1½ cups dried lentils, rinsed and
    picked over
¼ cup chopped fresh parsley, plus
    more for garnish
⅓ cup grated carrots (about 1 large
    carrot)
1 tbsp. plus 1 tsp. salt, divided

24 turns freshly ground black pep-
    per, divided
2½ cups beef stock (see index)
1 cup dry white wine
1 tbsp. Dijon mustard
4 lamb shanks (about 3 lb.), silver-
    skin and excess fat removed
6 cups fresh spinach, rinsed,
    stemmed, and patted dry

1. Preheat the oven to 300 degrees.

2. Heat the oil in a small skillet over medium-high heat. Add the onions and garlic and cook, stirring often, just until the vegetables are tender and translucent, 3 to 4 minutes. Remove from the heat.

3. In a large bowl combine the lentils, parsley, carrots, 1 tsp. of the salt, and 8 turns of the pepper. Stir in the sautéed onions and garlic, the stock, wine, and mustard. Mix well. Pour the lentil mixture into a 9" x 13" baking dish.

4. Season the lamb shanks, using ½ tsp. salt and 4 turns pepper for each, rubbing the seasoning into the meat with your hands.

5. Arrange the lamb shanks on top of the lentil mixture. Cover tightly with foil and bake for 2 hours. Remove the foil and continue baking until the meat is tender enough to fall off the bones when poked with a fork, and most of the liquid has been absorbed by the lentils. Remove from the oven.

6. Just before the lamb is done, bring 2" of water to a boil in a large pot with a steamer basket. Place the spinach in the basket. Sprinkle evenly with the remaining 1 tsp. salt and steam just until the leaves begin to wilt, about 20 seconds. Remove the spinach immediately and transfer it to a large serving platter. Ladle or spoon the lentils over the spinach, leaving a border of green. Arrange the lamb shanks on top, sprinkle with parsley, and serve.

Serves 4.

RUM AND COKE BAKED HAM
WITH RED-EYE GRAVY

This succulent ham goes perfectly with Blackeye Pea Pudding. Because its sauce is known as "red-eye gravy"* and the peas are blackeyes, this meal could be called "Irish Eyes." The whole deal makes a great Sunday dinner for the family.

2 cups nondiet cola
⅓ cup rum, light or dark
14 whole cloves
One 8-lb. fresh ham

1 large white unpeeled potato
12 turns freshly ground black pepper
½ cup strong, brewed coffee

1. Preheat the oven to 350 degrees. Combine the cola with the rum and cloves in a small bowl.

2. Line a large roasting pan with foil. Add several more layers of long sheets of foil and place the ham and potato in the center of these sheets. Pour the cola mixture over the ham, grind the pepper over all, and wrap loosely with the foil. Bake, basting every half-hour, 15 to 20 minutes per pound, about 2½ hours in all. Remove from the oven, transfer the ham to a serving platter, and keep warm.

3. Discard the potato and cloves, and pour the cooking juices, cola-rum mixture, and browned bits into a saucepan over medium-high heat. Bring to a boil and cook until slightly reduced and somewhat thickened, 1 to 2 minutes. Stir in the coffee, and cook another minute. Remove from the heat.

4. Slice the ham and serve with Blackeye Pea Pudding (see index), with the red-eye gravy spooned over the pudding.

Serves 10-12.

*Red-eye gravy is a traditional Southern American gravy that has been popular since the 1930s. As it reduces, a red eye seems to appear in the gravy.

BEER-BRAISED HONEY-MUSTARD PORK CHOPS WITH WHITE BEAN PUREE

At one time there were pork butchers in all the towns in Ireland, but today pork has been relegated to the meat counter in supermarkets, much as it is in America. The lightness of the bean puree is a wonderful contrast to the deep, complex flavors of this stove-top dish.

2 tbsp. olive oil, divided
½ cup chopped onions
½ tsp. minced fresh garlic
2 cups canned white beans (Great Northern or navy beans), drained and rinsed
¼ cup chopped fresh parsley
1½ tsp. rubbed sage
1¼ cups chicken stock, divided

1½ tsp. salt, divided
20 turns freshly ground black pepper, divided
8 loin or rib pork chops, about 1" thick
½ cup beer
¼ cup honey
2 tsp. dry mustard
1 tbsp. unsalted butter, cut into bits

1. To make the puree, heat 1 tbsp. of the oil in a medium saucepan over medium heat. Add the onions and garlic and cook, stirring occasionally, until tender and golden, 5 to 6 minutes. Stir in the beans, parsley, sage, and ¾ cup of the stock. Simmer over medium heat, stirring occasionally, until the flavors have married, 5 to 7 minutes.

2. Pour the bean mixture into the bowl of a food processor and puree. Return the mixture to the saucepan and stir in the remaining ½ cup stock, ½ tsp. of the salt, and 4 turns of the black pepper. Heat through and turn off the heat. Cover and keep warm.

3. Season the chops with the remaining 1 tsp. salt and 16 turns pepper.

4. In a large skillet heat the remaining 1 tbsp. oil over medium-high heat and brown the chops, 1 to 2 minutes on each side. Add the beer and bring to a bubble. Reduce the heat to low, cover, and simmer, turning the chops once, until they are tender, about 20 minutes in all. Remove the beer with a bulb baster to a bowl and reserve it. Increase the heat to medium and cook off most of the remaining liquid.

5. Stir the honey and mustard into the reserved beer, add the mixture to the skillet, and bring to a boil. Continue to cook over medium heat, turning the chops often, just until the meat has caramelized. Remove the chops and keep warm.

6. Swirl the butter into the remaining sauce a bit at a time, whisking until completely emulsified.

7. To serve, spoon a puddle of the puree on each plate, top with 2 pork chops, and nap with beer sauce.

Serves 4.

PIG IN A POKE WITH GREEN PEPPERCORN SAUCE

A "pig in a poke" is something that's hard to find, and since these elegant packages hide their filling of pork tenderloins, the name seemed appropriate.

PORK

2 whole pork tenderloins, 2 to 2½ lb. each
1 tbsp. olive oil
8 cups fresh spinach, rinsed and stemmed
1 cup feta cheese*
½ cup pine nuts, lightly toasted (see index)

½ tsp. fennel seeds
16 turns freshly ground black pepper, divided
3/4 cup (1½ sticks) unsalted butter
One 16-oz. pkg. fillo dough, thawed according to pkg. directions**

GREEN PEPPERCORN SAUCE

3 tbsp. unsalted butter, divided
1½ tbsp. minced scallions (green onions), green tops only
2 tbsp. brandy
1 cup beef stock (see index)

1 tbsp. all-purpose flour
1 tbsp. green peppercorns, divided
¼ tsp. salt
4 turns freshly ground black pepper
¼ cup heavy cream

1. To prepare the pork, remove membrane and all visible fat from the tenderloins.

2. Heat the oil in a skillet over medium-high heat and brown the meat on all sides, about 8 minutes. Remove the tenderloins from the skillet and drain on a rack set over a baking sheet.

3. Steam the spinach in a covered basket set on a pot of simmering water over medium-low heat until wilted, 2 to 3 minutes. Drain the spinach, place it in a food processor, and chop.

4. Combine the spinach, feta cheese, pine nuts, fennel seeds, and 8 turns of the pepper in a large bowl. Mix well with your hands.

5. Preheat the oven to 375 degrees.

6. Melt the butter in a small saucepan over low heat. As soon as the butter is melted, remove from the heat.

7. Remove the fillo dough from the package and cover it with a sheet of plastic wrap and a damp cloth (see index). Place one sheet of the dough on a flat surface and brush lightly with butter all the way to the edges (keep the remaining sheets of fillo covered so they won't dry out). Place another sheet of fillo on top of the first, brush it with butter, and continue until there are 12 layers of dough in all.

8. Spread half of the spinach mixture on one end of the top layer of dough, leaving a 2" border and covering one-quarter of the fillo sheet. Top with 4 turns of the pepper.

9. Place one tenderloin on top of the spinach mixture, fold the ends in, and brush with butter. Roll up, buttering the fillo with each turn. Brush the entire roll with butter, place seam side down on a wire rack over a baking pan, and cover with waxed paper. Repeat with the remaining fillo dough, spinach mixture, pepper, and tenderloin.

10. Bake until the dough is golden brown and crispy, 25 to 30 minutes. Remove from the oven and allow to cool for 10 minutes.

11. To make the sauce, in a small saucepan melt 2 tbsp. of the butter over medium heat. Add the scallions and cook, stirring occasionally, until soft, about 2 minutes. Stir in the brandy and stock and bring to a boil. Reduce the heat to low and cook until the mixture reduces to 3/4 cup. Strain and pour back into the saucepan.

12. In a small bowl mash the remaining 1 tbs. butter with the flour, forming a beurre manié, which is simply a butter and flour paste. Whisk half of the beurre manié into the sauce over medium heat until it is incorporated, then whisk in the remaining butter mixture until the sauce is thoroughly emulsified.

13. Crush 1 tsp. of the peppercorns with a meat mallet or a mortar and pestle. Stir both the crushed peppercorns and the whole peppercorns into the sauce. Reduce the heat to low and simmer, stirring occasionally, 5 minutes.

14. Stir in the salt, black pepper, and cream and heat through.

15. To serve, present the dish before slicing, as the crust is very pretty when it is intact. Cut in 1½" slices and serve on a pool of the sauce.

Serves 6-8.

*Feta cheese made from sheep's milk is very popular in Ireland. It is best when purchased moist from a tub, rather than commercially packaged.

**Once you begin working with the fillo pastry, work fast and keep buttering it. Don't prepare both crusts at once—do them one at a time so the second one doesn't dry out.

SHARAN'S IRISH BARBECUE WITH APPLE-BEER BASTE

Sharan Sheppard is originally from North Carolina, where barbecue is always chopped. Texans sneer at such shenanigans, because their barbecue is always sliced. In Ireland, both pork and cabbage are big favorites, but since I'm not sure whether barbecue even exists there, I think you can decide for yourself whether you want to chop or slice the meat before serving it.

BASTING SAUCE

½ cup apple jelly

½ cup ketchup

½ cup beer

¼ cup frozen apple juice
concentrate, thawed

2 tbsp. Worcestershire sauce

1 tsp. hot sauce

1 tsp. chili powder

½ tsp. garlic powder

PORK

2 cups applewood chips*

2 lb. pork tenderloins

1. To make the barbecue sauce, combine the apple jelly, ketchup, beer, apple juice concentrate, Worcestershire sauce, hot sauce, chili powder, and garlic powder in a small saucepan over low heat. Cook, stirring, until the jelly has melted and all of the ingredients are thoroughly blended. Remove from the heat and divide the sauce in half, pouring it into 2 small bowls.

2. Start heating your grill or oven. If you're using a charcoal grill, heat the coals until they've turned white. If you use a gas grill, set it at medium heat. If you're using your oven, preheat it to 350 degrees.

3. Soak the applewood chips in water for about an hour in advance, remove them from the water, and wrap them in heavy-duty foil, leaving a space open at the top to form a chimney. Place the foil package, chimney side up, on top of the coals. If you're using an oven, place the package of wood chips in a deep roasting pan and set the rack of the pan on top.

4. To prepare the pork, trim off the silvery membrane and any excess fat. Place the meat on the grill or the rack as close to the center as possible. Cover the grill or roasting pan and let the meat smoke (without sauce) for 5 minutes. Brush with some of the sauce, turn the meat, cover, and smoke 5 minutes. Continue this way, brushing and turning until the pork is thoroughly cooked and tender, for a total of approximately 25 minutes. Remove the meat to a cutting board and allow it to rest for 5 minutes.

5. Reheat the remaining sauce over low heat. Cut the meat Texas style in thin slices across the grain, or chop into bite-size pieces, if you prefer your Irish barbecue àla North Carolina. Serve with Apple-Scented Slaw and Onion Pudding (see index).

Serves 4-6.

*If you can't find applewood chips, use soaked hickory chips and add apple peels and cores to get the apple aroma.

HONEY BEER-BRAISED RIBS

Marinate these sticky-delicious ribs a day ahead. Then grill them on the barbie or easy-bake them in your oven.

½ cup dark beer
½ cup honey
1 tbsp. freshly squeezed lemon juice
½ tbsp. salt
1 tsp. chili powder

1 tsp. dried sage
¾ tsp. dry mustard
2 racks pork spareribs, about 2 lb. each

1. Combine the beer, honey, lemon juice, salt, chili powder, sage, and mustard in a small saucepan over low heat. Cook at a simmer, stirring often, until the ingredients are blended, about 5 minutes. Remove from the heat and cool slightly.

2. Place the ribs, meat side down, in a large roasting pan. Brush with the marinade and drizzle the rest into the pan. Cover and refrigerate overnight, turning the ribs over and basting with the marinade about halfway through.

3. To grill, remove the ribs from the refrigerator about 3 hours before serving. Pour the marinade into a saucepan over medium-low heat. Bring to a bubble, stirring, and remove from the heat. Prepare the coals, and when they're hot, move them to one side of the grill. Place the ribs on the side of the grill away from the coals. Grill slowly, turning the ribs and basting with the marinade every 20 minutes, until the ribs are fully cooked and tender, about 2½ hours in all.

4. If you are baking instead, preheat the oven to 350 degrees. Bake the ribs on a rack in the roasting pan, turning and basting with marinade every 20 minutes, until tender, 1 to 1½ hours in all.

5. Serve the ribs with Red Potato Salad with Warm Beer Dressing and Three-Cabbage Slaw or Onion Pudding (see index).

Serves 4.

BEERY BRATWURST
WITH SAUERKRAUT DUMPLINGS

Just add McGuire's Famous Irish-Fried Onion Rings (see index), and you'll have a rib-sticking winter meal worth raving about.

DUMPLING DOUGH

2 cups all-purpose flour

1 tsp. salt

1 large egg

½ cup milk

DUMPLING FILLING

2 tbsp. unsalted butter

½ cup chopped onions

¾ cup (packed) sauerkraut, rinsed and squeezed dry

½ tsp. granulated sugar

½ tsp. salt

4 turns freshly ground black pepper

½ cup dry white wine

2 tbsp. sour cream

BRATWURST

2 lb. bratwurst links, 8 to 10 links

2 tbsp. vegetable oil

1 cup green bell pepper strips

½ cup red bell pepper strips

⅔ cup chopped leeks

½ cup chopped celery

1 tbsp. minced fresh garlic

2 tsp. flour

1 tsp. fennel seeds

½ tsp. salt

8 turns freshly ground black pepper

3 cups beer, room temperature

3-4 qt. chicken stock (see index), or water

1. To prepare the dough, combine the flour and salt in a medium bowl. Whisk the egg until it's frothy, and combine it with the dry ingredients. Slowly stir in the milk until the mixture comes away from the sides of the bowl in a ball. Turn out the dough on a floured surface and knead until the consistency is smooth and satiny, about 8 minutes. Wrap the dough and refrigerate for at least 1 hour.

2. To make the filling, melt the butter in a large skillet over medium heat. Add the onions and cook until translucent, 4 to 5 minutes. Stir in the sauerkraut and cook, stirring, until golden, 4 to 5 minutes.

3. Stir in the sugar, salt, pepper, and wine, and bring to a bubble. Reduce the heat to low, cover, and cook, stirring occasionally, until all of the wine has evaporated, about 30 minutes. Keep your eye on this to prevent scorching.

4. Remove from the heat and turn the mixture into a bowl. Allow to cool for about 10 minutes. Stir in the sour cream, cover, and refrigerate for 1 hour.

5. To cook the bratwurst, heat a large skillet over high heat. Add the bratwurst, reduce the heat to medium, and cook, turning the sausages, until they are brown on all sides, about 6 minutes total. Remove the bratwurst from the skillet; drain off and discard the fat.

6. Place the skillet back over medium-high heat and add the oil. When the oil is hot, stir in the green and red peppers, leeks, and celery. Cook, stirring often, until the leeks are transparent, about 2 minutes. Stir in the garlic and cook until tender, about 1 minute.

7. Reduce the heat to medium and stir in the flour, coating the vegetables. Cook, stirring occasionally, until the flour turns golden brown, about 2 minutes. Stir in the fennel seeds, salt, and pepper.

8. Slowly stir in the beer—just a little at a time—stirring constantly to avoid lumps. Bring to a bubble and add the sausage. Reduce the heat to low, cover, and cook until the sausage is tender and the gravy is smooth and thick, about 1 hour.

9. To prepare the dumplings, remove the dough and the filling from the refrigerator. Flatten the dough on a lightly floured surface, until about ¼" thick. Use a biscuit cutter or the rim of an overturned glass to cut circles approximately 4" in diameter.

10. Place about 1½ tbsp. of filling in the center of each dough round. Fold each in half, sealing the edges with a little water. Use the tines of a fork to crimp the edges. Makes about 24 dumplings.

11. Bring the chicken stock or water to a boil in a wide pot. Slide in the dumplings, a few at a time, and bring back to a bubble. Reduce the heat to low, cover tightly, and cook until the dumplings bounce to the top, 10 to 12 minutes.

12. Remove the dumplings with a slotted spoon, and transfer them to the bubbling skillet of bratwurst, gently folding the dumplings into the gravy.

13. Serve in shallow bowls, allowing 4 to 6 dumplings per portion.
Serves 4-6.

IRISH RED PLATE

This delicious combination of sausage and red cabbage with pickled beets and horseradish is the kind of hearty fare you might find in the kitchen on a cold winter night in Dublin.

HORSERADISH VINAIGRETTE

1½ tbsp. prepared horseradish
1 tbsp. Dijon mustard
¼ tsp. salt

5 turns freshly ground black pepper
3 tbsp. balsamic vinegar
½ cup vegetable oil

RED PLATE

¼ cup (½ stick) unsalted butter
½ cup chopped onions
2 tsp. minced fresh garlic
½ cup peeled, chopped apples
3/4 cup pickled beet juice (from pickled beets, below)
5 cups shredded red cabbage

½ tsp. salt
1 tbsp. olive oil
2 lb. kielbasa sausage, cut into 6" pieces
1 cup dry white wine
2 cups pickled beets (see index)
½ cup minced parsley

1. To make the vinaigrette, combine the horseradish, mustard, salt, and pepper in a small bowl and whisk in the vinegar, whisking until the mixture is blended. Slowly stream in the oil, whisking constantly, until the vinaigrette is thick and emulsified. Set aside.

2. To make the red plate, melt the butter in a large, heavy pot over medium heat. Add the onions, garlic, and apples and cook until tender, about 5 minutes. Stir in the beet juice and cook, stirring and scraping the bottom of the pot to deglaze. Fold in the cabbage and salt and bring to a bubble. Cover, reduce the heat to low, and cook, stirring once to fold the cabbage into the juice, until the cabbage is tender, about 15 minutes.

3. While the cabbage is cooking, heat the oil in a large, heavy skillet over medium-high heat. Add the sausage to the skillet and cook, turning the sausage once or twice, until the meat is brown on all sides, about 6 minutes. Add the wine, and bring to a bubble. Cover and cook, shaking the skillet occasionally, until the wine has evaporated, 5 to 6 minutes. Remove from the heat.

4. Add the pickled beets to the vinaigrette, and toss to coat them.

5. To serve, arrange several pieces of kielbasa on each plate next to a mound of the cabbage and ⅓ cup of the vinaigrette-covered pickled beets. Sprinkle with the minced parsley.

Serves 6.

Under
Cover:

Savory Pies
and Tarts

Main-dish pies, or "potpies," have long been popular in many parts of the world—Ireland and America no exception. The surprise of finding a savory stew under a flaky crust seems to tickle many and appears to make eating even more fun, if that's possible.

The appeal of a potpie or savory tart also goes well with the particular charm of the pub. Eating comforting food in a cheerful place that keeps the cares of the world at bay is definitely agreeable.

Not only are savory pies a treat to eat, they are surprisingly easy to make. Some call for ready-made crusts, such as Lamb Meatball Pie with Fillo Crust and individual Steak and Mushroom Pies with their ready-to-use puff pastry. Others have potato crusts: Sheep Herder's Pie and Colcannon Torte. And Turkey Oyster Torte with Béchamel has a crust made of stuffing.

But the pastry crusts are not difficult, and they are rewarding. Try the Irish favorite, Chicken and Ham Pie, or Dilly Seafood Cobbler with Dill Pastry. Turnip and Scallion Flans with Canadian Bacon and Hollandaise Sauce have no pastry at all, and Vegetable Cheese Pizza Pie has a pizza crust, of course.

CHICKEN AND HAM PIE

This national favorite is frequently prepared in Irish homes, and it is also available for sale in many food stores for those who have no time to cook. Chicken and ham pies are a staple in Irish pubs.

4 large chicken breast halves
1 large onion, cut into rough chunks
1 celery stalk, cut into rough chunks
2 tsp. salt, divided
½ cup unsalted butter, divided
1 cup sliced white mushrooms
¼ cup chopped scallions (green onions)
⅓ cup all-purpose flour

1½ cups heavy cream, divided
3½ cups milk
¼ cup sherry
4 large egg yolks
8 turns freshly ground black pepper
2 cups diced cooked ham
1 cup fresh shelled green peas
1 recipe unbaked double pastry dough (see index)

1. Place the chicken breasts in a soup pot with the onions, celery, and 1 tsp. of the salt. Cover with water and bring to a boil over high heat. Reduce the heat to medium-low and simmer until the chicken is tender, 20 to 30 minutes. Remove the chicken from the pot. When it's cool enough to handle, remove the skin and bones, cut the meat into bite-size pieces, and set aside. You should have about 3 cups. Strain the cooking stock, discarding the solids and reserving 1½ cups. Freeze the rest for future use (see index).

2. Melt 2 tbsp. of the butter in a skillet over medium heat. Add the mushrooms and scallions and cook, shaking the skillet occasionally, until the onions are soft and translucent, 3 to 5 minutes. Place the vegetables on paper towels to drain.

3. Melt the remaining 6 tbsp. butter in the skillet over medium heat. Stir in the flour and cook over low heat, stirring constantly, for 1 minute. Gradually stir in 1 cup of the cream, the milk, sherry, and reserved chicken stock. Cook, stirring constantly, until the sauce begins to bubble and is thick enough to coat the back of a spoon, about 8 minutes.

4. Preheat the oven to 450 degrees.

5. Beat the egg yolks into the remaining ½ cup cream. Temper the mixture by gradually stirring ¼ cup of the hot sauce mixture into the egg-cream mixture, then slowly stir the tempered mixture back into the hot sauce, stirring constantly. Stir in the remaining 1 tsp. salt and the black pepper.

6. Fold in the chicken, ham, mushrooms, and peas and simmer over medium-low heat, stirring constantly, 1 to 2 minutes.

7. Fit one circle of dough into a 9" pie plate. Carefully pour the filling mixture into the shell. Cut decorative vents in the second dough circle, place it over the top, and crimp the edges all the way around to seal.

8. Bake until golden brown, about 15 minutes. Allow to cool slightly, then cut into wedges to serve.

Serves 8.

STEAK AND MUSHROOM PIES

These savory, individual "pubby" pies are easy to prepare and fun to eat. They can be made ahead and refrigerated until you're ready to bake them, so they're wonderful for a busy-day dinner or even a special dinner party.

⅓ cup unsalted butter
1 cup chopped onions
¼ cup chopped red bell peppers
2 tsp. minced fresh garlic
2 lb. beef tenderloin, trimmed of fat
   and cut into 2" cubes
½ cup all-purpose flour
4 cups sliced white mushrooms
⅓ cup dry red wine

¼ cup dry sherry
¼ cup chopped fresh parsley
2 tsp. salt
10 turns freshly ground black pepper
2 cups beef stock (see index)
½ lb. frozen puff pastry, thawed*
6 individual 1½-cup casseroles or
   ramekins

1. Melt the butter in a large, heavy pot over medium-high heat. Add the onions, red peppers, and garlic and cook, stirring occasionally, until the vegetables are tender, about 5 minutes. Add the beef and cook, shaking the pot and stirring occasionally, until the meat starts to brown all over, about 3 minutes.

2. Preheat the oven to 375 degrees.

3. Stir in the flour, coating the meat and onions, and cook, stirring often, until the flour starts to brown, 2 to 3 minutes. Fold in the mushrooms, red wine, sherry, parsley, salt, and pepper. Gradually stir in the stock and bring to a bubble, stirring. Cook, stirring often, until the meat is cooked through and the gravy is thickened, 10 to 12 minutes. Remove from the heat and divide the meat mixture among the 6 ramekins set on a baking sheet.

4. Lay the thawed pastry on a flat work surface. Cut it into 1" strips with a pastry cutter and arrange the strips in a lattice design over the ramekins. Bake until

the pastry is brown and puffy and the meat mixture bubbling, 12 to 15 minutes. If the pies have been refrigerated, they will need another 5 minutes in the oven.

Serves 6.

*Puff pastry can be purchased in the frozen foods section of most supermarkets. Thaw in your refrigerator and keep the dough cold: handle it as little as possible while you work on it, and don't allow it to sit at room temperature.

SHEEP HERDER'S PIE

This savory pie is just the sort of hearty fare one might expect to be served at an inn, along with a pint of ale. The pie can be made ahead and frozen; just thaw it slightly and add 10 minutes or so to the baking time.

2 cups peeled, sliced potatoes
1 cup peeled, sliced parsnips
2½ tsp. salt, divided
9 turns freshly ground black pepper,
    divided
3 tbsp. unsalted butter, divided
2 tbsp. chopped fresh parsley,
    divided
¼ cup heavy cream

2 tbsp. olive oil
1 cup minced onions
2 lb. ground beef
3 tbsp. all-purpose flour
2 cups (about 2 large) peeled,
    chopped tomatoes (see index)
1 tsp. dried thyme
½ tsp. dried sage
1 cup beef stock (see index)

1. Combine the potatoes, parsnips, and water to cover in a large saucepan over high heat. Bring to a boil, reduce the heat to medium, and cook until the potatoes and parsnips are fork-tender, 15 to 20 minutes. Remove from the heat and drain.

2. Mash the potatoes and parsnips in a bowl or process them through a ricer or food mill. Add 1 tsp. of the salt, 3 turns of the pepper, 2 tbsp. of the butter, 1 tbsp. of the parsley, and the cream, and beat all together with a wooden spoon. Transfer the mixture to a pastry bag fitted with a 1" fluted tip, and set aside.

3. Heat the olive oil in a large skillet over medium-high heat. Add the onions and cook until they begin to get limp, about 4 minutes. Add the meat and cook, breaking it up with a wooden spoon and shaking the skillet occasionally, until the meat loses all of its pink color, about 8 minutes. Drain off all of the fat.

4. Preheat the oven to 350 degrees.

5. Return the meat to the skillet over medium heat. Stir in the flour and cook, stirring, until the flour is golden brown, 2 minutes. Fold in the tomatoes, thyme, sage, and the remaining 1 tbsp. parsley, 1½ tsp. salt, and 6 turns pepper. Cook, stirring occasionally, until the tomatoes have started to liquefy and all of the ingredients are blended, 2 to 3 minutes.

6. Stir in the stock and cook, stirring constantly, until the entire mixture is thickened in gravy, 3 to 4 minutes. Pour into a 9" deep-dish pie pan. Melt the remaining 1 tbsp. butter.

7. Pipe the parsleyed potato-parsnips mixture over the meat: start in the center and pipe in a circular motion until the pie is completely covered with potatoes. Drizzle the melted butter over the top and bake until the potatoes are golden-brown and puffed, about 35 minutes.

Serves 6-8.

LAMB MEATBALL PIE WITH FILLO CRUST

Since Irish stew—made with lamb—is the national dish of Ireland, this savory pie of lamb meatballs and vegetables is sort of an Irish stew pie. You might call it the national savory pie of Ireland.

2 lb. ground lamb
2½ cups fresh bread crumbs
  (see index)
2 large eggs
1½ tsp. salt, divided
12 turns freshly ground black
  pepper, divided
¼ cup (½ stick) unsalted butter,
  divided
½ cup chopped onions
1 tsp. minced fresh garlic
2 cups sliced white mushrooms

¼ cup all-purpose flour
2½ cups chicken stock (see index)
1 cup dry red wine
1 tsp. dried rosemary
1 bay leaf
1 lb. new potatoes in their skins,
  scrubbed and halved or quartered
1 cup sliced carrots
1 cup fresh green peas
½ cup melted, unsalted butter
8 sheets fillo dough (see index)

1. In a bowl combine the lamb, bread crumbs, eggs, ½ tsp. of the salt, and 4 turns of the pepper. Mix with your hands just until thoroughly blended—over-handling will make the meatballs heavy. With light, gentle movements, shape meatballs about 1½" in diameter with your hands—don't pack. There should be about 35 meatballs.

2. Melt 2 tbsp. of the butter in a large skillet over medium heat. Add the meatballs in batches and cook them, shaking the skillet or turning them with a spatula, until they are brown on all sides, 6 to 7 minutes total. Remove the meatballs, transfer them to a bowl, and set aside.

3. In the same skillet, melt the remaining 2 tbsp. butter over medium heat. Add the onions, garlic, and mushrooms, and cook, stirring or shaking the skillet occasionally, until the vegetables are tender, about 5 minutes. Sprinkle the flour over the vegetables and cook, stirring to blend the flour in to the butter and vegetables, until the flour turns a light brown color, 2 to 3 minutes.

4. Preheat the oven to 350 degrees.

5. Slowly whisk in the stock and continue whisking until there is no flour visible. Stir in the wine, rosemary, bay leaf, remaining 1 tsp. salt, and 8 turns black pepper. Cook over medium heat, stirring often, until the gravy is thick and bubbling, about 6 minutes.

6. Fold in the potatoes, carrots, and peas. Fold in the reserved meatballs with their collected juices. Stir and cook until heated through. Remove the bay leaf.

7. Turn the mixture into a 9½" deep-dish pie plate. With a pastry brush, spread some of the melted butter over the edges of the pie plate. Place 1 sheet of fillo dough over the filling, allowing the ends to drape over the edge of the plate. Brush the fillo sheet, all the way to the draping ends, with butter. Continue with the remaining sheets, crisscrossing them and buttering each. Roll up the excess ends all the way around and crimp them with your fingers or a fork. Brush the edges with butter, covering them thoroughly. Pierce the top of the pie in several places with a sharp knife.

8. Bake until the crust is golden brown and the filling bubbly, 35 to 40 minutes. Serve with a crisp green salad.

Serves 8-10.

DILLY SEAFOOD COBBLER WITH DILL PASTRY

The word "cobbler" usually conjures up images of deep-dish fruit pies. In this savory version, chunks of briny seafood in a dilly cream sauce laced with sherry are substituted and topped with a flavor-echoing, dill-seasoned crust.

PASTRY

1 cup all-purpose flour
½ tsp. salt
1 tbsp. snipped fresh dill
3 tbsp. cold, firm solid vegetable
　shortening

3 tbsp. cold, firm butter
3 tbsp. (approx.) ice water

FILLING

6 tbsp. (¾ stick) unsalted butter
1 cup sliced, fresh white mushrooms
¼ cup chopped scallions (green
　onions)
6 tbsp. all-purpose flour
3 cups half-and-half
2 tbsp. snipped fresh dill
1½ tsp. salt
4 turns freshly ground black pepper
⅛ tsp. cayenne pepper
3 tbsp. dry sherry

4 cups mixed uncooked, fresh
　seafood (scallops, shrimp, lobster
　meat, oysters, firm-fleshed white
　fish), all peeled or shelled,
　deveined if necessary, drained,
　and cut into 1" pieces
2 tbsp. chopped fresh parsley,
　preferably Italian (flat leaf)
2 tbsp. freshly grated Parmesan
　cheese

　1. To make the pastry, combine the flour, salt, and dill in a large, chilled mixing bowl. Cut in the solid shortening and butter with a pastry blender, a fork, or two knives, working quickly, until the mixture resembles coarse crumbs.

　2. Sprinkle the ice water, 1 tbsp. at a time, into various sections of the mixture, stirring with a fork after each addition. Use only enough water to barely moisten, without making the mixture sticky, and mix only until it can be gathered into a ball. Wrap the dough ball in plastic wrap and refrigerate for 1 hour. For more tips on making perfect pastry, see index.

　3. Remove the dough from the refrigerator and turn out onto a lightly floured work surface. Roll out the pastry dough (see index) to ½" thickness and cut with a pastry wheel into strips 2" wide. Preheat the oven to 400 degrees.

　4. To make the filling, melt the butter in a large skillet over medium heat. Add

the mushrooms and scallions and cook until soft, about 5 minutes. Stir in the flour and cook, stirring occasionally, until the flour is incorporated and golden, about 4 minutes. Stir in the half-and-half, dill, salt, black pepper, and cayenne and cook, stirring occasionally, until the mixture is thick and has a soft pudding texture, 6 to 7 minutes.

5. Stir in the sherry, and fold in the seafood and parsley. Mix well and just heat through. Pour into a shallow, 2-qt. casserole or pie dish. Sprinkle the Parmesan cheese on top.

6. Cover the pie with the pastry strips, laying them about ¾" apart in one direction and then a layer of strips across, to form a lattice. Bake until the pastry is brown and the filling bubbly, about 30 minutes. Allow the cobbler to cool slightly before cutting it into wedges and serving.

Serves 4-6.

TURKEY OYSTER TORTE WITH BECHAMEL

The crust for this torte is actually a savory dressing or stuffing mixture, making the dish an interesting variation on the ubiquitous stuffed turkey. You probably shouldn't serve it for Thanksgiving, or you might get lynched by the traditionalists—and there are many of us. But this is delicious and will be welcomed any other time of the year.

TURKEY
One 2½-lb. fresh breast of turkey, with skin
2 tbsp. salt
12 turns freshly ground black pepper

2 medium onions, quartered
2 stalks celery, with leaves, quartered

DRESSING
½ cup (1 stick) unsalted butter
1 cup minced onions
½ cup minced celery
8 cups cubed day-old French bread, including crusts (1")
1½ cups chicken stock (see index)
½ cup milk

2 large eggs, lightly beaten
1 tsp. salt
6 turns freshly ground black pepper
1 tsp. dry rubbed sage
¼ tsp. dried thyme
1 tbsp. vegetable oil
1 cup drained, freshly shucked oysters

BÉCHAMEL

Reserved pan drippings from the turkey

Melted butter (about 2 tbsp.), if necessary

3 tbsp. all-purpose flour

2½ cups chicken stock (see index)

1½ tsp. salt

½ tsp. ground white pepper

1 cup heavy cream

Whole Cranberry Sauce

Minced fresh parsley for garnish

Fresh sage sprigs for garnish

1. Preheat the oven to 350 degrees.

2. To cook the turkey, place the turkey breast in a baking pan and season all over with the salt and pepper, rubbing the seasonings in with your hand. Arrange the onions and celery pieces around the turkey in the pan. Cover tightly with a fitted lid or foil and bake until the turkey juices run clear when the meat is pricked with a fork, about 1½ hours. Remove from the oven, transfer the turkey to a platter or slicing board, and allow it to cool. Remove the vegetables from the pan but reserve the drippings. When the turkey is cool, trim off the skin and slice the meat into ¼" slices. Leave the oven at 350 degrees.

2. To make the dressing, melt the butter in a skillet over medium heat. Add the onions and celery and cook, stirring or shaking the skillet often, until the vegetables are tender, about 6 minutes. Remove from the heat.

3. In a large bowl, combine the bread cubes, stock, milk, eggs, salt, pepper, sage, thyme, and the cooked onions and celery, as well as the butter in the skillet. Blend well with a wooden spoon or your hands, until the dressing is thoroughly mixed.

4. Brush the bottom and sides of a 10" springform pan with the oil. Turn about three-fourths of the dressing into the pan and pat it into the bottom and up the sides, forming a 1" "crust."

5. Arrange a layer of half the turkey slices on the bottom crust. Spread the oysters over the turkey, and top the oysters with the remaining turkey slices. Spread the remaining dressing evenly over the top, and press the edges to seal.

6. Cover the torte tightly with foil and bake at 350 degrees for 45 minutes. Remove the foil and continue baking until the top is golden brown and firm to the touch, about 15 minutes. Remove from the oven and allow the torte to cool on a rack for about 5 minutes. Remove the pan and transfer the torte to a serving platter.

7. To make the Béchamel, pour the drippings into a measuring cup. Add melted butter, if needed, until there is ½ cup. Pour the drippings into a medium saucepan and place over medium heat until it begins to sizzle. Stir in the flour and cook, stirring constantly, until you have a golden-brown roux, 7 to 8 minutes.

8. Gradually whisk in the stock until the gravy is smooth. Add the salt and white pepper. Cook over medium heat, stirring constantly, until the gravy begins to thicken, 5 to 6 minutes. Slowly stir in the cream and bring to a bubble. Reduce the heat to low and cook, stirring occasionally, until the flavors are thoroughly blended and the consistency is creamy, about 5 minutes. Remove from the heat.

9. Cut the torte into 8 wedges. Coat the bottom of each serving plate with some of the Béchamel and place a wedge of the torte on top. Arrange a mound of cranberries at the side, sprinkle the top of each wedge with parsley, and add a sprig of sage.

Serves 8.

COLCANNON TORTE

Also called "champ," colcannon is one of Ireland's most traditional and best-known dishes, a basic mixture of potatoes and cabbage. In this reinvented version, colcannon comes to the table as a crisp, golden-brown cake that's cut into wedges.

5 cups peeled, diced potatoes
4 tsp. salt, divided
2 slices bacon, diced
4 cups chopped red cabbage
½ cup chopped scallions (green onions)

¼ cup water
¾ cup heavy cream
4 turns freshly ground black pepper
3 tsp. unsalted butter, divided

1. Place the potatoes and 3 tsp. of the salt in a large pot. Cover with cold water and bring to a boil over high heat. Reduce the heat to medium-low and simmer until the potatoes are tender, about 15 minutes.

2. Preheat the oven to 350 degrees.

3. In a large, deep skillet, fry the bacon over medium-low just to render out the fat. Don't let the bacon get too crisp. Remove and drain on paper towels.

4. In the hot bacon fat over medium heat, sauté the cabbage and scallions until the cabbage is just golden, stirring and shaking to coat the vegetables with the bacon drippings, about 4 minutes. Add the ¼ cup water, cover, and reduce the heat to low. Steam until the cabbage is tender, about 10 minutes. Drain and toss with the remaining 1 tsp. salt.

5. When the potatoes are tender, drain and mash with a potato masher until

slightly lumpy. Add the cream and beat with a whisk or wooden spoon just until fluffy and creamy. Don't beat too long, or they'll get starchy. Fold in the black pepper and mix thoroughly.

6. Use 1 tsp. of the butter to grease an 8" pie pan. Spread half the potato mixture in the pan and cover with the cabbage mixture. Fold the reserved bacon into the remaining potatoes and spread over the cabbage, sealing it with the rim of the pie pan.

7. Melt the remaining 2 tsp. butter and drizzle over the top. Bake until golden brown, about 25 minutes. Remove from the oven and let set for 5 minutes. Cut the torte into 8 wedges and serve.

Serves 8.

SUMMER SQUASH TART

This savory tart is a perfect way to treat your lucky guests at a lazy, mid-summer's day luncheon. Just add a light green salad and tall glasses of iced tea.

PASTRY
¾ cup whole-wheat flour, plus more
    for rolling
⅔ cup all-purpose flour

¼ tsp. salt
⅓ cup plus 2 tbsp. solid shortening
3 tbsp. ice water

TOPPING
½ cup grated aged asiago cheese*
1 cup bread crumbs, preferably fresh
    (see index)
2 tbsp. chopped fresh parsley

1 tsp. chopped fresh basil
¼ cup (½ stick) melted butter
6 slices crisp-cooked bacon,
    crumbled

FILLING
2 cups sliced yellow squash
    (1" strips)
½ cup sliced zucchini (1" strips)
½ cup sliced small pattypan squash
    (1" strips)**
¼ cup chopped onions
1¼ tsp. salt, divided

6 turns freshly ground pepper, divided
½ cup water
3 large egg yolks
1½ cups milk
½ cup sour cream
1 tsp. dried basil
½ cup grated Cheddar cheese

1. To make the pastry, sift the whole-wheat flour, all-purpose flour, and salt into a large bowl. Using a pastry blender, a fork, or two knives, cut in the shortening until the mixture resembles coarse crumbs.

2. Sprinkle the ice water, 1 tbsp. at a time, into various sections of the mixture, stirring with a fork after each addition. Use only enough water to barely moisten, without making the mixture sticky, and mix only until it can be gathered into a ball. Wrap the dough ball in plastic wrap and refrigerate for 1 hour. For more tips for making perfect pastry, see index.

3. Preheat the oven to 400 degrees. Sprinkle the work surface lightly with wheat flour and roll out the pastry to a circle about ¼" thick. Fit the pastry dough into a 10" tart pan, cover with parchment or foil, and fill with rice or beans. Bake for 15 minutes until the pastry is partially baked, and remove from the oven. Remove and discard the beans and paper and allow the pastry to cool on a rack. Reduce the oven heat to 350 degrees.

4. To make the tart topping, in a bowl combine the cheese, bread crumbs, parsley, and basil. Add the butter and work it in well with your hands. Add the bacon and mix again. Set aside.

5. To make the filling, combine the yellow, zucchini, and pattypan squash with the onions, ½ tsp. of the salt, 3 turns of the pepper, and the water in a saucepan over medium-high heat. Bring to a boil, reduce the heat to medium-low, and cover the saucepan. Cook until the squash is tender, about 20 minutes. Uncover, increase the heat to medium-high, and cook, stirring constantly, until the liquid has cooked off, about 5 minutes.

6. Drain the squash mixture in a colander, transfer to a food processor, and puree until fairly smooth and thick. Return the mixture to the saucepan over low heat and cook, stirring constantly, until any excess liquid is gone, 4 to 5 minutes. Remove from the heat and set aside to cool.

7. In a small bowl whisk together the egg yolks and ½ tsp. salt.

8. Heat the milk in a small saucepan over medium heat until bubbles appear, about 4 minutes. Add the milk, a little at a time, to the egg yolks, whisking constantly. Return the mixture to the saucepan over low heat and cook, stirring occasionally, until it becomes thick and custardlike, about 8 minutes. Pour into a bowl, cover, and refrigerate 20 minutes.

9. In a large bowl combine the squash, custard, sour cream, basil, Cheddar cheese, the remaining ¼ tsp. salt, and 3 turns pepper and mix well with a wooden spoon. Pour into the tart shell, crumble the topping over the tart, and bake

until brown and bubbly, about 25 minutes. Garnish with chopped fresh chives, if desired.

Serve 4-6 for lunch.

*Asiago cheese can be bitter if young; always try to use aged asiago.

**Pattypan is a pretty, scalloped-edge summer squash, pale green to white in color. Pattypans are available in small or large sizes, but the small ones are the most tender and tasty.

TURNIP AND SCALLION FLANS WITH CANADIAN BACON AND HOLLANDAISE SAUCE

These individual flans make a pretty presentation and should be served on separate plates from the main course.

2½ tbsp. olive oil, divided
3 tbsp. chopped scallions (green onions), white part only
2 cups peeled, diced turnips
½ cup chopped scallions, green part only, plus more for garnish
2 tbsp. chopped fresh parsley
1 tbsp. granulated sugar
⅛ tsp. cayenne pepper
1 tsp. salt, divided
12 turns freshly ground black pepper, divided

½ cup dry white wine
½ cup heavy cream
1 tbsp. grated Swiss cheese
1 cup half-and-half
2 large whole eggs
2 large egg yolks
Softened unsalted butter for greasing
8 slices Canadian bacon (¼" thick)
1 cup hollandaise sauce (see index)

1. Heat 1½ tbsp. of the oil in a skillet over medium heat. Add the chopped white scallion bulbs and cook until tender, 4 to 5 minutes. Add the turnips and cook, stirring or shaking the skillet occasionally, until the turnips begin to soften, about 7 minutes. Fold in the ½ cup chopped green scallion tops. Sprinkle the parsley, sugar, cayenne, ½ tsp. of the salt, and 8 turns of the black pepper over the turnips. Stir in the wine and cover the skillet. Reduce the heat to low and

cook, uncovering to stir once or twice, until the turnips are tender and the liquid cooked in, 20 to 30 minutes.

2. Preheat the oven to 325 degrees.

3. When the turnip mixture is cooked, remove it from the heat and allow it to cool for several minutes. Turn the mixture into the bowl of a food processor and puree. Transfer to a bowl, cover, and chill while you prepare the custard.

4. In a bowl combine the cream with the cheese, half-and-half, whole eggs, egg yolks, the remaining ½ tsp. salt, and 4 turns black pepper. Beat with a whisk until well blended and foamy. Remove the turnip mixture from the refrigerator, turn it into the custard, and mix well with a wooden spoon.

5. Generously butter 8 individual ½-cup ramekins. Fill each ramekin ¾ full with the turnip/custard mixture. Place a large baking pan on the center rack of the oven and fill it with about 1" water. Place the ramekins in the water (the water should reach about halfway up the sides of the ramekins; if it doesn't, carefully add more). Bake until the flans are set, 25 to 30 minutes. Place the ramekins on a rack to cool slightly.

6. Fry the Canadian bacon in the remaining 1 tbsp. oil in a skillet over medium heat until it is golden, 2 to 3 minutes each side. Drain on paper towels.

7. Place one slice of Canadian bacon on each plate. To remove the flans from the ramekins, gently loosen the sides with a sharp knife and invert on top of the bacon. Top each with 2 tbsp. hollandaise and garnish with chopped scallion greens.

Serves 8 for a side dish.

VEGETABLE CHEESE PIZZA PIE

Believe it or not, the Irish like pizza almost as much as Americans do, and it can be found by the slice in many pubs. This one could even be called healthy, because of all the tasty vegetables. To keep it from being too healthy, serve it with a pitcher of ice-cold beer.

1 cup whole-milk ricotta cheese
2 tbsp. freshly grated Parmesan cheese
½ tsp. ground nutmeg
1 small zucchini, peeled and julienned
1 cup peeled, julienned eggplant, blotted with paper towels
1¼ tsp. salt, divided
1 tbsp. plus 1 tsp. olive oil, divided
2 medium onions, in 1/4" slices
2 medium green bell peppers, in ¼" slices
One 14 ½-oz. can whole peeled tomatoes, drained, seeded, and chopped

1 tbsp. minced fresh basil
2 tsp. minced fresh or ¾ tsp. dried oregano leaves
1 tbsp. minced fresh garlic, divided
8 turns freshly ground black pepper, divided
4 cups (one 10-oz. pkg.) fresh spinach, rinsed, stemmed, and patted completely dry
1 Basic Pizza Crust or whole-wheat crust (see index)
1½ cups coarsely grated Gruyère cheese

1. In a small bowl combine the ricotta with the Parmesan cheese and nutmeg. Mix well and set aside. Spread the zucchini and eggplant on paper towels and sprinkle with ½ tsp. of the salt. Allow the julienned vegetables to sit until you're ready to assemble the pizza.

2. Heat ½ tbsp. of the oil in a large, deep skillet over medium heat. Add the onions and bell peppers and cook, shaking the skillet occasionally, until the vegetables are limp but not brown, about 5 minutes. Turn the onions and bell peppers into a bowl to cool.

3. Preheat the oven to 450 degrees.

4. Place the skillet back over medium heat and add another ½ tbsp. olive oil. When the oil is hot, add the tomatoes, basil, oregano, ½ tbs. of the garlic, ½ tsp. salt, and 4 turns of the black pepper. Cook, stirring often, until most of the liquid has cooked in and disappeared, about 8 minutes. Transfer to another bowl to cool.

5. Place the skillet back over medium heat and add the remaining 1 tsp. oil.

When the oil is hot, add the remaining ½ tbsp. garlic, and cook until the garlic begins to get soft, about 1 minute. Add the spinach, the remaining 4 turns black pepper, and the remaining ¼ tsp. salt. Cook, stirring once or twice, until the spinach is limp and all of the liquid is gone, about 5 minutes. Turn the spinach onto a plate to cool.

6. To assemble the pizza, spread the ricotta cheese mixture over the par-baked crust. Spread the spinach mixture over the cheese, gently fanning the leaves and spreading them open with your fingers. Spoon the tomato mixture in small blobs over the top of the spinach—don't spread the sauce. Arrange the onion-bell pepper mixture over this and sprinkle with ¾ c. of the Gruyère cheese. Toss the julienned zucchini and eggplant together, and spread a thin layer of this mixture over the cheese. Top with the remaining Gruyère.

7. Bake until the cheese is melted, brown, and bubbly, and the crust is golden brown, 15 to 20 minutes.

Serves 4.

Noodles
And:

Pasta
and Crepes

You might think it strange to find a chapter like this in a book on Irish pub cooking. But the fact is that in Ireland, as in restaurants all over the world, there is a trend toward the latest in food fashions. Moreover, the Irish love pasta, as do the Italians, Americans, Asians, and people everywhere. Pasta is here to stay.

It's no wonder that pubs, with their fingers on the pulse of the people—so to speak—and their eagerness to please, picked up the scent of the worldwide noodle-mania. Pasta is no longer relegated to the ubiquitous bowl of spaghetti in the neighborhood Italian bistro but is found on menus in almost every type of restaurant known to man and woman.

In the United States alone, there are more than 150 pasta shapes available, and the amount of pasta consumed every year, placed end to end, could circle the equator nine times. No one has the figures yet for pasta consumption in Ireland, a country roughly the size of West Virginia. But I do know that it has become a popular menu item both in restaurants and in the home.

BASIL SHRIMP ON NOODLES

This dish, with its sophisticated appeal, is more pub than country-style Irish. Once the shrimp are peeled and deveined the rest is a snap, so you can whip it up in almost no time.

½ cup (1 stick) unsalted butter
2 tsp. minced fresh garlic
2 lb. large shrimp, peeled, deveined, rinsed, and patted dry
1 tbsp. chopped fresh parsley
2 tbsp. chopped scallions (green onions)

1 tsp. salt
1 tsp. paprika
¼ cup (4 tbsp.) chopped fresh basil, divided
4 cups cooked egg noodles or fettuccine

1. Melt the butter in a skillet over medium heat. Add the garlic and cook, shaking the skillet occasionally, until the garlic is soft, about 2 minutes.

2. Stir in the shrimp, parsley, scallions, salt, paprika, and 2 tbsp. of the basil. Cook, shaking the skillet occasionally, until the shrimp are pink on both sides, 3 to 4 minutes.

3. Toss the shrimp mixture with the noodles and serve garnished with the remaining 2 tbsp. chopped basil.

Serves 4-6.

WINEY MUSSELS IN JUNIPER TOMATO SAUCE OVER ANGEL HAIR

This slightly alcoholic dish has an irresistibly tangy sauce enhanced by the unusual appeal of juniper berries.

48 mussels
3 tbsp. olive oil
⅔ cup minced onions
1 tbsp. minced fresh garlic
1 tbsp. crushed juniper berries
1 tbsp. gin
3 cups peeled, seeded, coarsely chopped Roma tomatoes (see index)
2 tbsp. red wine vinegar
1 tsp. granulated sugar
¼ cup minced fresh parsley, preferably Italian (flat-leaf)

2 tsp. salt
14 turns freshly ground black pepper, divided
One 16-oz. pkg. angel hair pasta
2 cups dry white wine
1 cup water
3 sprigs fresh parsley
¼ cup chopped scallions (green onions)
2 tbsp. freshly grated Parmesan cheese

1. Begin soaking and debearding the mussels (see index).

2. To prepare the sauce, heat the oil in a large, heavy saucepan over medium heat. Add the onions, garlic, and juniper berries and cook, stirring occasionally, until the onions are tender, about 5 minutes. Stir in the gin and cook until the liquid is absorbed, about 45 seconds.

3. Stir in the tomatoes, vinegar, and sugar and bring to a bubble. Reduce the heat to medium-low and cook, stirring occasionally, until the mixture becomes a thick sauce, 35 to 40 minutes. Stir in the chopped parsley, salt, and 8 turns of the black pepper and cook, stirring, until heated through, 1 to 2 minutes.

4. While the sauce is cooking, prepare the pasta according to package directions and keep it warm.

5. Combine the wine, water, parsley sprigs, scallions, and the remaining 6 turns pepper in a large pot over high heat. Bring to a boil and cook at a brisk bubble for 5 minutes.

6. Add the mussels, cover the pot, and cook just until the mussels open, 3 to 5 minutes. Remove the mussels from the cooking liquid and discard any that haven't opened. Allow them to cool slightly, and carefully remove the mussels from their shells. Toss the mussels with the sauce.

7. To serve, turn the pasta onto a serving platter. Top with the mussels and sauce, and sprinkle with Parmesan.

Serves 6.

CHICKEN AND ROASTED-VEGETABLE ZITI

This dish makes a hearty family dinner. Everything but the pasta is roasted for a sweet-smoky flavor.

5 tbsp. olive oil
1½ tsp. minced fresh garlic
2 whole chicken breasts, with skin and bones
2 tsp. salt, divided
16 turns freshly ground black pepper, divided
1 cup sliced onions (¼" thick)
2 cups sliced portobello mushrooms (½" thick)

3 cups julienned red and yellow bell peppers (about 3 large peppers)
2½ cups cherry tomatoes (about 1 lb.)
1 lb. dried ziti pasta
1 cup heavy cream
¼ tsp. dried red pepper flakes
¾ cup freshly grated Romano cheese (about 5 oz.), divided
½ cup minced cilantro, plus more for garnish

1. Preheat the oven to 350 degrees.

2. Heat the oil in a small saucepan over medium heat. Add the garlic and cook, stirring or shaking the skillet once or twice, until the garlic is soft and a light golden color, 2 to 3 minutes. Remove from the heat.

3. Place the chicken breasts, skin side up, on a 10" x 15" baking sheet. Sprinkle the skin with 1 tsp. of the salt and 4 turns of the black pepper. Brush with some of the garlicky olive oil. Roast for 15 minutes.

4. Remove the baking sheet from the oven and arrange the onions, mushrooms, and bell peppers around the chicken. Sprinkle the vegetables with 6 turns of the black pepper and the remaining 1 tsp. salt. Drizzle with some of the oil, coating the vegetables well. Return to the oven and roast about 15 minutes, turning the vegetables over once halfway through. Remove from the oven.

5. Remove the chicken and set aside to cool slightly. Add the tomatoes to the baking sheet, drizzle with the remaining oil, and roast until the vegetables are brown and caramelized, about 15 minutes longer.

6. Meanwhile, cook the pasta in boiling salted water according to package directions. Remove the skin and bones from the chicken and julienne or shred the meat.

7. In the same saucepan in which the oil was heated, combine the cream, red pepper flakes, and ½ cup of the Romano cheese over medium heat. Bring to a boil, stirring constantly. Reduce the heat to low and cook, stirring often, until the mixture coats the back of a spoon, about 5 minutes.

8. Combine the roasted vegetables, chicken, pasta, and cilantro in a large bowl and toss well. Add the sauce and toss again. Divide among 8 pasta bowls and sprinkle with remaining black pepper and Romano cheese. Garnish with additional cilantro and serve.

Serves 8 generously.

CHICKEN PILLOWS WITH IRISH RAREBIT

The "pillows" in this tempting dish might be suggestive of ravioli, but may I remind you that this is an Irish cookbook, and so they are pillows. Won-ton skins make the airiest ravioli and guarantee a fuss-free preparation.

½ lb. boneless, skinless chicken breast
1 large onion, quartered
1 stalk celery, halved, with leaves
1½ tbsp. salt, divided
6 slices crisp-cooked bacon, drained and coarsely crumbled
½ cup minced ham
¼ cup heavy cream
8 turns freshly ground black pepper
1 16-oz. pkg. won-ton wrappers*

3 tbsp. unsalted butter
3 tbsp. all-purpose flour
1½ cups beer, divided
1 lb. sharp or extra sharp Cheddar cheese (or a combination of the two), shredded
1 tbsp. Worcestershire sauce
1 tsp. dry mustard
¼ tsp. Hungarian hot paprika
2 qt. water
¼ cup minced fresh parsley

1. Place the chicken, onion, celery, and 1 tsp. of the salt in a large saucepan. Cover with cold water and bring to a boil over medium-high heat. Reduce the heat to low and simmer until the chicken is tender, about 15 minutes.

2. Drain the chicken and cut it into large chunks. Discard the onion and celery. Place the chicken in the bowl of a food processor. Pulse until the chicken is minced, but not ground, about 15 seconds. Add the bacon and pulse 2 to 3 times, about 5 seconds each. Add the ham and pulse 2 to 3 times. Add the cream and pulse until the mixture is well combined, 4 to 5 pulses. Turn the mixture into a bowl and stir in the pepper and ½ tsp. of the salt.

3. Separate the won-ton wrappers as needed, making sure you peel off the thinnest single wrappers (they tend to stick together). Keep the wrappers you're not working with covered with a damp cloth. Have a pastry brush nearby and a little bowl of water. Place one won-ton wrapper on a flat surface. Lightly brush the edges with water. Place 1 tbsp. of the filling mixture in the center and top with another wrapper, pressing the edges tightly together. Trim the edges with a pastry wheel so that each pillow measures about 2" square. There will be about 25 pillows. As you make them, place the pillows on a baking sheet and cover with wax paper.

4. To prepare the sauce, start heating some water in the bottom half of a double boiler over medium heat.

5. Place the top saucepan of the double boiler over medium-high heat. Melt the butter in this pan. Stir in the flour and cook, stirring constantly, until you have a light golden roux, 3 to 4 minutes. Stir in ¾ cup of the beer and cook, stirring constantly, until slightly thickened, 2 to 3 minutes.

6. Place the saucepan over its lower half, where the water is by now simmering. Into the thickened beer stir the cheese, Worcestershire, mustard, and paprika. Cook, stirring often, until the cheese has melted and the sauce is well blended, 15 to 20 minutes. Gradually stir in the remaining 3/4 cup beer and cook, stirring often, until the alcohol has cooked off, about 5 minutes. Cover and keep warm until the pillows are cooked.

7. While the cheese is melting, begin heating the 2 qt. water and the remaining 1 tbsp. of salt in a large saucepan over high heat. When the water comes to a rapid boil, reduce the heat to medium-low to keep the water at a simmer. Cook the pillows in 2 or 3 batches: Slip the pillows into the simmering water and cook, turning once or twice with a slotted spoon, until tender, 3 to 4 minutes. If you crowd the pillows they may fall apart.

8. To serve, spoon some of the sauce into the bottom of each plate, top with 3 or 4 chicken pillows, and garnish with minced parsley.

Serves 8 for a first course or 6 for a main course.

*Won-ton skins or wrappers can be found in many supermarkets and any Asian specialty food store.

CURRIED PUMPKIN TORTELLINI

Chutney is an Indian relish usually made of fruits, vegetables, vinegar, and spices. The most common one found in America is "Major Grey's," which is a mango chutney. In small amounts, chutney acts as a booster rocket for spicy dishes, such as this one. And the applejack brandy gives the sauce an unusual twist.

2 tbsp. vegetable oil
¾ cup chopped onions
1 tsp. minced garlic
2 tsp. curry powder, divided
2 tbsp. chutney
3 cups chicken stock (see index), divided
1 tbsp. salt
4 turns freshly ground black pepper

One 15-oz. can (1¾ cups) pumpkin puree
¼ cup applejack brandy
1½ tsp. freshly squeezed lemon juice
½ cup heavy cream
One 7-oz. pkg. tricolor tortellini
½ cup freshly grated Parmesan cheese
¼ cup chopped fresh parsley

1. Heat the oil in a small skillet over medium heat. Add the onions, garlic, and 1 tsp. of the curry powder, and cook until the onions are translucent, about 5 minutes. Transfer to a food processor. Add the chutney and ½ cup of the stock and puree until smooth. Turn the mixture into a large saucepan.

2. Place the saucepan over medium-high heat and stir in the salt, pepper, pumpkin, applejack brandy, lemon juice, the remaining 1 tsp. curry powder, and the remaining 2½ cups stock. Bring to a bubble, reduce the heat to low, and cook, stirring occasionally, until the flavors have blended and the sauce is thick and slightly reduced, about 30 minutes. Stir in the cream and heat through.

3. While the sauce is simmering, cook the tortellini in salted water according to package directions, and drain.

4. To serve, divide the tortellini among 4 shallow bowls. Top with the sauce, Parmesan, and chopped parsley.

Serves 4.

MACARONI AND MANY CHEESES

If macaroni tastes good with one kind of cheese, think how wonderful it would be with a whole bunch, lending their distinctive flavors to the homely, but much-loved, macaroni elbow.

½ cup unsalted butter, plus more for the casserole
One 16-oz. pkg. elbow macaroni
½ cup all-purpose flour
1 qt. milk
4 cups shredded cheese, a mixture of Cheddar, fontina, Swiss, Muenster, provolone, asiago, a bit of crumbled blue, a bit of Parmesan Reggiano—or the cheeses of your choice
2 tsp. salt
¼ tsp. ground white pepper
¼ cup minced fresh parsley
1½ tsp. paprika

1. Preheat the oven to 350 degrees. Grease a deep, 4-qt. casserole and set aside. Cook the macaroni al dente according to package directions, and drain thoroughly.

2. Melt the ½ cup butter in a large saucepan over medium heat. Stir in the flour and cook, stirring often, until the flour is a light brown color, about 3 minutes. Slowly whisk in the milk and cook, stirring constantly, until the sauce is thick and bubbly, 6 to 7 minutes.

3. Stir in 2 cups of the mixed cheeses, the salt, and pepper and cook, stirring, over medium heat, until the cheese is completely melted and incorporated, 4 to 5 minutes. Stir the parsley into the cheese sauce and remove from the heat.

4. Pour one-third of the cheese sauce into the casserole. Add a layer of half the macaroni and sprinkle with ¾ cup of the remaining uncooked shredded cheese. Pour another one-third of the sauce over, add the remaining macaroni and sprinkle with ½ cup of the uncooked shredded cheese. Pour the remaining cheese sauce over this, and sprinkle the top with the remaining ¾ cup shredded cheese and the paprika.

5. Bake until brown and bubbly, 35 to 40 minutes. Serve warm.
Serves 8-10.

CHEESE AND SPINACH CREPES IN CREAM SAUCE

These light and lovely crepes are always elegant for a luncheon, dinner, or cocktail party.

SAUCE
3 tbsp. unsalted butter, divided
2 tbsp. all-purpose flour
¼ tsp. salt
1 cup milk

2 tbsp. minced onions
1 tbsp. paprika
¼ cup heavy cream

CREPES
3 large eggs
½ tsp. salt
2 cups all-purpose flour
2 cups milk

6 tbsp. (¾ stick) unsalted butter, melted, divided
2 tbsp. unsalted butter, room temperature

FILLING
Two 10-oz. pkg. fresh spinach, stemmed, rinsed, squeezed dry between towels, and chopped
½ cup crumbled feta cheese
½ cup ricotta cheese
3 large eggs, beaten

¼ cup toasted pine nuts (see index), coarsely chopped
½ tsp. salt
¼ tsp. ground nutmeg, preferably freshly ground
4 turns freshly ground black pepper

GARNISH
1 cup freshly grated Parmesan cheese
¼ cup minced chives

2 tbsp. whole, toasted pine nuts
1 tbsp. paprika

1. To make the sauce, melt 2 tbsp. of the butter in a small saucepan over medium heat. Add the flour and cook, stirring constantly, until the flour is golden, about 4 minutes. Stir in the salt.

2. Whisk in the milk and reduce the heat to low. Cook, stirring occasionally, until the mixture is very thick and resembles cold gravy, about 5 minutes.

3. Meanwhile, heat the remaining 1 tbsp. butter in a small skillet. Add the onions and paprika and cook, stirring often, until the onions are soft, about 3

minutes. Fold the onions into the cream sauce. Stir in the heavy cream and heat through. Turn off the heat, cover the saucepan, and keep warm.

4. To make the crepes, beat the eggs in a large bowl. Beat in the salt. Gradually stir in the flour and milk, alternating additions of each. Stir in 4 tbsp. (1/4 cup) of the butter. Cover and refrigerate for 1 hour.

5. Remove the batter from the refrigerator. Heat a crepe pan or skillet over medium-high heat. When the pan is hot, lightly brush it with some of the remaining 2 tbsp. butter. Pour about 1/4 cup of the batter into the center of the pan, tipping the pan to get a circle 4 to 5" in diameter. Cook until the edges begin to bubble, about 2 minutes. Flip carefully and cook for about 3 seconds. Transfer to a plate and keep warm. Repeat with the remaining batter, brushing with butter as needed. You should get between 12 and 14 crepes from the batter.

6. Combine all of the filling ingredients in a large bowl and mix well.

7. Preheat the oven to 350 degrees. Grease a 9" x 13" baking dish with the 2 tbsp. room-temperature butter.

8. Place one crepe on a work surface. Spread 1/4 cup of the filling down the center of the crepe, and fold over the sides. Place seam side down in the baking dish. Repeat with the remaining crepes.

9. Cover the baking dish with foil and bake 10 minutes. Remove the foil, pour the sauce over the crepes, and sprinkle with the grated cheese. Return to the oven uncovered and continue baking until brown and bubbly, 10 to 15 minutes longer.

10. Allow 2 to 3 crepes for a main-course serving. Garnish each serving with a sprinkling of chives, pine nuts, and a pinch of paprika.

Serves 4-6.

And With
It All:

Side Dishes

As important as the main course itself is the side dish or dishes that accompany it. When a side is a slap-dash serving of frozen vegetables, a half-hearted dish of boiled rice, or a plain baked potato, it does nothing to enhance the rest of the meal. Watch those lackluster vegetables return to the kitchen uneaten. An unappetizing side might even make the main course seem less attractive, by association.

I believe in interesting, even exciting side dishes to help make every meal you serve complete. This chapter presents such wonderful delights as creamy Gaelic Garlic Mashed Potatoes or Horseradish Potato Mash; crispy Wild Rice Pancakes; savory Cabbage Bread Pudding, Corn Pudding, or Blackeye Pea Pudding; crunchy-good McGuire's Famous Irish-Fried Onion Rings; Parsnip Croquettes with Garlicky Carrot Salsa; Applejack Squash and Apple Puree; and more!

Put the same care and planning into your side plates as you do your main dishes and you will be amply rewarded by the leprechauns.

GAELIC GARLIC MASHED POTATOES

Garlic, called gairleog by the Irish, is so revered in Ireland that the first Sunday in August is designated Garlick Sunday. Here the pungent bulb is roasted for its sweetness and combined with the ever-present potato for a heavenly, creamy side dish—McGuire's version of the traditional dish of champ. *

2 large heads garlic, unpeeled
¼ cup olive oil
6 cups peeled, diced potatoes
½ cup (1 stick) unsalted butter,
    room temperature

½ to ¾ cup heavy cream
1 tsp. salt
16 turns freshly ground black pepper

1. Preheat the oven to 200 degrees.
2. Place the garlic on a sheet of foil, pour the oil over them, and wrap in the foil. Bake until very tender, 1 to 1½ hours. Remove and set aside.
3. Meanwhile, place the potatoes in a large pot over high heat. Cover the potatoes with cold water and boil until tender, about 15 minutes. Drain.
4. Turn the potatoes into a large bowl and mash until well mashed but slightly lumpy. Slice the roasted garlic heads crosswise and squeeze out the soft garlic into the potatoes, whipping with a whisk. Whisk in the butter, cream, salt, and pepper just until all of the elements are completely incorporated. Take care not to overbeat, or the potatoes will become gluey. Serve immediately.**
Serves 8.

*Champ—also known in Ireland as poundies, pandy, and cally—is that country's favorite and traditional way of serving mashed potatoes. It was enjoyed on meatless days such as Fridays and during Lent. On Halloween it was the custom to place two portions of champ on the farm gate for the fairies.

**If you prepare the mashed potatoes ahead of time, keep them covered in the top half of a double boiler over simmering water until you're ready to serve.

HORSERADISH POTATO MASH

The poor people of 17th- and 18th-century Ireland revered the potato, because it was their main sustenance. A big bowl of potatoes was set in the middle of the floor of the home, and the family—including livestock and household pets—all ate from the same bowl. The family would dip their potatoes into dishes of salt and pepper and sometimes even buttermilk. This tangy horseradish potato dish is a far cry from a bowl of boiled potatoes. It's especially good served with Burgundy-Soused Roast (see index).

6 medium potatoes, peeled and
   cubed
¼ cup (½ stick) unsalted butter in
   pats, room temperature
1 cup milk

½ cup heavy cream
½ tsp. salt
¼ tsp. white pepper
2 tbsp. prepared horseradish

1. Place the potatoes in a large saucepan and cover with cold water. Bring to a boil over medium-high heat, cover the pot, and reduce the heat to medium. Cook until the potatoes are tender, about 15 minutes. Remove the pot from the heat and drain the potatoes thoroughly.

2. With a potato masher, mash the potatoes to the lumpy stage.

3. Return the empty saucepan to the stove over low heat to evaporate any remaining water. When the pan is dry, add the mashed potatoes. Fold in the butter pats with a large wooden spoon until they are thoroughly melted and incorporated. Stir in the milk, cream, salt, white pepper, and horseradish. Beat well with the wooden spoon. If you prefer your potatoes smoother, beat with an electric mixer.

Serves 6.

POTATO DUMPLINGS
WITH WILD MUSHROOM CREAM

This rich, rib-sticking side dish is best when accompanying a simple piece of broiled or grilled meat or fish and a green salad with a light vinaigrette dressing.

MUSHROOM CREAM

¼ cup (½ stick) unsalted butter

2 tbsp. minced onions

1 lb. sliced fresh wild mushrooms, morels, chanterelles, shiitakes, or your choice

¼ cup all-purpose flour

¼ cup beef or chicken stock (see index)

⅓ cup dry white wine

1 cup heavy cream

½ tsp. salt

4 turns freshly ground black pepper

⅓ cup grated Gruyère cheese

2 tbsp. minced fresh parsley

DUMPLINGS

2 lb. medium-size potatoes

3 large egg yolks

2 tsp. salt

6 turns freshly ground black pepper

1 cup or more all-purpose flour

2 qt. chicken stock (see index)

¼ cup chopped chives

1. To make the cream, melt the butter in a saucepan over medium heat. Add the onions and mushrooms and cook until they begin to get soft, about 3 minutes. Stir in the flour and cook, stirring gently, until the flour is incorporated and golden, about 3 minutes.

2. Stir in the stock, wine, cream, salt, and pepper and cook, stirring often, until the flavors have married and the sauce is thickened, about 8 minutes. Fold in the cheese and parsley and simmer, stirring occasionally, until the cheese has melted and the sauce is thick and bubbly, 3 to 5 minutes. Set aside, cover, and keep warm.

3. To make the dumplings, combine the unpeeled potatoes with water to cover in a large saucepan over high heat. Bring to a boil, reduce the heat to medium-low, cover, and cook until the potatoes are tender, 25 to 30 minutes. Drain, cool, and peel the potatoes. Process the potatoes through a food mill, ricer, or sieve and turn the riced potatoes into a large bowl.

4. Fold in the egg yolks, salt, and pepper. Add the flour slowly, mixing in well with your hands. If the mixture is too sticky, add more flour 1 tbsp. at a time until the mixture is smooth and cohesive and resembles a soft pie dough.

5. Bring the stock to a boil in a large pot over high heat.

6. Meanwhile, divide the potato dough into fourths. Roll each piece with your hand into a log shape about ¾" thick. Cut each log of dough with a floured knife into 1" pieces. Pinch the ends of each small piece with the floured tines of a fork.

7. When the stock is at a rapid boil, slip the dumplings in and cook until they float to the top, 10 to 12 minutes. Do not cover! Remove the dumplings with a slotted spoon to 6 shallow bowls. Cover each portion with Wild Mushroom Cream, sprinkle with chives, and serve.

Serves 6.

POTATOES AND WILD MUSHROOMS AU GRATIN

The potato is almost synonymous with Ireland. According to legend, Sir Walter Raleigh planted the first potatoes in Ireland in 1585, and the nutritious vegetable was soon grown by almost all of Ireland's farmers; a family could be fed for an entire year by just a half-acre of the crop. Today, in pubs all over the world, potatoes are mashed, creamed, fried, boiled, or served in bubbly casseroles such as this one.

5 cups peeled, thinly sliced potatoes
    (about ⅛" thick)
1 tbsp. plus 1½ tsp. salt, divided
6 tbsp. unsalted butter, divided
2 cups fresh, sliced wild mushrooms,
    a mixture of chanterelles, shiitakes,
    lobster mushrooms, or your
    choice

¼ cup all-purpose flour
1½ cups milk
½ tsp. white pepper
2 tbsp. chopped fresh parsley,
    divided
1½ cups grated Colby or Cheddar
    cheese, divided
1 cup fresh bread crumbs (see index)

1. Combine the potatoes with 1 tbsp. of the salt and water to cover in a large saucepan over high heat. Bring to a boil, reduce the heat to medium, and cook until the potatoes are firm-tender, 10 to 12 minutes. Drain the potatoes and set aside.

2. Preheat the oven to 350 degrees.

3. While the potatoes are cooking, melt 2 tbsp. of the butter in a large skillet

over medium-high heat. Add the mushrooms and cook, shaking the skillet once or twice, until the mushrooms are tender, 3 to 5 minutes. Remove the mushrooms with a slotted spoon and set aside.

4. Melt the remaining 4 tbsp. butter in a medium saucepan over medium-high heat. Whisk in the flour and cook, whisking, until the flour turns a light golden brown color, 3 to 4 minutes. Slowly stream in the milk, whisking constantly. Cook, whisking, until the sauce is thickened, about 7 minutes. Stir in the white pepper and the remaining 1½ tsp. salt, and remove from the heat.

5. Pour about one-quarter of the sauce into a deep, 2-qt. casserole. Arrange one-third of the potatoes over the sauce, and spread about a third of the mushrooms over the potatoes. Sprinkle about 1 tsp. of the parsley and ⅓ cup of the cheese over the mushrooms. Repeat with two more layers: ¼ of the sauce, ⅓ of the potatoes and the mushrooms, 1 tsp. parsley, and ⅓ cup cheese. Use the remaining sauce to blanket the top. Combine the bread crumbs with the remaining ½ cup cheese and 1 tbsp. parsley and sprinkle this mixture evenly over the sauce.

6. Bake, uncovered, until the bread crumbs are brown and the cheese bubbly, about 25 minutes. Remove from the oven and allow the casserole to rest for about 5 minutes. Serve with Irish Whiskey Steak (see index).

Serves 6-8.

BRANDIED YAMS

Brandied and candied, these sweets would wow 'em at Thanksgiving, accompanying the big roasted bird. Or serve them with any roasted meat or fowl.

4 lb. sweet potatoes or yams	2 tbsp. unsalted butter
⅔ cup brown sugar (packed)	¼ cup raisins
¼ cup water	¼ cup brandy

1. Preheat the oven to 350 degrees.
2. Scrub the potatoes, place them in a large saucepan, and cover with cold water. Bring to a boil over high heat and cook until barely soft, 15 to 20 minutes. Drain and let the potatoes sit until they're cool enough to handle.
3. Peel the potatoes and cut them into 1" rounds. Arrange the slices in a square 9" baking pan.

4. Combine the sugar, water, butter, and raisins in a small saucepan over medium-high heat. Bring to a boil and cook, stirring once, over medium heat, 5 minutes. Remove from the heat and allow to cool slightly. Stir in the brandy.

5. Pour the mixture over the potatoes and bake, uncovered, basting once or twice with the syrup in the pan, until brown and bubbly, about 30 minutes.

Serves 6-8.

WILD RICE PANCAKES

These are wonderful served with Staggering Skillet Steaks with Winey Wild Mushrooms, but then, they are delicious with almost everything.

½ cup firm-cooked wild rice
½ cup long-grain white rice
1 tbsp. minced onions
⅓ cup plus 2 tbsp. milk, divided
1 large egg

1½ tbsp. self-rising flour
½ tsp. salt
2 tbsp. chopped fresh parsley
2 tbsp. vegetable oil, divided

1. Combine all of the rice, onions, and ⅓ cup of the milk in a saucepan over low heat. Cook until all of the milk is absorbed and the rice is soggy, 15 to 20 minutes.

2. In a small bowl beat the egg. Beat in the flour, salt, and remaining 2 tbsp. milk. Fold this mixture into the rice and stir in the parsley.

3. Heat 1 tbsp. of the oil in a large, heavy skillet over medium-high heat. Fry the pancakes in batches: Drop the rice batter ¼ cup at a time into the oil, flattening each to a 3" circle (approximately). Cook until the pancakes are brown on the bottom, about 4 minutes. Turn them carefully with a long spatula and brown them on the second side, about 3 minutes. As the oil disappears, add the remaining 1 tbsp., and allow it to get hot before continuing to fry the remaining pancakes.

4. Drain the pancakes on paper towels and serve with Staggering Skillet Steaks with Winey Wild Mushrooms (see index), spooning some of the mushrooms over the pancakes.

Serves 4.

LEMON RICE BUNDT

This lightly lemoned rice dish makes a beautiful presentation when unmolded from its Bundt pan. Serve it with Veal Scallops and Artichokes, arranged as described below.

6½ cups chicken stock (see index)
3 tbsp. olive oil, divided
¼ cup minced onions
1 tsp. minced fresh garlic
2 cups long-grain white rice
½ cup freshly squeezed lemon juice
  (about 4 lemons)

2 tsp. salt
8 turns freshly ground black pepper
½ cup freshly grated Parmesan
  cheese
Zest of 1 lemon
Lemon slices for garnish

1. Bring the stock to a boil in a saucepan over high heat. Reduce the heat to low and simmer to keep the stock hot.

2. Heat 2 tbsp. of the oil in a large, deep skillet over medium heat. Add the onions and garlic and cook until soft and translucent, 3 to 4 minutes. Stir in the rice, coating it with the oil. Cook, shaking the pan or stirring once or twice, until the rice is golden, about 2 minutes.

3. Increase the heat to medium-high and stir in the lemon juice. Cook, stirring constantly, until all of the liquid is absorbed, about 2 minutes. Stir in ¾ cup of the hot stock and cook, stirring constantly, until the liquid has been absorbed. Continue adding stock this way, stirring constantly, until all of the stock has been used and is absorbed into the rice, about 25 minutes. Remove from the heat and fold in the salt, pepper, Parmesan, and lemon zest.

4. Grease a Bundt pan with the remaining 1 tbsp. oil. Spoon the rice into the pan, packing it well. Place a serving platter upside down over the top of the Bundt pan and quickly invert it to unmold the rice.

5. Serve with Veal Scallops and Artichokes (see index), arranging the veal and artichokes around the rice and spooning the sauce over all. Garnish with lemon slices.

Serves 8-10.

SHARAN'S CREAMED CORN

A sweet and delicious vegetable dish for almost any main course, this is also the main ingredient in Corn Pudding.

6 large ears fresh corn
¼ cup water
¼ cup (½ stick) unsalted butter
½ tsp. granulated sugar

½ cup milk
2 tsp. cornstarch
½ tsp. salt
3 turns freshly ground black pepper

1. Remove the husks and silk tassels from the corn, and cut the kernels from the cobs (you should have about 3 cups of kernels).
2. Combine the corn with the water, butter, and sugar in a large saucepan over medium heat. Bring to a bubble, cover, and cook until the corn is tender, about 10 minutes.
3. Meanwhile, whisk the milk, cornstarch, salt, and pepper together in a bowl until smooth. Whisk the mixture into the cooked corn, cover, and cook, stirring occasionally, until thick and bubbly, 3 to 5 minutes. Remove from the heat and serve or use to prepare Corn Pudding.
    Serves 3-4 (makes 2½ cups total).

CORN PUDDING

Corn has always been a staple vegetable in Ireland, in the past most often ground into meal or flour and baked into bread. Today corn is used as a vegetable as well, sometimes in creative ways, other times in traditional dishes, such as this rich, creamy pudding.

6 tbsp. unsalted butter, divided
1 cup chopped onions
1 cup chopped red bell peppers
¾ cup milk
3 large eggs, lightly beaten

3 tbsp. all-purpose flour
1 tbsp. granulated sugar
¼ tsp. salt
¼ tsp. cayenne pepper
1¼ cups Sharan's Creamed Corn

1. Preheat the oven to 350 degrees.
2. Melt 2 tbsp. of the butter in a small skillet over medium-low heat. Add the

onions and cook until translucent, about 5 minutes. Add the bell peppers and cook until tender, shaking the skillet once or twice, 4 to 5 minutes. Remove from the heat.

3. In a small bowl, combine the milk and eggs and whisk lightly until well combined. Use 1 tbsp. of the butter to grease a 1-qt. casserole dish.

4. Melt the remaining 3 tbsp. butter in a large saucepan over medium heat. Stir in the flour and cook, stirring constantly with a wooden spoon, until the roux is golden in color and bubbly, 5 to 6 minutes. Stir in the sugar, salt, and cayenne pepper. Slowly add the milk-egg mixture, beginning with just a little at a time, stirring constantly until incorporated. Cook, stirring constantly, over medium heat, until the sauce is thick enough to coat a spoon, 5 to 8 minutes. Fold in the creamed corn and the onion-bell pepper mixture.

5. Pour the entire mixture into the casserole and bake until brown and bubbly, 45 to 55 minutes. Serve immediately.

Serves 4.

McGUIRE'S POLENTA

Polenta is cornmeal that is cooked to a light creaminess then baked or fried. Serve fried slices of polenta for breakfast with maple syrup poured over them or with bacon and eggs. Or serve for dinner with Scallops in Saffron Cream (see index).

3 cups water	1 tbsp. salt
1 cup yellow cornmeal	1 tbsp. vegetable oil

1. Preheat the oven to 375 degrees.

2. Combine the water, cornmeal, and salt in a large saucepan over medium heat. Bring to a boil and cook, stirring constantly, until the mixture is oatmeal thick, about 20 minutes.

3. Grease a 9" x 5" loaf pan with the oil and pour the cornmeal mixture into the pan. Bake until firm, 30 to 35 minutes. Place on a wire rack and allow to cool completely before removing from the pan.

4. For fried polenta, remove the mixture from the loaf pan when it reaches room temperature, wrap it in plastic, and refrigerate for several hours or overnight. When you're ready to serve it, slice the polenta and fry it in olive oil or a mixture of olive oil and butter. Serve immediately.

Makes 1 loaf.

BLACKEYE PEA PUDDING

This unusual pudding completes the "Irish Eyes" dinner of Rum and Coke Baked Ham with Red-Eye Gravy (see index).

3 cups crumbled cornbread
4 slices plain wheat or sourdough
   bread, torn in chunks
3 cups milk
2 tbsp. vegetable oil
½ cup chopped onions
½ cup grated Cheddar cheese

½ tsp. salt
8 turns freshly ground black pepper
3 large eggs, beaten
2 cups cooked blackeye peas
Softened butter or vegetable oil
   spray

1. In a large bowl, combine the cornbread and wheat or sourdough bread. Pour the milk over the bread, and allow it to sit until all of the milk is soaked up, 15 to 20 minutes.

2. Preheat the oven to 350 degrees.

3. Heat the oil in a small skillet over medium heat. Add the onions and cook until they are translucent and soft, 5 to 6 minutes. Remove from the heat.

4. Fold the onions into the bread mixture. Stir in the cheese, salt, and pepper. Fold in the eggs, then the blackeye peas, and stir until the mixture is well blended.

5. Grease a 9" x 13" x 2" deep baking dish with the butter or oil spray. Turn the batter into the dish and bake until the pudding is firm and golden brown, about 45 minutes. Remove from the oven and allow the pudding to sit for about 15 minutes. Turn out of the loaf pan and serve.

Serves 10-12 generously.

ONION PUDDING

Here's a quick and easy side dish that may become a family favorite. Serve it with Baked Trout with Mushrooms and Almonds, McGuire's Panéed Turkey Cutlets, Sharan's Irish Barbecue, Honey Beer-Braised Ribs, or whatever suits your fancy.

½ cup (1 stick) unsalted butter, plus more for greasing
6 cups thinly sliced onions (about 6 large onions)
¼ cup granulated sugar

3 tbsp. all-purpose flour
2 tsp. baking powder
2 tsp. salt
6 large eggs, beaten
2 cups heavy cream

1. Melt the butter in a large saucepan over medium heat. Add the onions and reduce the heat to medium-low. Cook, stirring occasionally, until the onions are caramelized and sweet, about 45 minutes. Remove from the heat.

2. About 15 minutes before the onions are finished cooking, preheat the oven to 350 degrees.

3. In a small bowl combine the sugar, flour, baking powder, and salt. Fold in the eggs and cream and blend well. Fold in the onions and stir until thoroughly incorporated.

4. Butter a deep, 2-qt. casserole and pour the pudding mixture into it. Bake until golden brown and firm to the touch, 30 to 40 minutes. A knife inserted in the center of the pudding should come out clean.

sServes 6-8.

McGUIRE'S FAMOUS IRISH-FRIED ONION RINGS

There's a good reason these tender, crispy onion rings are famous, and when you taste them, you'll know why. Baskets of them go like wildfire at McGuire's.

6 cups saltine crackers (about 120 crackers)
1 tsp. onion powder
1 tsp. garlic powder
½ tsp. paprika
½ tsp. freshly ground black pepper
1 large egg

1½ cups Irish ale
½ tsp. salt
2 cups all-purpose flour
4 cups vegetable oil
4 cups fresh yellow onion rings (½" thick, about 3 large onions)

1. Place the saltines in a food processor and pulse until you have coarse crumbs, or place the crackers in a large plastic bag and crush with a rolling pin. Place the crumbs in a large bowl and combine with onion powder, garlic powder, paprika, and black pepper.

2. In another bowl, beat the egg with the ale and salt. Slowly mix in the flour, stirring well until the mixture resembles a thick pancake batter.

3. Heat the oil in a large, deep skillet until it sizzles when a bit of water is dropped in. Dip each onion ring into the batter, then the cracker mixture. Drop into the hot oil and cook, turning once, until golden brown, 1 to 1½ minutes. (You will probably need to fry these in batches; don't coat onion rings until right before you drop them in the oil.) Remove from the oil and drain on paper towels before serving.

Serves 6 generously.

> *Lest your kissing should be spoiled,*
> *your onions must be thoroughly boiled.*
> —Deane Swift, *The Progress of Poetry*

CABBAGE BREAD PUDDING

Serve this unusual, savory bread pudding with Soused Corned Beef in Horseradish Sauce (see index) for a delicious twist on the original—corned beef and cabbage.

½ baguette (unsliced) French bread, torn into chunks
½ loaf (unsliced) dark pumpernickel, torn into chunks
4 cups milk
6 slices bacon, quartered
1 cup chopped onions (about 1 medium-large onion)

2 tsp. minced fresh garlic
1 small green cabbage, cut into chunks and leaves pulled apart
3 large eggs
1 tbsp. caraway seeds
2 tbsp. unsalted butter

1. Preheat the oven to 350 degrees.

2. Place all of the bread chunks in a large bowl. Add the milk, mix well, and soak until the bread has absorbed all of the milk, about 15 to 20 minutes.

3. Place the bacon in a skillet over medium-high heat and cook until the fat begins to render, about 2 minutes. Add the onions and garlic and cook, stirring occasionally and turning the bacon, until the bacon is crisp and the onions tender, 6 to 7 minutes.

4. Stir in the cabbage and toss to cover all of the pieces with bacon drippings. Reduce the heat to medium-low, cover the skillet, and steam the cabbage until tender, 10 to 15 minutes. Remove from the heat and stir the contents of the skillet into the bread mixture.

5. Beat the eggs in a small bowl. Fold the beaten eggs into the bread-cabbage mixture. Stir in the caraway seeds and blend until thoroughly combined.

6. Melt the butter in two 8" baking pans, coating the bottom and sides of the pans. Turn the bread mixture into the pans and spread it evenly. Bake until the pudding tests done with a toothpick, about 30 minutes. Remove from the oven and cut the bread pudding into wedges.

Serves 8-12.

PARSNIP CROQUETTES
WITH GARLICKY CARROT SALSA

Root vegetables have long been an important staple in Irish cooking. This dish comes to dinner as a side—or to your best party.*

¼ cup olive oil, divided
4 cloves garlic, slivered
2 cups peeled, grated carrots
½ cup coarsely chopped red or yellow bell peppers
½ cup coarsely chopped red onions
¼ cup freshly squeezed lime juice
1½ tsp. salt, divided
8 turns freshly ground black pepper, divided

1 lb. parsnips, peeled and sliced thick (about ½")
2 large eggs, beaten
⅛ tsp. ground nutmeg, preferably freshly ground
1 tbsp. chopped fresh parsley
½ cup fresh bread crumbs (see index)
Vegetable oil for frying

1. To prepare the salsa, heat 1 tbsp. of the olive oil in a small skillet over medium heat. Add the garlic and cook, shaking the skillet, until the garlic slivers are soft and a pale golden color—not brown—about 2 minutes. Transfer to a bowl and add the carrots, bell peppers, onions, lime juice, ½ tsp. of the salt, 4 turns of the black pepper, and the remaining 3 tbsp. olive oil. Toss well and serve chilled or at room temperature.

2. To make the croquettes, combine the parsnips with water to cover and the remaining 1 tsp. salt in a saucepan over high heat. Bring to a boil, reduce the heat to medium-low, and cover the saucepan. Cook until the parsnips are soft, 20 to 25 minutes. Drain the parsnips, turn them into a bowl, and mash until they resemble mashed potatoes. Beat in the eggs, nutmeg, parsley, and the remaining 4 turns black pepper. Fold in the bread crumbs and mix with a wooden spoon just until the mixture is thoroughly blended.

3. Heat about an inch of vegetable oil in a large, heavy skillet. Shape the parsnip mixture into croquettes using a ⅓-cup measure. When the oil is very hot, add the croquettes and fry them in batches until golden brown, 4 to 5 minutes each side. Drain on paper towels.

4. Serve as a side dish with a spoonful of Carrot Salsa on top.
Serves 6.

*For a party dish, form balls (instead of croquettes), using 1½ tbsp. of the mixture for each. Deep fry the parsnip balls in hot oil until golden brown, about 3 minutes. Drain and serve warm on doily-lined platters, with toothpicks, and pass the salsa for dipping.

APPLEJACK SQUASH AND APPLE PUREE

This is a good winter side dish, since winter is the season of the acorn squash. The vegetable is difficult to peel when uncooked, but the process is easily mastered once the squash has been baked. This popular gourd, with its dark green skin and pumpkin-colored flesh, has a rich flavor that makes it a heavenly complement for almost any roasted meat or fowl; I love it with Stuffed Quail with Pilsner Sauce (see index).

2 acorn squash, halved vertically and pitted
4 large baking apples, halved and cored

½ tsp. salt
2 tbsp. applejack brandy
2 tbsp. heavy cream
1 tbsp. unsalted butter

1. Preheat the oven to 350 degrees.
2. Place the squash and apples cut side down in a foil-lined pan. Bake until the squash is soft, 30 to 40 minutes. Remove from the oven and allow to cool slightly.
3. Remove the peel from the squash and apples and place their pulp in a food processor. Puree until smooth and pour into a saucepan over medium heat. Stir in the salt, brandy, cream, and butter and simmer, stirring often, until the alcohol has evaporated, about 5 minutes.
Serves 4-6.

TOMATO-ARTICHOKE GRATIN

A creamy, herby casserole, this dish makes a great vegetarian brunch, a first course for dinner, or a lovely side course to accompany almost any roast or chop.

Two 14½-oz. cans whole tomatoes
14 oz. frozen artichoke hearts (about one and a half 9-oz. pkg.), thawed (reserve any liquid)
1 tsp. salt, divided
8 turns freshly ground black pepper, divided
6 tbsp. unsalted butter, divided, plus more for greasing
1½ tsp. minced fresh garlic
¼ cup all-purpose flour
1 tsp. dried sage, divided
1½ cups milk
1½ cups medium-fine cornbread crumbs (see index)*
1 cup grated Gruyère cheese

1. Preheat the oven to 350 degrees.

2. Drain the tomatoes and artichokes, reserving and combining their liquids. Measure out ½ cup of this liquid and set aside. Quarter the tomatoes and discard their seeds. Quarter the artichoke hearts. Combine the tomatoes and artichoke hearts in a bowl and toss with ½ tsp. of the salt and 4 turns of the pepper.

3. Melt 4 tbsp. of the butter in a large saucepan over medium heat. Add the garlic and cook, shaking the saucepan often, until the garlic is soft and golden, 2 to 3 minutes. Stir in the flour and cook, stirring constantly, until the flour is golden, about 4 minutes.

4. Gradually stir in the ½ cup reserved tomato-artichoke liquid, ½ tsp. of the sage, the remaining ½ tsp. salt, and 4 turns pepper. Cook, stirring, until the mixture begins to thicken, 2 to 3 minutes. Slowly stir in the milk and cook, stirring often, until the mixture becomes a cream gravy, 2 to 3 minutes. Remove from the heat and fold in the tomatoes and artichoke hearts.

5. Butter an 8-cup gratin pan or shallow casserole dish. Pour the tomato-artichoke mixture into the dish. Combine the cornbread crumbs with the cheese and the remaining ½ tsp. sage and spread the mixture evenly on top of the gratin. Melt the remaining 2 tbsp. butter and drizzle over the topping. Bake until the gratin is golden brown and bubbly, 25 to 30 minutes. Serve hot or warm.

Serves 8 for a first course or side dish and 6 for a main course.

*To make cornbread crumbs, place broken-up cornbread in the bowl of a food processor and process until you have medium-fine crumbs.

RUBIES AND EMERALDS

Here's an attractive and delicious way to enjoy healthy vegetables. Take care not to overcook them since vegetables taste most delicious and are best for you when they are just tender.

1 qt. water
2 cups fresh broccoli florets
10 to 12 asparagus spears
2 tbsp. olive oil
2 tsp. minced fresh garlic
¼ cup minced red bell peppers

2 tbsp. pine nuts
6 cups fresh spinach leaves (10 oz.), rinsed, stemmed, and patted dry
1 tsp. salt
4 turns freshly ground black pepper

1. Bring the water to a boil in a large saucepan fitted with a steaming basket. Place the broccoli and asparagus in the basket and steam until the vegetables just start to get tender, about 1 minute. Drain and set aside.

2. Heat the oil in a large skillet over medium heat. Add the garlic and bell peppers and cook for 1 minute. Add the pine nuts and cook, shaking the pan often, until the nuts are golden, 1 to 2 minutes.

3. Add the spinach and cook, tossing it to coat the leaves with the oil, about 30 seconds. Add the broccoli, asparagus, salt, and black pepper. Cover and steam until the vegetables are tender, 4 to 5 minutes. Toss the vegetables once, taking care not to break the asparagus, and serve immediately.

Serves 4-6.

PICKLED BEETS

Make these delicious beets at least 3 weeks before you plan to use them. Serve them as a snack with drinks or as a side dish with broiled fish or use them in Irish Red Plate (see index).

4 lb. fresh whole beets, unpeeled
2 cups granulated sugar
2 tbsp. mixed pickling spices

2 tsp. pickling salt*
1 cup white wine vinegar

1. Combine the beets with cold water to cover in a large pot over high heat. Bring to a boil, reduce the heat to medium, and cook until the beets are tender, about 30 minutes. Drain in a colander and allow the beets to sit until cool enough to handle. Peel and quarter the beets, and drop them into 4 pint-size Mason jars.

2. To make the pickling juice combine the sugar, pickling spices, salt, and vinegar in a saucepan over medium-high heat. Bring to a boil, stirring almost constantly to dissolve the sugar. Reduce the heat to medium-low and cook at a slow bubble until the flavors have blended, about 5 minutes.

3. Pour the pickling juice evenly over the beets, leaving a ½" space at the top. Use the handle of a wooden spoon or a rubber spatula to push the beets gently under the juice, eliminating any air pockets. Cap the jars to seal them, and screw on the lids tightly.

4. Place the jars in a large stockpot and add enough water to come up to the lids on the jars. Bring to a boil over high heat, reduce the heat to a bare simmer, and let the jars heat for 30 minutes. Remove the jars from the pot and allow them to sit at room temperature until the caps "pop," about 2 hours. (If a cap doesn't pop, press down on the center of the lid. If the lid moves, it wasn't sealed properly. You can return the jar to the pot and heat for another 10 minutes or refrigerate once the jar is cool.)

5. Allow the beets to stand for 3 weeks. Refrigerate any opened jar; they will keep for months in the refrigerator.

Makes 2 qt.

*Pickling salt is available in boxes in grocery stores and supermarkets.

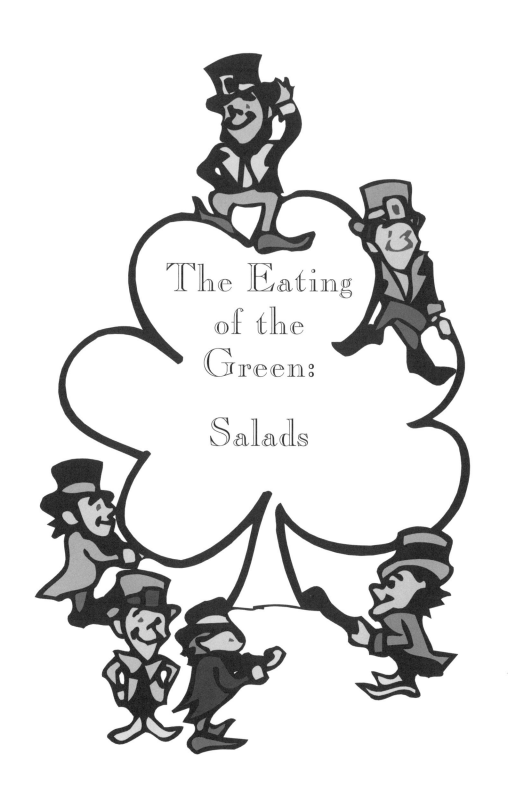

The Eating
of the
Green:

Salads

In this age of healthier eating, we are constantly pummeled with all sorts of negative information regarding our evil eating ways. As a result, restaurants have felt pressure to offer healthier alternatives to their usual fare. Pubs are no exception, and today one can wander into the local tavern and have a huge bowl of salad for lunch instead of a hamburger and fries. If the pub knows its stuff, the chosen salad will have lots of delicious things in it and the customer never misses eating the heavy food.

In this chapter we present salads that are unique, smoky, tangy, beefy, fruity, and some that are pasta based. Some are hearty one-dish meals; others are meant to be served as side dishes.

Try, for instance, the refreshing Cold Smoked Salmon and Bow Ties with Caper-Dill Dressing; spicy-sweet Asparagus Salad with Pear Salsa and Roquefort, with the surprise of mint, ginger, and pickled jalapeños; Shrimp and Pasta-Shell Salad with Walnut Dressing in a light dressing with chopped, toasted walnuts; or hearty Red Potato Salad with Warm Beer Dressing to accompany a picnic or barbecue.

Now we're not claiming that these are necessarily fat free, but they are a tasty way to eat your vegetables—and lots of other good things, as well.

APPLE-SCENTED SLAW

This tangy-sweet, snap-to-make slaw is delicious with Sharan's Irish Barbecue or Beer-Braised Honey-Mustard Pork Chops with White Bean Puree (see index).

3 cups finely shredded cabbage
¾ cup finely shredded carrots
⅓ cup fresh thin onion rings
¾ cup frozen apple juice
  concentrate, thawed

¼ cup apple cider vinegar
1 tbsp. vegetable oil
½ tsp. celery salt
½ tsp. Dijon mustard
8 turns freshly ground black pepper

1. Combine the cabbage with the carrots and onions in a large mixing bowl. Set aside.

2. In a blender or food processor, combine the apple juice concentrate, vinegar, oil, celery salt, mustard, and pepper. Pulse until thoroughly blended. Pour over the cabbage mixture, cover, and refrigerate 3 to 4 hours.

Serves 4-6.

RED CABBAGE APPLE CONFIT

This tart, tangy side dish is delicious with pork and with Rosemary-Scented Irish Stew (see index).

1 head red cabbage, finely shredded
2 Granny Smith apples, peeled and
  shredded
¼ cup balsamic vinegar

2 tbsp. vegetable oil
½ tsp. salt
6 turns freshly ground black pepper

1. Combine the cabbage and apples in a bowl. Stir in the vinegar, oil, salt, and pepper. Cover and chill. Serve chilled or at room temperature.

Serves 6-8.

THREE-CABBAGE SLAW

This delicious and pretty cole slaw is easy to make and the recipe can be doubled or tripled to serve a crowd.

2 tbsp. brown sugar
¼ cup apple cider vinegar
½ lb. red cabbage, coarsely shredded
½ lb. green cabbage, coarsely shredded
½ lb. savoy cabbage, coarsely shredded

1 small unpeeled apple, thinly sliced and julienned
½ tsp. salt
6 turns freshly ground black pepper

1. In a small saucepan over low heat combine the brown sugar and vinegar, stirring until thoroughly mixed and heated through. Remove from the heat.
2. In a large bowl combine the cabbages and apples. Pour the sugar-vinegar mixture over all, and toss well with the salt and pepper. Refrigerate until thoroughly chilled.
Serves 4.

ASPARAGUS SALAD
WITH PEAR SALSA AND ROQUEFORT

A mélange of bright, lively flavors makes this salad a standout. It's a wonderful salad course with a roast or chops, and it's an unforgettable main course for a summer lunch.

2 qt. water
1 tbsp. plus ½ tsp. salt, divided
18 stalks fresh asparagus
Large bowl of ice water
3 fresh pears
2 tbsp. freshly squeezed lemon juice
1 tsp. minced pickled jalapeño peppers
¼ cup minced red onions
2 tbsp. chopped fresh mint

½ tsp. ground ginger
6 cups mixed salad greens
6 tbsp. olive oil
6 tbsp. crumbled, good-quality Roquefort cheese
6 tbsp. chopped walnuts, toasted (see index)
12 turns freshly ground black pepper, or to taste

1. Early in the day, bring the water with 1 tbsp. of the salt to a boil in a large pot over high heat. While the water is heating, trim the ends from the asparagus. When the water reaches a boil, add the asparagus and blanch for 3 minutes. Remove the asparagus and immediately submerge in the ice water. When the asparagus stalks are cool and the color bright, remove from the ice water and refrigerate to chill thoroughly.

2. Prepare the salsa. Peel and cube the pears (about ¼" cubes), and toss them in a bowl with the lemon juice. Add the jalapeños, onions, mint, ginger, and the remaining ½ tsp. salt and blend thoroughly with the pears. Cover and refrigerate for at least 1 hour, stirring once or twice.

3. Just before serving, toss the salad greens in a large bowl with the olive oil, coating the greens thoroughly. Divide the greens among 6 salad plates. Top each serving with 3 asparagus spears and 2 to 3 tbsp. of Pear Salsa. Sprinkle each salad with 1 tbsp. Roquefort, 1 tbsp. toasted walnuts, and 2 to 3 turns black pepper, and serve. For a main-course lunch dish, divide the greens among 3 plates and double the asparagus, salsa, Roquefort, walnuts, and pepper per plate.

Serves 6 for a side dish and 3 for lunch.

RED POTATO SALAD WITH WARM BEER DRESSING

You've probably never tasted potato salad like this. And despite all of the potato dishes in Ireland, the Irish have probably never tasted anything like this, either.

2½ lb. unpeeled red potatoes
½ cup thinly sliced red onions
¼ cup chopped fresh parsley
6 tbsp. olive oil, divided
½ cup minced yellow onions
¾ cup dark beer or ale, preferably stout
¼ cup balsamic vinegar
2 tsp. granulated sugar
1 tbsp. Dijon mustard
1 tsp. salt
20 turns freshly ground black pepper
2 tbsp. chopped fresh chives

1. In a large pot over high heat, cover the potatoes with water and bring to a boil. Cook until tender, 20 to 25 minutes. Drain and cut the potatoes, unpeeled, into ¼" slices. Place the potatoes in a large bowl.

2. Add the red onion slices and the parsley and gently toss them all together.

3. In a saucepan heat 2 tbsp. of the oil over medium heat. Add the minced onions and cook until soft and golden, 4 to 5 minutes. Increase the heat to

medium-high, stir in the beer, vinegar, and sugar, and bring to a boil. Cook over medium-high heat, stirring often, about 5 minutes.

4. Pour the beer mixture into a food processor and add the mustard. With the food processor running, slowly stream in the remaining 4 tbsp. oil and puree until emulsified. Stir in the salt and pepper.

5. Pour the dressing over the potatoes and red onions and toss gently, being careful not to break the potato slices.

6. Sprinkle with chopped chives and serve warm.

Serves 6-8.

AL SILVER'S WILTED SPINACH, BACON, AND PASTA SALAD

Al Silver was one of the first customers at McGuire's and has been a regular ever since. Al has his very own, very rickety, chair at the bar. The chair bears a brass plate with his name, and Al gets a little grumpy if he arrives to find someone else in it. Every Friday, Al used to be found sitting at the bar digging into his usual—McGuire's spinach salad. We added a pasta twist, but we though Al would enjoy this new wrinkle on his old favorite.

8 oz. tricolor rotini
10 slices bacon (about ½ lb.)
½ cup vegetable oil
¼ cup red wine vinegar
2 tbsp. granulated sugar
½ tsp. dry mustard
½ tsp. salt

12 turns freshly ground black pepper
10 oz. fresh spinach, rinsed, stemmed, and patted dry
½ cup chopped scallions (green onions)
½ cup sliced white mushrooms

1. Prepare the pasta according to package directions. Drain, and set aside to cool slightly.

2. Cook the bacon in a heavy skillet over medium heat, turning once, until very crisp, about 8 minutes. Remove the bacon and drain on paper towels. Reserve 2 tbsp. of the bacon drippings, and transfer this to a small saucepan.

3. Stir the vegetable oil, vinegar, sugar, mustard, salt, and pepper into the bacon drippings in the saucepan over low heat. Bring to a bubble, stirring occasionally. Turn off the heat and cover to keep warm.

4. In a large salad serving bowl, combine the pasta, spinach, scallions, and

mushrooms. Pour the warm dressing over the salad and toss well. Crumble the bacon over the top and serve immediately.

Serves 6-8 for a generous main course.

BEEFY PASTA SALAD WITH SNAPPY
CAESAR DRESSING AND CROUTONS

This main-course salad makes a great case for a cool yet hearty meal. In warm weather it would be a refreshing change for dinner.

DRESSING

2 large eggs
¼ cup coarsely chopped celery
¼ cup coarsely chopped onions
2 oz. anchovy paste

1 tbsp. Dijon mustard
½ tbsp. freshly squeezed lemon juice
4 turns freshly ground black pepper
1 cup vegetable oil

CROUTONS

Olive oil for frying

Six 1" slices French bread, cut in 1" cubes or roughly torn

SALAD

1 tsp. salt
1 tsp. black pepper
1 tsp. garlic powder
1½ lb. boneless top sirloin of beef

One 16-oz. pkg. penne pasta, cooked al dente, drained, and cooled
1 cup freshly grated Romano cheese
½ cup minced fresh parsley

1. To make the dressing, combine the eggs, celery, onions, anchovy paste, mustard, lemon juice, and pepper in the bowl of a food processor. Process until the mixture is smooth, about 45 seconds. With the processor running, slowly stream in the oil and continue to process until the dressing is thoroughly emulsified, about 15 seconds. Turn the mixture into a bowl or container, cover, and refrigerate for about 1 hour.

2. To make the croutons, heat 2" of oil in a skillet over medium-high heat. When the oil is very hot, add the bread cubes in batches. Fry, turning once, until golden brown, 20 to 30 seconds. Remove with a slotted spoon and drain on paper towels.

3. Preheat oven broiler or prepare a charcoal grill.

4. To make the salad, in a small bowl combine the salt with the pepper and garlic powder, and blend well. Rub the mixture into the beef, covering the meat

all over. Grill or broil the meat until medium-rare, 5 to 6 minutes on each side. Allow the meat to cool to room temperature, then cut into ¼" slices.

5. Place the cooked, cooled pasta in a large bowl. Add ⅓ cup of the dressing and toss. Add the beef, cheese, parsley, and another ⅓ cup of the dressing, and toss well. Add additional dressing if you like, or pass the rest at the table. Top the salad with the croutons, and serve.

Serves 10-12 for a main course.

IRISH-ASIAN PORK AND GREENS WITH CITRUS DRESSING AND GOAT CHEESE CROSTINI

The unusual combination of flavors in this salad makes it an exotic delight. Serve it as the main attraction at a special luncheon, or treat your family with it for dinner on a summer night.

DRESSING
½ cup orange juice
¼ cup freshly squeezed lemon juice
1 tbsp. minced shallots

½ tsp. minced fresh garlic
1¼ tsp. salt
½ cup olive oil

SALAD
½ cup soy sauce
¼ cup dry sherry
¼ cup brown sugar
1 tbsp. rice wine vinegar
1 tbsp. crushed star aniseed*
1 tbsp. orange zest
1 tsp. minced fresh gingerroot
¾ cup chopped scallions (green onions), divided
2 lb. trimmed pork tenderloin, cut into ¾" strips

6 cups rinsed romaine lettuce, torn into bite-size pieces
1½ cups rinsed, trimmed watercress
1 cup thinly sliced fennel bulbs
1 cup shredded green cabbage
½ cup all-purpose flour
1 tsp. salt
4 turns freshly ground black pepper
Vegetable oil for frying

CROSTINI
Eight 2" French baguette slices
Olive oil
3 oz. goat cheese, room temperature

1 tbsp. minced fresh chives
2 tbsp. grated Parmesan cheese

GARNISH

3 oranges, peeled and sectioned   1 cup toasted sliced almonds

1. A day ahead, prepare the dressing. Combine the orange juice and lemon juice in a small saucepan over medium-high heat. Bring to a boil, reduce the heat to medium-low, and cook until the flavors are infused and the mixture slightly reduced, about 10 minutes. Stir in the shallots, garlic, salt, and pepper, and slowly whisk in the olive oil. Continue to whisk until the mixture is thoroughly emulsified, and pour into a small bowl. Allow the dressing to cool to room temperature, cover tightly, and refrigerate overnight.

2. Also a day ahead, prepare the marinade. In a bowl combine the soy sauce, sherry, brown sugar, vinegar, star anise, orange zest, ginger, and ¼ cup of the scallions. Stir well to blend the ingredients. Arrange the pork strips in a flat baking dish and pour the marinade over the meat, turning the strips to coat them. Cover and refrigerate overnight, turning the strips once.

3. About 45 minutes before serving, combine the romaine, watercress, fennel, cabbage, and remaining scallions in a large bowl. Remove the pork from the refrigerator and drain off the marinade. Combine the flour with the salt and pepper in a shallow bowl. Start heating about 1" of the vegetable oil in a large skillet over medium-high heat.

4. Dredge the pork strips in the seasoned flour and when the oil is very hot, add them to the skillet (you may have to do this in batches) and fry until brown on all sides, 4 to 5 minutes. Drain the pork on paper towels. While the last batch is frying, preheat the oven to 400 degrees.

5. Prepare the crostini: Place the baguette slices on a baking sheet and brush lightly with olive oil. Toast until golden on both sides, about 6-8 minutes, turning once and brushing the second side with a bit of olive oil. While the bread is toasting, combine the goat cheese and chives and mash until well blended. Remove the bread from the oven and turn on the broiler. Spread the cheese mixture on the baguette slices, sprinkle with Parmesan, and broil until the cheese is brown and bubbly, about 4 minutes.

6. Remove the dressing from the refrigerator and stir well. Pour the dressing over the greens and toss until all of the greens are covered.

7. Divide the greens among 8 serving plates. Arrange the orange sections over the greens and sprinkle with the almonds. Arrange the pork strips on top of the salad and add one crostini to each plate before serving.

Serves 8 for a main course.

*Star anise is native to China and is not related to the anise family. It comes from the brown pods in a star-shaped cluster and is available in Asian food markets. If you can't find star anise, substitute five-spice powder.

SMOKED CHICKEN SALAD

This dish is easy to prepare whether or not you own a barbecue grill. The marriage of aromatic smoking woods with fresh tarragon brings the salad out of the realm of the usual. For a super, out-of-the-ordinary sandwich, mound the chicken salad on No-Rise Swiss-Cheese Applesauce Bread.

Mesquite or hickory chips
2½ lb. chicken parts, with skin and bones
1 cup coarsely chopped celery
1 cup coarsely chopped peeled red apples
½ cup toasted slivered almonds

2 tbsp. chopped fresh tarragon
1 cup mayonnaise
1 tbsp. Dijon mustard
1 tbsp. tarragon-infused white wine vinegar
½ tsp. salt
8 turns freshly ground black pepper

1. Soak the chips in water. Build a charcoal fire to one side of the barbecue grill.* When the fire has burned low, add the chips and place the metal grill over them.

2. Arrange the chicken pieces, skin side up, on the grill on the side away from the fire. Cover with the top of the grill and allow the chicken to smoke 1½ to 2 hours. Remove the chicken to cool.

3. Remove the skin and bones from the chicken and cut the meat into bite-size pieces. Toss the chicken in a large bowl with the celery, apples, almonds, and tarragon.

4. In a small bowl combine the mayonnaise with the mustard, vinegar, salt, and pepper, and mix well. Toss this mixture with the chicken, cover, and refrigerate.

5. Serve over a bed of mixed baby greens, including arugula, endive, and watercress, if available. Or serve as sandwiches between thick slabs of fresh No-Rise Swiss-Cheese Applesauce Bread (see index).

Serves 6 for lunch.

*To create a device for smoking the chicken indoors, use a wok lined with foil. Add about 4 cups of soaked wood chips, and cover tightly with more foil. Place the wok over high heat on your stove and heat for 10 to 12 minutes. Remove the foil from the top of the chips and place a rack over them. Brush the rack with oil and place the chicken on the rack. Cover the wok tightly and smoke over high heat for 30 minutes. Remove the wok from the heat and allow it to sit, still covered, off the heat for 30 minutes longer.

SCALLOPS AND SHELLS

The sweetness of fresh sea scallops against the tangy, nutty flavor of the dressing may make this one of your favorite cool pasta salads. When you purchase sea scallops, make sure you see the little notch on the side of each scallop, so you know you're not buying stamped-out pieces of fish.

¾ cup plus 2 tbsp. walnut oil*
¼ cup freshly squeezed lemon juice
    (2 to 3 lemons)
1 tsp. minced fresh garlic
1 tsp. salt plus more to taste, if
    desired
6 turns freshly ground black pepper
    plus more to taste, if desired

1½ lb. sea scallops
One 16-oz. pkg. pasta shells, cooked
    al dente and drained
1 cup chopped red bell peppers
¼ cup chopped fresh parsley
½ cup chopped walnuts, toasted (see
    index)

1. In a small bowl, combine ¾ cup of the walnut oil, the lemon juice, garlic, 1 tsp. of the salt, and 6 turns of the black pepper. Set this dressing aside.

2. Heat the remaining 2 tbsp. oil in a large skillet over medium heat. Pat the scallops dry and squeeze out any excess liquid. Cook, stirring often, until the scallops are a light golden color on both sides and just cooked through, 2 to 3 minutes total. Remove from the heat and turn the scallops into a large bowl.

3. Add the pasta shells, red peppers, parsley, walnuts, and the dressing. Toss well, add salt and pepper to taste, if desired, and chill for 3 to 4 hours before serving.

Serves 8 for a main course.

*Walnut oil is available in gourmet and specialty food shops. You can make your own by adding ¼ cup of walnut pieces to 2 cups olive oil.

SHRIMP AND PASTA-SHELL SALAD
WITH WALNUT DRESSING

This is a slightly simpler version of Scallops and Shells, this time for shrimp lovers.

One 8-oz. pkg. pasta shells
3/4 cup walnut oil*
¼ cup freshly squeezed lemon juice
½ tsp. salt
4 turns freshly ground black pepper

2 lb. large shrimp, peeled and
   deveined
½ cup chopped walnuts, toasted
   (see index)
¼ cup chopped fresh parsley

1. Prepare the pasta shells according to package directions. Drain, and set aside.

2. In a small bowl, combine the oil, lemon juice, salt, and pepper.

3. Bring a large pot of water to a boil over high heat. Add the shrimp, return to a boil, and cook just until the shrimp turn pink and lose their translucence, about 1 minute. Drain and cool to room temperature.

4. Transfer the shrimp to a large bowl, toss with the dressing, cover, and refrigerate for 1 hour. Add the cooked pasta, chopped walnuts, and parsley, toss again, and serve.

Serves 4-6 for a main course.

*Walnut oil is available in gourmet and specialty food shops. You can make your own by adding ¼ cup of walnut pieces to 2 cups olive oil.

COLD SMOKED SALMON AND BOW TIES WITH CAPER-DILL DRESSING

This is a hot-weather treat for lunch or dinner, featuring the Irish "king of the sea"—the salmon.

One 12-oz. pkg. bow tie pasta
⅓ cup olive oil
¼ cup minced scallions (green onions)
2 tbsp. freshly squeezed lemon juice
⅓ cup freshly snipped dill
1 tbsp. capers
½ tsp. salt plus more to taste, if desired

4 turns freshly ground black pepper plus more to taste, if desired
6 oz. smoked salmon, chopped in ½" pieces
1 cup cherry tomatoes, halved or quartered
1 medium red onion, in thin rings
¼ cup chopped chives

1. Cook the bow ties according to package directions. Drain and turn the bow ties into a large bowl.

2. In a jar with a tight-fitting lid combine the oil, scallions, lemon juice, dill, capers, ½ tsp. salt, and 4 turns of the black pepper. Cover and shake well until thoroughly blended. Adjust salt and pepper to taste.

3. Add 3 tbsp. of the dressing to the pasta, and toss well. Add the salmon, tomatoes, red onions, and ¼ cup of the dressing and toss well. Cover and refrigerate for at least 2 hours.

4. Garnish the salad with chopped chives and serve with remaining dressing on the side.

Serves 8-10 for a main course.

Celebrations:

Passionate
Potables

When McGuire's first opened, everyone pitched in wherever they were needed, and Molly often found herself tending bar. The fact that Molly knew nothing at all about mixing drinks never deterred her; with her usual optimism and perseverance she would get quick bits of advice from people who knew their way around a bar, and she actually handled things quite well.

Today, McGuire's bar is in the very capable hands of experienced mixologists. There are many regular customers who show up not just for the drinks but the warmth and camaraderie as well.

Even before he dreamed of the dazzling microbrewery now in place at the pub, McGuire wanted to have a beer wagon to put outside the old place. He managed to buy one from a man for $75, including the horse. Trigger, the "wonder horse," was a stubborn old cuss. McGuire kept him out in the rugby field in back but brought him to the street to hitch him up to the beer wagon for rides. Occasionally Trigger could even be found wandering through the pub.

Today the bar at McGuire's is still a source of good-natured mischief—a bit more tame perhaps, but just as much fun as in the old days. The drinks are frosty and generous and the company cheering.

Here is everything you'll need for your own happy hours—but don't forget to provide the coffee for departing guests.

BLOODY McGUIRE

A tradition at McGuire's Irish Pub, this drink bears a strong resemblance to the ubiquitous Bloody Mary. I think this version, which features Irish whiskey instead of vodka, is ever so much better. Increase the recipe depending on the number of guests at your party.

1 cup tomato juice
1½ tsp. freshly squeezed lemon juice
¾ tsp. Worcestershire sauce
¼ tsp. seasoned salt
¼ tsp. celery salt

2 to 3 turns freshly ground black
   pepper
One dash hot sauce
¼ cup Irish whiskey
2 lemon slices

1. Combine the tomato juice, lemon juice, Worcestershire, seasoned and celery salt, pepper, and hot sauce. Stir well and chill.
2. Just before serving, add the whiskey and pour over ice. Garnish each drink with a lemon slice.
Serves 2.

> *My love she's handsome,*
> *My love she's bonny:*
> *She's like good whisky*
> *When it is new.*
> —James Joyce

McGINTY'S IRISH MARGARITA

McGinty the Irish Goat was the pet of Molly and McGuire years ago, when McGuire's was still a small pub at another site. McGinty was often walked on a leash, as if he were the family dog. But most of the time he roamed freely through the pub, cadging drinks from the customers, who were very fond of him. McGinty's preference was for margaritas. This one's pretty potent, but McGinty could hold it.

3 tbsp. frozen lime juice concen-
    trate, thawed
1 cup water
1 oz. orange juice
½ fresh lemon, juice only
2 oz. gold tequila

1 oz. Cointreau, Triple Sec, or other
    orange liqueur
½ oz. Grand Marnier, or other
    cognac
½ fresh lime, juice only

1. In a shaker, combine the lime juice concentrate with the water, orange juice, and lemon juice. Mix well and stir in the tequila, orange liqueur, and Grand Marnier. Squeeze in the fresh lime juice, cover, and shake well. Pour over ice in a glass with or without the rim coated in Kosher salt, and serve.
    Serves 1.

Variation: For a frozen margarita, use only 1 oz. of tequila, add 3 cups of ice, and pour the mixture into a blender. Blend on high until thick and frosty. Pour into a glass rimmed with Kosher salt or not, and serve.

O'TOOLE'S WALLBANGER*

Be certain the walls are padded before you try this one. Sure, O'Toole himself is still in a body cast.

Crushed ice
⅓ cup orange juice
2 tbsp. vodka
1 tbsp. Irish Mist liqueur

1 tbsp. Galliano liqueur
1 fresh orange segment
1 green maraschino cherry

1. Fill a 14-oz. glass with crushed ice. Combine the orange juice, vodka, and Irish Mist. Pour over the ice and stir.
2. Float the Galliano on top, garnish with the orange segment and cherry, and serve.
Serves 1.

*The Harvey Wallbanger®, namesake of O'Toole's favorite drink, is sometimes called an Italian Screwdriver. Rumor has it that it was the favorite drink of professional surfer Tom Harvey in the sixties. Harvey would drink until he was unable to walk without hitting a wall and, well, you know the rest.

Harvey Wallbanger is a trademark of 21 Brands, Inc., importers of Galliano liqueur.

IRISH WAKE

This may knock you dead, but then everyone enjoys an old-fashioned Irish Wake.

Crushed ice
1 tbsp. gold rum (premium)
1 tbsp. "151" rum*
½ cup freshly squeezed orange juice

1 tbsp. blue Curaçao
1 orange slice
1 green maraschino cherry

1. Fill a 12-oz. glass with crushed ice. Combine the gold rum, "151" rum, and orange juice, and pour the mixture over the ice. Pour the Curaçao over the top and stir gently. Spear the orange slice and cherry on a toothpick for a garnish.
   Serves 1.

*The 151 refers to the proof of the rum; standard rum is 80 proof, and 151 is—don't ask!

BELFAST BOMBER

Word has it that this refresher is the IRA's official recipe and its best secret weapon. Whether or not that's true, I think enough Belfast Bombers would render anyone's enemies harmless.

Crushed ice
1 tbsp. gold rum
1 tbsp. light rum
½ cup freshly squeezed orange juice

2 tbsp. cherry-flavored brandy
1½ tsp. grenadine
2 maraschino cherries

1. Fill a 16-oz. glass with crushed ice. Combine the gold rum, light rum, and orange juice, and pour the mixture over the ice.
2. Combine the brandy and grenadine. Pour this mixture on top and stir gently. Top with the cherries, and serve.
   Serves 1.

HOT LIMERICK TODDY

This is just what the doctor ordered for a cold winter night.

1 lemon
2 tsp. honey
3 oz. Irish whiskey

1 oz. Irish Mist liqueur
1½ cups (approx.) hot water
2 cinnamon sticks

1. Squeeze half the lemon into each of two 8-oz. mugs or glasses with handles. Stir 1 tsp. of the honey into each glass. Add 1½ oz. of the whiskey and ½ oz. of the Irish Mist to each, and fill with hot water. Stir well, add a cinnamon stick to each drink, and serve.
Serves 2.

BAILEYS FLOAT

Keep in mind that this "ice-cream-soda-esque" drink is definitely not for kids. It's not for dieters, either.

3 scoops vanilla ice cream
¼ cup Baileys Irish Cream

¾ cup cola

1. Place the ice cream in a tall soda glass, pour the Baileys over the ice cream, and fill the glass with cola. Serve with a spoon and a straw.
Serves 1.

*The well-known Baileys Irish Cream was developed by Gilbey's in 1974. It is a combination of fresh Irish dairy cream with a butterfat content of 48 percent, triple-distilled whiskey, and pure vanilla and cocoa extracts. There are other brands of Irish cream that came on the market after Gilbey's developed it, but I am most fond of Baileys.

MULLIGAN'S CELEBRATION

Pub-regular Mulligan is apt to celebrate almost anything, and he always parties with this delicious potable.

¼ cup Baileys Irish Cream   1½ tbsp. Amaretto
1½ tbsp. vodka

1. Combine the ingredients in a shaker. Fill the shaker to the top with ice and shake well. Pour into a fluted champagne glass, garnish with a green cherry, if you like, and serve.
   Serves 1.

IRISH GOODNIGHT

Sharan and Dair, one of the bartenders, like to whip up new drinks together. Then, of course, they must test them. Well, somebody has to. This one is definitely not for dieters.

2 cups milk   2½ oz. Irish Mist
⅔ cup cocoa   ¼ cup whipped cream
⅔ cup granulated sugar

1. Combine the milk, cocoa, and sugar in a saucepan over medium-low heat. Bring to a bubble, reduce the heat to low, and simmer, stirring, 2 to 3 minutes. Skim off any skin that might form on top of the mixture.
2. Pour 1¼ oz. of the Irish Mist into each of two 12-oz. mugs or glasses with handles. Pour half the hot cocoa mixture into each glass, and mix well. Top with a dollop of whipped cream, and enjoy.
   Serves 2.

BLARNEY BULLDOG

Both delicious and potent, this drink is pure fun.

¾ cup (3 scoops) vanilla ice cream
3 tbsp. Kahlua coffee-flavored
    liqueur

2 tbsp. vodka
¼ cup heavy cream
¼ cup root beer

1. Place the ice cream in a 16-oz. stemmed glass.
2. Combine the Kahlua, vodka, and cream, and pour the mixture over the ice cream. Slowly pour the root beer over the top (it will fizz up) and serve with an iced-tea spoon.
Serves 1.

McGUIRE'S FROZEN IRISH COFFEE

An old Irish toast comes along with this delicious, bittersweet drink:

Health and long life to you,
Land without rent to you,
A child every year to you,
And may you die in Ireland.

1½ tbsp. Irish whiskey
1½ tbsp. Kahlua coffee-flavored
    liqueur
½ cup strong, freshly brewed hot
    coffee, cooled to room tempera-
    ture

1½ cups vanilla ice cream, slightly
    softened
¼ cup heavy cream
4 tbsp. whipped cream
Crème de menthe for garnish

1. Combine the whiskey and Kahlua in a blender. Add the coffee, ice cream, and heavy cream and pulse on high speed for 3 to 4 seconds about 4 times, or until the consistency is like a milk shake and the ingredients are well blended.
2. Pour into two 10-oz. glasses, top with the whipped cream, and garnish with crème de menthe.
Serves 2.

McGUIRE'S IRISH COFFEE

An old, old recipe for Irish coffee goes like this:

Cream, rich as an Irish brogue
Coffee, strong as a friendly hand
Sugar, sweet as the tongue of a rogue
Whiskey, smooth as the wit of the land

Although some insist that Irish coffee was first created in San Francisco, this old recipe may be proof that it's really from some authentic pub on the "old sod."

1½ tbsp. Irish whiskey
1½ tbsp. Kahlua coffee-flavored
    liqueur

1 cup freshly brewed hot coffee
2 tbsp. whipped cream
Crème de menthe for garnish

1. Combine the whiskey and Kahlua in a large (10-oz.) coffee mug or heat-proof Irish-coffee glass. Slowly stir in the coffee. Mound the whipped cream on top and drizzle with crème de menthe. Don't stir, or you'll miss the delightful sensation of drinking the hot coffee and Irish whiskey through the coolness of the whipped cream.
    Serves 1.

Sweet
Sign-Offs:

Heavenly Desserts

And who among us has not a sweet tooth? The Irish have always loved their desserts and have a long history of traditional baked sweets—including dark cakes studded with raisins and candied fruits, whiskey or porter, seeds, and nuts; tarts of shortcrust pastry filled with apples or berries; and cookies of shortbread, oats, or honey.

The pubs have glamorized many favorites of the dessert category—mainly from the Irish countryside, where the aromas of rich puddings, fruit-laden pies, seductive cakes, cookies, and finger-sweets fill the air.

Try some of the heavenly sweets in this chapter: creamy, fruity Date and Irish Mist Rice Pudding with Irish Mist Whipped Cream; Fudge Nut Brownie Cake Smothered in Orange Liqueur Mousse; dazzling Almond Praline Torte; traditional, caraway-seeded Carvie Cake with Port-Wine Glaze; Emerald Eyes, cookies punctuated with green maraschino cherries; a summertime fruit treat—Raspberry Plum Tart with Chambourd Custard and Plum Wine Cream; dreamy Chocolate Eclairs bursting with Baileys Custard.

Whatever your pleasure, one of these desserts is sure to make it heavenly for you.

TIPSY APRICOT CHOCOLATE CAKE

Fruit and whiskey abound in many Irish cakes, pies, and tarts. Combining apricot preserves and whiskey with a deep chocolate cake and rich chocolate frosting is just about irresistible.

Vegetable oil
⅔ cup self-rising all-purpose flour
⅓ cup cocoa powder
3 large eggs, divided
2 tbsp. warm water
4 tbsp. whiskey, divided
1 cup apricot jam, room temperature, divided

1 cup plus 1 tbsp. heavy cream, divided
½ lb. dark chocolate (1 cup when melted)
1 tbsp. unsalted butter
Shaved milk chocolate (see index) for garnish
Whipped cream for garnish

1. Preheat the oven to 375 degrees. Line the bottom of an 8" cake pan with a parchment or wax paper circle. Lightly oil the paper and the sides of the pan, and set aside.

2. Sift the flour and cocoa together into a bowl, combining them well. Beat 2 of the eggs until thick and lemon colored, about 5 minutes. Slowly fold the flour mixture into the eggs, doing it in three increments. With the third, add the warm water.

3. Pour the batter into the oiled cake pan and bake until the cake shrinks slightly from the sides of the pan, about 25 minutes. Remove from the oven and set on a rack to cool.

4. When the cake is completely cool, use a serrated knife to cut it horizontally into three layers. Place the bottom layer of the cake on a serving platter. Sprinkle with 1 tbsp. of the whiskey, allowing it to sink into the cake, and spread ½ cup of the jam over that.

5. Whip 1 cup of the cream until soft peaks form. Spread half the whipped cream over the jam. Place the second layer on top, sprinkle on another 1 tbsp. of whiskey, spread with the remaining jam, and top with the remaining whipped cream. Place the third layer on top of all.

6. To prepare the frosting, melt the chocolate in the top of a double boiler over simmering water. When the chocolate is completely melted, remove it from the heat. Stir in the butter and the remaining 2 tbsp. whiskey.

7. Beat the remaining egg with the remaining 1 tbsp. cream, and fold this into the chocolate mixture, blending well. Spread the chocolate frosting evenly over the top and sides of the cake.

8. Garnish with shaved chocolate and additional whipped cream.
Makes 1 cake, 8-12 servings.

CHOCOLATE HAZELNUT CAKE
WITH GLAZED PEARS AND FRANGELICA

The hazelnut, which is the closest thing to the national nut of Ireland, is revered for its distinctive flavor and is widely available throughout Ireland. Fresh hazelnuts couple deliciously with Frangelica liqueur and dark chocolate in this sinful cake.

1 tbsp. unsalted butter, softened
1 cup hazelnuts
2 oz. (bulk) bittersweet chocolate, broken in chunks
½ cup plus 3 tbsp. plus ½ tsp. granulated sugar, divided
5 large egg yolks, divided

5 large egg whites
¼ tsp. salt
3 tbsp. Frangelica, divided
2 tbsp. champagne
½ cup half-and-half
2 firm, ripe pears
2 tbsp. unsalted butter

1. Preheat the oven to 350 degrees. Use some of the softened butter to grease an 8" cake pan. Line the pan with parchment and grease the paper with the rest of the softened butter.

2. In a food processor, grind the hazelnuts into a fine powder. Add the chocolate and ¼ cup of the sugar and process until the chocolate is in fine pieces, 30 to 45 seconds.

3. In a bowl beat 4 of the egg yolks with another ¼ cup of the sugar until thick, about 3 to 4 minutes. Stir in the nuts and chocolate until the mixture becomes thick and heavy.

4. In a separate bowl, beat the egg whites with the salt until stiff peaks form. Gently fold about one-third of the egg whites into the mixture in the first bowl, then fold in the remaining egg whites. Pour this cake batter into the pan and bake until a toothpick tests dry and clean, 30 to 35 minutes. Remove from the oven and cool on a wire rack for about 5 minutes.

5. In a small bowl, combine 2 tbsp. of the Frangelica with the champagne and ½ tsp. of the sugar. Stir until the sugar is completely dissolved.

6. Use a skewer or a sharp knife to poke holes all over the top of the cake, approximately ½" apart. Pour the Frangelica mixture over the cake until all of the holes are filled. Cover loosely and chill for 1 hour. Turn the cake out of its pan onto a serving plate, cover, and return to the refrigerator.

7. Meanwhile, whisk together 1 tbsp. of the sugar, the remaining egg yolk, and remaining 1 tbsp. Frangelica in a small bowl. Heat the half-and-half in a small

saucepan just until small bubbles form. Whisk a little of the warm half-and-half into the Frangelica mixture, then turn the mixture back into the saucepan. Cook, stirring, over medium heat until bubbles form, about 3 minutes (don't let the sauce boil). Pour the sauce into a small bowl, cover, and chill for at least 1 hour.

8. Just before serving, peel and core the pears and cut them into thin slices. Melt the butter in a small skillet over medium heat. Add the pears and cook, shaking the skillet occasionally, on both sides until they are soft, about 2 minutes. Sprinkle with the remaining 2 tbsp. sugar and cook, shaking the pan occasionally, until the sugar is caramelized and the pears are golden brown, 2 to 3 minutes.

9. To serve, remove the cake from the refrigerator. Spoon a puddle of Frangelica sauce onto each plate, top with a slice of cake, and add a small mound of pears to the side of the cake.

Makes 1 cake, 8 generous servings.

FUDGE NUT BROWNIE CAKE SMOTHERED IN ORANGE LIQUEUR MOUSSE

If McGuire ever removed his brownie pie from the pub's menu, he'd probably have an uprising on his hands. He knows better, and so it remains—the darling of all of the pub's very popular desserts. Orange mousse adds a wonderful touch in this cake version.

BROWNIE CAKE

1⅓ cups vegetable oil, plus more for greasing
6 squares unsweetened chocolate
2¼ cups all-purpose flour
3 cups granulated sugar
1 tbsp. baking powder

1 tsp. salt
1 cup coarsely chopped nuts (walnuts or pecans)
6 large eggs
1 tbsp. vanilla extract

ORANGE MOUSSE

2¾ cups orange juice
½ cup granulated sugar
2½ tsp. unflavored gelatin
2 tbsp. freshly squeezed lemon juice
23 oz. solid white chocolate, divided

¾ cup sour cream
2 tbsp. Grand Marnier or Triple Sec, divided
2 cups heavy cream, chilled
¼ cup cocoa powder

1. Preheat the oven to 350 degrees.

2. Lightly grease a 10" springform pan with vegetable oil. Set the pan aside.

3. Melt the chocolate in the top of a double boiler over simmering water.

4. Meanwhile, combine the flour, sugar, baking powder, salt, and nuts in a large bowl, and mix well.

5. In another bowl, beat together the eggs, vanilla, and 1⅓ cups oil. Add this mixture to the dry ingredients, blending well with a wooden spoon. Fold in the melted chocolate.

6. Pour the batter into the oiled springform pan and bake until moist but springy to the touch, about 45 minutes. Remove from the oven.

7. Carefully remove the outer ring from the springform pan, wash, and dry it thoroughly.

8. Using a serrated knife, trim off 1" around the entire edge of the cake. Snap the washed ring back on the springform pan (the cake will be smaller than the pan) and refrigerate.

9. To prepare the mousse, combine the orange juice and sugar in a heavy saucepan over high heat. Bring to a boil, lower the heat to medium, and let the mixture bubble slowly until it has reduced to 1½ cups, about 30 minutes.

10. Sprinkle the gelatin over the lemon juice and stir until blended. Allow the mixture to sit until slightly thick and tacky to the touch, 1 to 2 minutes. Stir the lemon mixture into the orange juice.

11. Break up 14 oz. of the white chocolate, stir it into the orange juice mixture, and whisk until melted. Blend some of the hot mixture into the sour cream and then turn all of the sour cream into the saucepan, stirring carefully. Stir in 1 tbsp. of the liqueur.

12. Refrigerate the mixture for 1 hour, whisking every 15 minutes; the mixture should be cold but not firm.

13. Beat the cream until stiff. Beat in the remaining 1 tbsp. of liqueur. Gently fold the cream into the orange mixture, blending well.

14. Pour the mousse mixture around the cake, filling the sides first. Use a knife to fill in and poke out any air pockets. Cover the top of the cake with the mousse, and refrigerate overnight.

15. Remove the cake from the refrigerator. Run a knife around the edges of the pan, then release the spring and remove the ring. Place the cake on a serving platter.

16. Use a vegetable peeler to shave the remaining white chocolate into thin curls, and arrange the curls over the top and sides of the cake. Dust with the cocoa and serve.

Makes 1 cake, 10-12 servings.

MOLLY'S IRISH COFFEE-CREAM CAKE AND CHOCOLATE SILK FROSTING

This is hardly what you would call a coffee cake, so don't confuse it with the plain cake one normally has with a cuppa java. A seductive, irresistible sweet, it makes a near-intoxicating finale for every special dinner in your repertoire. The recipe looks long and complicated, but as Molly told me, it's really easy to make and worth a little extra time for the results. And she was right!

CAKE

½ cup unsalted butter
1 cup granulated sugar
2 large eggs
½ cup buttermilk
1 tsp. pure vanilla extract

1½ cups all-purpose flour
1 tsp. baking powder
½ tsp. baking soda
½ tsp. salt

IRISH WHISKEY GLAZE

1 cup granulated sugar
¼ cup water
½ cup unsalted butter

¼ cup Irish whiskey
1 tbsp. pure vanilla extract

COFFEE CREAM

4 oz. white chocolate
½ cup unsalted butter
¼ cup confectioners' sugar

1 tbsp. instant coffee powder
1 tsp. hot water
2 large eggs

FROSTING

1 cup plus 2 tbsp. granulated sugar
¼ cup water
4 oz. unsweetened chocolate pieces
4 oz. semisweet chocolate pieces

5 large eggs, room temperature
½ cup unsalted butter, cut in cubes
½ cup slivered almonds, toasted (see index)

1. Preheat the oven to 350 degrees.

2. For the cake, cream the butter and sugar together in a bowl with an electric mixer until light and fluffy. Stir in the eggs, buttermilk, and vanilla, and mix well.

3. Sift together the flour, baking powder, baking soda, and salt. Add the dry mixture to the wet mixture and combine well with a spoon.

4. Grease and flour a 9" x 13" baking pan. Pour in the batter and bake until the cake tests done with a toothpick, 35 to 40 minutes.

5. While the cake is baking, prepare the Irish Whiskey Glaze: Combine the sugar and water in a saucepan over medium-high heat, and bring to a boil. Stir in the butter, and continue to stir until it has melted. Stir in the whiskey and vanilla, and remove from the heat.

6. Remove the cake from the oven and carefully remove it from its pan with a sharp knife. Using a wooden or metal skewer, poke holes all over the top of the cake and pour the whiskey glaze over it, letting the glaze seep into the holes. Allow the cake to cool completely.

7. While the cake is cooling, prepare the coffee cream: Melt the chocolate in the top of a double boiler over medium heat. Pour the chocolate into the bowl of a food processor. Add the butter and sugar, and process until smooth.

8. Dissolve the coffee in the hot water and add to the mixture in the food processor. Add the eggs and process until smooth. Spread the cream on the top of the cooled cake. Refrigerate for 1 hour.

9. While the cake is being refrigerated, prepare the frosting. Combine the sugar and water in a saucepan over medium-high heat and bring to a boil, stirring until the sugar has dissolved and the mixture has turned into a syrup.

10. Place all of the chocolate pieces in the bowl of a food processor and run the machine just until the chocolate is minced. With the processor running, pour in the hot sugar syrup, scraping the sides of the bowl.

11. Add the eggs one at a time, then the butter cubes in 5 increments, processing after each addition. Continue processing until the mixture is smooth and silky.

12. Remove the cake from the refrigerator and spread the frosting over the entire cake. Sprinkle with the almonds and return to the refrigerator. Allow the cake to come to room temperature before serving.

Makes 1 cake, 12-16 servings.

Note: As with most legends, the story of how and where Irish coffee was invented is endlessly disputed. One story has it that the first Irish coffee was made and served at the Buena Vista Bar in San Francisco, California, in 1952. But according to food historian Doris Reynolds, the recipe originated at the Pig in the Poke Tavern in Waterford, Ireland. For the McGuire's Irish Coffee recipe, see the index.

APPLE BROWN BETTY CHEESECAKE

Chef Sharan Sheppard says this cake is "rich as hell, but wonderful," so serve it with care to people who don't need to watch their weight.

BOTTOM CRUST

1 cup graham cracker crumbs
1 cup fresh bread crumbs (see index)
½ cup coarsely ground almonds

¼ cup granulated sugar
6 tbsp. melted, unsalted butter
½ tsp. pure vanilla extract

FILLING

1 lb. cream cheese, softened
1 lb. whole-milk ricotta cheese
1½ cups granulated sugar

5 large eggs
¾ cup heavy cream
1¼ tsp. pure vanilla extract

APPLE TOPPING

3 cups peeled, sliced Granny Smith or other tart apples
1½ tbsp. freshly squeezed lemon juice (about 1 large lemon)

2 tbsp. granulated sugar
½ tsp. ground cinnamon

OATMEAL-ALMOND TOPPING

1 cup all-purpose flour
¾ cup uncooked oatmeal
¼ cup sliced almonds

1 cup dark brown sugar
1 cup (2 sticks) unsalted butter, softened

1. To make the crust, combine the graham cracker crumbs, bread crumbs, almonds, and sugar in a bowl. Use your hands to work the butter and vanilla into the dry ingredients. Press the mixture into the bottom of a 9" x 13" baking pan.

2. To make the filling, beat the cream cheese and ricotta cheese together with an electric mixer in a large bowl. When the cheeses are well blended, beat in the sugar gradually, and continue to beat until the mixture is light and fluffy, about 5 minutes.

3. Beat in the eggs one at a time, beating well after each egg. Beat in the cream and vanilla until thoroughly incorporated.

4. To make the apple topping, in a bowl, sprinkle the apple slices with the lemon juice. Combine the sugar and cinnamon and toss the mixture with the apples.

5. To make the oatmeal-almond topping, combine the flour, oatmeal, almonds, and brown sugar in a bowl. Mix well with a wooden spoon or your hands. Add the butter and work it into the mixture until it is crumbly but cohesive.

6. Preheat the oven to 350 degrees.

7. Pour the filling over the bottom crust. Arrange the apple topping in a thin layer over the filling, covering it completely. Use your hands to crumble the oatmeal topping over all.

8. Place the cake pan in a larger pan. Carefully add enough water to come about one-third of the way up the side of the cake pan.* Bake until the cake is firm and a cake tester or toothpick comes out clean, about 1 hour.

9. Remove the cake from the oven and allow it to come to room temperature. Cover and chill 4 hours to overnight. Allow to come to room temperature before serving.

Serves 10-12.

*You'll have an easier time with this or any water bath (bain-marie) if you place the pans on the pulled-out oven rack before adding the water.

CARVIE CAKE WITH PORT-WINE GLAZE

In Ireland, seedcake—or carvie cake—usually means caraway seeds. The trick is to use just enough and not too many seeds because of their strong flavor. In the last century, when elegant ladies came to call of a morning or afternoon, they were often served a seedcake similar to this one, accompanied by a wee glass of port.

CAKE
2 cups (4 sticks) unsalted butter, plus more for greasing, room temperature
2½ cups granulated sugar
4 cups all-purpose flour
1 tsp. baking powder
½ tsp. ground cinnamon

½ tsp. ground nutmeg
8 large eggs
⅔ cup buttermilk
1 cup candied peel (mixed cherries, citron, orange peel, etc.)
¼ cup caraway seeds

GLAZE
1 cup sifted confectioners' sugar   ¼ cup port

1. Preheat the oven to 325 degrees.
2. Lightly grease a Bundt pan with butter and set aside.
3. In a large bowl cream the 2 cups butter with the sugar until the mixture is light, fluffy, and pale in color.
4. Sift the flour, baking powder, cinnamon, and nutmeg together into a bowl. In a separate bowl beat the eggs until frothy. Slowly stir the eggs into the butter-sugar mixture.
5. Begin folding the flour mixture into the egg mixture, alternating each increment of flour with one of buttermilk until all is well combined. Fold in the candied fruit and caraway seeds.
6. Pour the batter into the Bundt pan and smooth the top until it is level. Bake until a skewer or toothpick inserted in the cake comes out clean, about 1 hour.
7. Meanwhile, prepare the glaze by combining the sugar and port in a small saucepan over low heat. Simmer, stirring, until the alcohol has cooked off, about 5 minutes.
8. Remove the cake from the oven. Immediately remove the cake from the pan and place it on a wire rack over wax paper.
9. Use a small skewer to poke holes all over the top of the cake, and slowly pour the warm glaze over, allowing it to soak into the cake. Allow the cake to cool before serving.

Makes 1 cake, about 10-12 servings.

ALMOND PRALINE TORTE

Although this torte is somewhat time consuming to build, it's really quite easy and the result is worth every minute spent.

1 tbsp. vegetable oil
1¼ cups plus ⅔ cup plus 2 tbsp. granulated sugar, divided
6 tbsp. water, divided
1 cup sliced almonds, toasted (see index)
Parchment paper
9 large egg whites, divided
¾ tsp. cream of tartar, divided

1 tsp. almond extract, divided
1 cup confectioners' sugar
4 oz. white chocolate
1 tsp. light corn syrup
Candy thermometer
1 cup unsalted butter, room temperature
2 tbsp. Amaretto
1 tsp. vanilla extract

1. Grease a large baking sheet with the oil, and set it aside.

2. To prepare the praline, combine ¾ cup of the sugar with 3 tbsp. of the water in a small saucepan over medium heat. Cook, stirring, until the sugar dissolves, 2 to 3 minutes. Increase the heat and boil, without stirring, until the mixture turns light brown in color, 5 to 7 minutes. Remove from the heat and stir in the almonds.

3. Pour the mixture immediately onto the oiled baking sheet, spread it out, and allow it to cool. When it is cool, mince this praline mixture. Place ½ cup of the praline crumbs in a food processor and grind it into a powder.

4. Preheat the oven to 225 degrees. Use an 8" cake pan to trace 3 circles on parchment paper. Cut out the circles and lay them flat on baking sheets.

5. In a bowl beat 5 of the egg whites with ½ tsp. of the cream of tartar until soft peaks form. Gradually beat in ½ cup of the sugar, and beat until the mixture is stiff. Beat in ½ tsp. of the almond extract. Fold in the confectioners' sugar and the ½ cup powdered praline.

6. Spoon one-third of the meringue mixture onto each of the 3 circles of parchment. Spread it to the edges, and place the baking sheets in the oven for 45 minutes. Turn the baking sheets around and bake until golden brown, about 1 hour more. Remove from the oven and cool the 3 meringue layers completely.

7. To prepare the Amaretto buttercream frosting, melt the white chocolate over simmering water in the top of a double boiler. Allow the chocolate to cool slightly.

8. In a small saucepan over medium heat combine ⅔ cup of the sugar with the

remaining 3 tbsp. water and the corn syrup. Cook, stirring, until the sugar dissolves. Increase the heat and boil until a candy thermometer reads 238 degrees, or until it reaches the soft-ball or Gummi-bear stage, about 5 minutes.

9. Using an electric mixer beat the remaining 4 egg whites with the remaining 1/4 tsp. cream of tartar until soft peaks form. Gradually beat in the remaining 2 tbsp. sugar.

10. Pour the hot syrup mixture in a steady stream into the egg whites. Beat until the mixture is cool, about 1 or 2 minutes. Beat in the butter 2 tbsp. at a time. Beat in the chocolate, Amaretto, vanilla, and the remaining 1/2 tsp. almond extract until all is thoroughly blended together. Chill until thickened to the consistency of rich cake icing, about 45 minutes.

11. To assemble, place a meringue layer on a serving plate and frost with about one-quarter of the buttercream. Add another meringue layer and spread another one-quarter of the buttercream over that. Repeat with the remaining layer and frost the top and sides with the remaining buttercream.

12. Press the chopped almond praline mixture into the top of the torte and refrigerate overnight. Before serving, allow the torte to come to room temperature, then slice.

Makes 1 torte, 10-12 servings.

RASPBERRY PLUM TART WITH CHAMBOURD CUSTARD AND PLUM WINE CREAM

This is strictly a summer treat because of the fresh fruit. There seem to be many steps but it's definitely not difficult to make.

PASTRY
1¼ cups all-purpose flour
¼ cup granulated sugar
⅛ tsp. salt
3 large egg yolks
½ tsp. pure vanilla extract

6 tbsp. unsalted butter, cubed, room temperature
Parchment paper
Pie weights or dried beans

CUSTARD
3 large egg yolks
¼ cup granulated sugar
1 cup heavy cream

2 tbsp. Chambourd (black currant) liqueur
1 tsp. pure vanilla extract

PLUM WINE CREAM
4 large egg yolks
3 tsp. granulated sugar
2 cups heavy cream

2 tbsp. plum wine
1 tsp. pure vanilla extract

FRUIT TOPPING
1 cup fresh raspberries
½ cup sliced red plums

1½ tbsp. freshly squeezed lemon
  juice

GLAZE
1 cup red currant jelly

1 tbsp. Chambourd liqueur

GARNISH
Fresh mint sprigs

1. To make the pastry, sift together the flour, sugar, and salt into a large bowl. In a small bowl beat together the egg yolks and vanilla. Make a well in the center of the flour mixture and add the beaten egg yolks and the butter cubes. Using your fingers, work all of the ingredients together, cutting the wet into the dry, until the mixture resembles coarse crumbs.

2. Gather the dough into a rough ball and transfer it to a lightly floured work surface. Knead the dough with the heel of your hand (see index for general kneading directions) until it pulls together into one piece, 8 to 10 minutes. Shape the dough into a ball and cover with plastic wrap. Refrigerate until the dough ball is firm, about 2 hours.

3. Remove the dough from the refrigerator. Preheat the oven to 400 degrees.

4. Carefully roll out the dough on a lightly floured surface. As the dough gets thinner, it becomes more difficult to roll, so you may have to patch it in spots. Roll until it is large enough to fit a 9½" x 2"-deep tart pan.

5. Arrange the dough in the tart pan, flute the edges, and place a sheet of parchment over the dough. Cover the paper with pie weights or dried beans. Fold foil around the edges of the dough to keep them from burning, and bake until firm, about 15 minutes. Remove the weights and parchment and prick the bottom of the tart shell with the tines of a fork. Continue to bake until the tart shell is a light golden brown, 10 to 15 minutes. Remove from the oven and cool on a wire rack.

6. To make the custard, in a small bowl beat together the egg yolks and sugar until thick and light.

7. Heat the cream in a saucepan over medium-high heat until it bubbles. Slowly whisk the cream, little by little, into the egg yolks and return the mixture to the saucepan. Reduce the heat to low and cook, whisking constantly, until the mixture begins to bubble, 6 to 7 minutes. Continue to cook, whisking, until the custard is thick, about 2 minutes longer. Remove from the heat. Stir in the Chambourd and vanilla.

8. Pour the mixture into a bowl and cover with plastic wrap, pressing the wrap tightly against the surface to prevent a crust from forming.

9. To make the cream, in a medium bowl beat the egg yolks until frothy, add the sugar, and continue beating until thick and lemon colored.

10. Heat the cream in a saucepan over medium heat and bring to a bubble. Remove from the heat and temper a bit of the hot cream into the egg yolks, taking care not to let the eggs curdle. Turn the yolks into the cream in the saucepan and turn it to low heat. Cook, stirring constantly, until the mixture is thick enough to coat the back of a spoon. Remove from the heat.

11. Push the mixture through a strainer into a clean bowl. Stir in the wine and vanilla. Pour into an airtight container and chill for 2 hours.

12. To make the fruit topping, rinse and pick over the raspberries and allow them to dry on several layers of paper towels.

13. In a small bowl, toss the plum slices with the lemon juice.

14. Make the glaze just before assembling the tart. Melt the jelly in a small saucepan over low heat until thoroughly liquefied, about 5 minutes. Stir in the Chambourd, mix well, and cook, stirring, 2 minutes longer. Turn off the heat and keep warm.

15. To assemble, use a pastry brush to lightly coat the bottom of the tart shell with some of the glaze. Allow the glaze to set, about 5 minutes.

16. Pour the Chambourd custard into the pastry and smooth the top. Arrange a circle of raspberries around the outer edge of the tart. Arrange the plum slices inside the raspberries, and arrange the remaining raspberries in the center. Carefully brush the hot glaze over the fruit, taking care not to disrupt the arrangement. Brush the edges of the pastry to give the whole tart a shine. Add mint sprigs and chill the tart until the glaze is completely set, about 30 minutes.

17. To serve, place 2 tbsp. of the Plum Wine Cream on each plate and top with a wedge of the tart.

Makes 1 tart, 6-8 servings.

CHOCOLATE ECLAIRS WITH BAILEYS CUSTARD

Maybe the only way an eclair could get any better would be to have its silky custard made with Irish cream, as this one is.

PASTRY
½ cup all-purpose flour
½ tsp. granulated sugar
¼ tsp. salt

½ cup water
¼ cup (½ stick) unsalted butter
2 large eggs

CUSTARD
1¼ cups milk
¼ cup Baileys Irish Cream
1 large egg
⅓ cup granulated sugar

1½ tbsp. cornstarch
¼ tsp. salt
2 tbsp. pure vanilla extract
1 tbsp. unsalted butter, softened

FROSTING
2 tbsp. unsalted butter
2 tbsp. half-and-half

¼ cup semisweet chocolate morsels
1 cup confectioners' sugar

BAILEYS DRIZZLE
6 tbsp. confectioners' sugar

1 tbsp. Baileys Irish Cream

1. Preheat the oven to 400 degrees.

2. To make the eclair pastry, sift the flour, sugar, and salt together into a small bowl and set aside.

3. Combine the water and butter in a saucepan over medium-high heat and bring to a boil, stirring once or twice to blend the butter into the water. Reduce the heat to medium, add the flour mixture all at once, and stir until the mixture forms a smooth ball. Remove the saucepan from the heat and allow the dough to cool for 5 minutes.

4. Beat in the eggs one at a time, continuing to beat with a wooden spoon until the dough is smooth. Spoon the dough into a pastry bag. Pipe the dough onto an ungreased cookie sheet in rectangles or oblong shapes measuring approximately 4½" x 2".

5. Bake until the pastry shells are puffed and golden brown, about 40 minutes. Remove the pastry shells from the oven and allow them to cool completely on a wire rack.

6. While the pastry cools, prepare the custard: Combine the milk, Baileys, and egg in the top of a double boiler set over simmering water. Whisk the mixture until well blended. Whisk in the sugar, cornstarch, and salt. Cook, stirring constantly, until the mixture is thickened and bubbles form, 8 to 10 minutes. Stir in the vanilla and butter and heat, stirring, until the butter is thoroughly incorporated. Remove from the heat and allow the custard to cool.

7. To make the frosting, combine the butter and half-and-half in a saucepan over medium-low heat. Cook, stirring, until the butter has melted, about 3 minutes. Stir in the chocolate and cook, stirring constantly, until the chocolate is melted and the mixture smooth, 4 to 5 minutes. Gradually beat in the sugar with a wooden spoon until the frosting is smooth and all of the sugar incorporated. Turn off the heat.

8. For the "drizzle," combine the sugar and Baileys in a small bowl and stir until smooth.

9. To assemble the eclairs, use a sharp knife to slice the pastry shells lengthwise. Spoon the custard into the bottom halves and replace the tops. Spread the chocolate frosting over the tops and drizzle with the drizzle in a decorative zigzag. Refrigerate before serving.

Makes 6 eclairs.

CHOCOLATE WHISKEY BALLS

These are so gorgeous, no one will believe you made them yourself. So have someone on-site with a video camera to prove you did. The best part is that they're so easy to make.

½ cup (1 stick) unsalted butter, room temperature
1 tbsp. heavy cream
4 tbsp. Irish whiskey, divided
1 lb. (3½ cups) confectioners' sugar
Eye dropper

¾ lb. good-quality bulk semisweet chocolate
Double boiler
Candy dipper*
½ cup pecan halves

1. Using an electric mixer, combine the butter, cream, and 2 tbsp. of the whiskey in a medium bowl until smooth. Slowly and gradually add the sugar, beating after each addition, until the mixture is stiff and lumpless.

2. Using your hands, roll the mixture into 1" balls, placing the balls on a cookie sheet as you go.

3. With the end of a wooden spoon, press a well into the center of each ball, taking care not to go all the way through. Put the remaining whiskey into a small cup (a ¼-cup measure works well). Use an eye dropper or similar tool to add 2 to 3 drops (no more, or it will become runny) whiskey into each well. Pinch the tops of the balls closed. Refrigerate for at least 1 hour.

4. Break the chocolate into the top of a double boiler over simmering water. When the chocolate has melted, use a candy dipper to dip the balls into the chocolate one at a time, covering them evenly, and return them to the cookie sheet. Press a pecan half gently into the top of each ball and refrigerate until thoroughly chilled.

Makes 24 balls.

Variations:

1. Substitute Irish cream for Irish whiskey.

2. Use half dark chocolate and half white chocolate and melt them in separate pots. Dip half the balls in each and decorate them by drizzling some of the dark on the white, and vice versa.

*A candy dipper can be purchased at most kitchen shops. If you prefer, you can use a toothpick and a fork to maneuver the balls in the chocolate.

EMERALD EYES

On St. Patrick's Day, when Irish eyes are smiling everywhere, these cookies will make a lot of your own favorite faces light up.

½ cup (1 stick) unsalted butter, softened
½ cup solid shortening
3 oz. cream cheese, softened
1 cup granulated sugar
1 large egg
1 tsp. pure almond extract

2½ cups all-purpose flour
½ tsp. salt
1/4 tsp. baking soda
1½ cups minced pecans
One 12-oz. jar green maraschino cherries, drained and cherries halved

1. Using an electric mixer, cream together the butter, shortening, and cream cheese in a bowl until the mixture is light and fluffy, about 4 minutes. Slowly beat in the sugar until thoroughly incorporated, about 1 minute. Add the egg and almond extract and beat 1 minute longer.

2. Sift the flour, salt, and baking soda into another bowl, and fold the dry ingredients into the wet, blending thoroughly with a wooden spoon. Cover the bowl and refrigerate for 1 hour.

3. Remove the cookie dough from the refrigerator and preheat the oven to 350 degrees. Place the nuts in a shallow bowl or plate. Form the dough into about 4 dozen 1" balls and roll them in the nuts. Place the balls on cookie sheets 2" apart, and press a cherry half into the center of each.

4. Bake until the cookies are light golden brown and firm to the touch, 12 to 15 minutes. Cool on a wire rack and store in an airtight container.

Makes about 4 dozen cookies.

OUR OWN BREAD PUDDING
WITH IRISH WHISKEY SAUCE

A similar dish, known as Bread and Butter Pudding, has been enjoyed in Ireland for centuries. The added feature of the whiskey sauce turns a homely (but scrumptious) dessert into a dinner-party attraction.

PUDDING

1 loaf Irish Soda Bread (see index)

4 cups milk

3 large eggs, lightly beaten

1½ cups granulated sugar

2 tbsp. pure vanilla extract

1 cup raisins

8 oz. Del Monte Dried Fruit Mix

3 tbsp. melted, unsalted butter

SAUCE

1 cup granulated sugar

½ cup (1 stick) unsalted butter

½ cup heavy cream

¼ cup Irish whiskey

1. To make the pudding, tear the soda bread into large chunks and place in a large bowl. Pour the milk over the bread and allow it to soak until the milk has been completely absorbed, about 30 minutes.

2. Meanwhile, preheat the oven to 350 degrees.

3. In another bowl combine the eggs, sugar, and vanilla, and beat well. Fold the egg mixture thoroughly into the soaked bread. Stir in the fruits.

4. Grease a 9" x 13" baking pan with the melted butter. Pour in the bread mixture, spreading it evenly. Bake until the pudding is brown and firm, about 30 minutes.

5. While the pudding is baking, make the sauce. Combine the sugar, butter, and cream in a saucepan over medium-high heat. Bring to a boil, reduce the heat to medium, and cook, stirring occasionally, 5 minutes. Stir in the whiskey and cook until some of the alcohol has cooked off and the flavors are blended, about 4 minutes. Remove from the heat.

6. To serve, slice or spoon out the pudding onto plates, and top with the sauce. Serves 8.

DATE AND IRISH MIST RICE PUDDING WITH IRISH MIST WHIPPED CREAM

Puddings are a big deal in Ireland and were at one time considered the soft sweetness in lives that were otherwise filled with hardship. Today milk and honey rice puddings are served throughout Ireland—in pubs and homes alike. This recipe takes a bit of license with the original, using half-and-half for added richness, chopped dates for a special flavor, and Irish Mist for a kick.

½ cup uncooked long-grain white rice
2 cups half-and-half
1 cup plus 2 tbsp. heavy cream, divided
¼ cup granulated sugar
2 large egg yolks

1 tsp. pure vanilla extract
⅓ cup coarsely chopped dates
4 tbsp. (¼ cup) Irish Mist liqueur, divided
Six ¾- to 1-cup custard cups or ramekins

1. Combine the rice, half-and-half, ½ cup of the cream, and the sugar in a large saucepan over medium heat. Bring to a bubble and cook, stirring occasionally, until the rice is cooked and most of the liquid is absorbed, about 30 minutes.

2. In a small bowl beat the egg yolks until frothy. Beat in the vanilla and whisk until thoroughly blended. Stir a little of the hot rice mixture into the egg yolks, then a little more. Turn the tempered egg yolks into the saucepan and stir well into the

rice. Cook over medium heat, stirring occasionally, until the mixture has thickened and has a custardlike texture, 5 to 6 minutes. Stir in the dates, 3 tbsp. of the Irish Mist, and 2 tbsp. of the cream and cook 2 minutes longer. Remove from the heat.

3. Pour the mixture into the custard cups, filling each about half full. Cover the cups or ramekins with plastic wrap and refrigerate for at least 2 hours.

4. To prepare the topping, beat the remaining ½ cup cream in a bowl with an electric mixer until soft peaks form when the beaters are pulled up. Fold in the remaining 1 tbsp. Irish Mist and continue to beat 1 more minute. Spoon some of the whipped cream on top of each cup of rice pudding and serve.

Serves 6.

IRISH ZABA WHIP

This stunning dessert may remind you of Italian zabaglione, but it actually comes straight from the heart of the Blarney Stone. Dazzle your guests by serving it in your prettiest stemware.

3 large egg yolks
2 tbsp. confectioners' sugar
2 tbsp. Irish Mist liqueur
1 tbsp. Amaretto
8 oz. Mascarpone cheese

¼ cup cold water
2 tbsp. coffee liqueur
1 tbsp. instant coffee powder
12 ladyfingers, broken into thirds
1-oz. square milk chocolate, grated

1. Combine the egg yolks and sugar in a bowl and beat with an electric mixer until thick and pale yellow, about 5 minutes. Gradually beat in 1 tbsp. each of the Irish Mist and Amaretto. Add the Mascarpone and continue beating until the mixture is smooth and well blended, about 3 minutes.

2. In a separate bowl combine the water, coffee liqueur, instant coffee, and the remaining 1 tbsp. Irish Mist.

3. Arrange 3 ladyfinger sections in the bottom of each of six 12-oz. wine glasses. Sprinkle the ladyfingers with ½ tbsp. of the coffee mixture. Spoon enough of the cheese mixture to fill the glass halfway up. Sprinkle with about one-twelfth of the grated chocolate. Repeat the whole process: 3 pieces of ladyfinger, ½ tbsp. coffee mixture, cheese mixture almost to the top, grated chocolate last. Do the same with the remaining glasses.

4. Cover the glasses and refrigerate for at least 2 hours before serving.

Serves 6.

WHISKEY PRALINE ICE CREAM

Some people balk at the prospect of making homemade ice cream, believing it's a complicated process and thinking they have to go out and buy an ice-cream freezer. Not true on both counts: this heavenly, creamy treat is easy to make and can be frozen in a bowl in your freezer. Of course, if you already have an ice-cream freezer, by all means, use it. One tip for whiskey enthusiasts: don't add more than the 3 tbsp. in the recipe, or you'll have trouble getting the ice cream to freeze.

1½ cups half-and-half
1 cup heavy cream
⅓ cup white granulated sugar
⅓ cup brown sugar (packed)

3 tbsp. Irish whiskey
1 tsp. pure vanilla extract
1 cup coarsely chopped pecans

1. Combine the half-and-half, cream, white sugar, and brown sugar in a medium saucepan over medium-low heat. Cook, stirring constantly, until the sugars have dissolved, about 4 minutes.

2. Stir in the whiskey and vanilla and cook, stirring, until the alcohol evaporates, 2 to 3 minutes (if the alcohol doesn't fully evaporate, the ice cream won't freeze properly). Fold in the pecans and stir well.

3. Pour the mixture into a container and refrigerate for 1 hour. Place the bowl in your freezer and stir the hardening ice cream every 20 minutes or so, until the ice cream sets. If you have an ice-cream freezer, turn the refrigerated ice cream into the ice-cream freezer and follow the manufacturer's directions.

Makes 1½ pt.

St. Pat
Tricks:

Tips, Techniques,
Stocks, Etc.

As Saint Patrick himself knew, you can't do a successful job unless you do it properly. And so I've included some tips and techniques to help you complete a variety of recipes in this book and ensure their success.

In addition, you'll find recipes for making the stocks used in other recipes. Probably one of the most important elements separating an "okay" dish from a memorable one is a homemade stock. They are easy to make and can be stored in your freezer, ready to thaw for use whenever you need them.

So take the extra step, employ the correct techniques, prepare good stocks, and your reputation as a fine cook will be greatly enhanced.

St. Pat Tricks, Tips, and Techniques

Some of the recipes in this book refer you to this chapter for help in preparing certain ingredients. Use the following techniques as a guide to show you how to:

MAKE FRESH BREAD CRUMBS

1. Place 8 slices white or whole-wheat bread on a baking sheet in a 200-degree oven until dry, turning once, 30 to 40 minutes.
2. Slice off and discard the crusts and roughly cube or break the toast.
3. Place in a food processor and process until you have fine bread crumbs, about 30 seconds.

Makes 1 cup.

PEEL TOMATOES OR PEARL ONIONS

1. Bring a pot of water to a boil.
2. Fill a bowl with ice and cold water.
3. Drop tomatoes one at a time—or onions in batches—into the boiling water, just until the skins split (for tomatoes), 15 to 30 seconds, or until the skins soften (onions), about 1 minute.
4. Immediately remove the tomatoes or onions with tongs and transfer into the ice water. When cool enough to handle, slip off the skins.

CUT FRESH CORN

1. Remove corn husks and silk tassels.
2. Stand an ear vertically on its end. Using a short, sharp paring knife, slice the kernels off evenly from top to bottom.
3. If the ears are long, scrape off the bottom half, turn the ears, and scrape off the remaining corn kernels.

ROAST PEPPERS

1. With a gas stove or grill: Spear each pepper on a long-handled fork and hold it over the flame, turning to blacken all sides.

2. With an oven: Heat the broiler and line a baking sheet with foil. Cut peppers in half, and place them cut side down on the foil. Broil until the peppers are blackened, about 5 minutes.

3. To cool the peppers, place them in a brown paper bag and close the top, or wrap them in plastic wrap. When they are cool, the skins will slip easily off the peppers. Remove the seeds.

ROAST GARLIC

1. Preheat the oven to 350 degrees.

2. Line a baking dish with a sheet of aluminum foil large enough to wrap over the garlic, or use a terra-cotta garlic roaster. Place whole, unpeeled heads of garlic in the middle of the foil or in the roaster. Toss each head in olive oil and cover loosely with the foil, or place the cover on the garlic roaster.

3. Bake until the garlic is soft to the touch, about 30 minutes. Remove from the oven, trim off the ends of the garlic, and squeeze out the pulp, which should resemble soft butter. Spread on crostini or crackers or use in recipes requiring roasted garlic.

4. Any garlic not being used immediately can be stored in the refrigerator for up to 2 weeks. Leave these garlic heads untrimmed, skin on, and store in airtight containers or wrap tightly in plastic wrap to avoid infusing everything else in your refrigerator with garlic.

MAKE ROASTED-GARLIC BUTTER

1. When your roasted garlic is cool enough to handle, squeeze out the pulp. Combine with softened butter, adding roasted garlic to taste.

CLARIFY BUTTER

1. Cut up 3 sticks (3/4 lb.) of butter, place in a small saucepan over low heat, and heat until all of the butter is melted.

2. Remove the saucepan from the heat and allow the melted butter to stand until the milky solids have settled on the bottom, about 5 minutes.

3. Carefully skim off the foam that has risen to the top and strain the clear yellow liquid into a bowl or container, discarding the solids. The clear yellow liquid is the clarified butter.

Makes about 1 cup.

Note: Clarified butter, sometimes called "drawn butter" when served with seafood, burns less easily than unclarified butter.

PICK OVER CRAB MEAT

1. Place a piece of parchment paper on a flat surface and turn the crab meat onto the paper. Using your fingers, spread the crab meat into a thin layer, picking out any pieces of cartilage and shell you find.

CLEAN CLAMS AND MUSSELS

1. Scrub clams and mussels under cold water with a stiff brush, scraping off sand and barnacles. Mussels are easily debearded with a small, sharp knife by trimming the fuzzy beards at the lips of the shells.

2. Place mollusks in a large bowl in your sink and cover with cold water and ice. Allow the clams and mussels to soak, replacing ice if necessary, for about 45 minutes.

3. Drain the mollusks through a strainer, discarding the soaking water. Rinse any collected sand out of the bowl. Rinse the mollusks and repeat the process.

SKIM FAT

1. To skim fat from stocks for immediate use, allow the stock to cool to room temperature.

2. Fill a large strainer or a chinoise with ice and place over a large container. Pour the stock through the ice. The ice will catch and congeal the fat. If you don't get it all on the first try, pour the stock through again.

3. If you don't need the stock right away, refrigerate it overnight in a covered container. The fat will congeal and can be more easily removed the next day. The stock can then be frozen in small containers.

KNEAD DOUGH

1. To keep your dough light, flour a board lightly. Too much flour on the board will toughen the dough.

2. Yeast dough should be a little sticky when you first turn it out of the bowl to knead it.

3. Fold the dough over toward you once. Press with the heels of both hands. Move the dough about one-quarter turn, fold, press, and turn again. Continue kneading this way until the dough becomes smooth, shiny, and elastic in texture and is no longer sticking to the board or your hands, about 10 minutes.

4. Place the dough in a deep, well-greased bowl and turn the dough around in the bowl until it is lightly greased all over. Moisten a dishtowel with warm water, wring out thoroughly, and cover the bowl with the cloth. Place the covered bowl in a warm place and let the dough rise to double its original size, 1 1/2 to 2 hours. Don't allow the dough to rise to more than double its bulk.

5. Uncover the bowl and punch down the dough. If you're using all-purpose flour, knead the dough again right in the bowl for about 3 minutes. Cover again and allow the dough to rise a second time to double its bulk. If you use enriched bread dough, you won't have to knead the dough a second time.

MAKE PIE PASTRY

SINGLE CRUST
1 cup sifted flour
½ tsp. salt
¼ cup plus 2 tbsp. unsalted butter or
  shortening

2-3 tbsp. ice water

DOUBLE CRUST
Double the ingredients

1. For light, flaky pastry, keep one important rule in mind: cold. What this means is having your butter and/or solid shortening cold and firm and being sure the water you use is ice water. To be really orthodox about this, prechill the bowl you will use, the flour, and the rolling pin. My mother had a metal rolling pin with a hollow center, and she filled this with ice before rolling. Her pie crusts were the flakiest anywhere. If you have to handle the dough with your hands, do it quickly, so your body heat won't warm it up. And always refrigerate the ball of dough for at least 1 hour before rolling it out. (Separate the dough into two balls for a double crust.)

2. Turn out the dough on a lightly floured work surface, or between two sheets of lightly floured wax paper. (The latter technique makes it easier to apply the pastry to the pie without its tearing.) Lightly flour your hands and the rolling pin (unless you're rolling the dough between sheets of wax paper). Use the heel of one hand to flatten the ball of dough into a circle about 6 or 7" in diameter. Try to smooth or seal any small tears at the edges.

3. Roll the dough from the center outward, always rolling out only, never back and forth. Turn the dough slightly as you go, so that it will be evenly rolled out, until the circle is larger than your pie plate by about 4" all around. Transfer the dough to the pie plate draped over the rolling pin, or, if you're using wax paper, remove the top sheet, transport the dough on the bottom sheet, and invert it onto the pie plate.

4. Gently press the dough into the bottom and sides of the pie plate and cut off any excess—leaving about a ¾" overhang—with kitchen shears. Lightly fold the overhang back on itself on the edge of the pie plate, and create a decorative edge if you like— either fluting it or pressing all around it with the tines of a fork. Use the fork to prick the bottom of the crust. Follow directions for each recipe. Or wrap the unbaked pie crust (airtight) in plastic wrap and foil and freeze for up to 3 or 4 months.

WORK WITH FILLO DOUGH

1. Open a package of fillo dough and lay the dough flat on a clean, dry work surface.

2. Cover the fillo immediately with plastic wrap, and place a moist dishtowel over the plastic.

3. Work quickly, separating each single sheet of fillo from the pack, keeping the rest covered until needed.

TEST ICING OR PRALINES (SOFT-BALL STAGE)

1. The most accurate way for you to test the various stages of things sugary is to get yourself a good candy thermometer. When a confection is at the soft-ball stage the candy thermometer should read about 240 degrees (bend down to read the thermometer at eye level or you'll get an inaccurate reading).

2. To test visually, remove the pot from the heat and drop a bit of the syrup or candy mixture into a small bowl of ice water. When you lift the ball out of the water it should automatically flatten somewhat. If it disintegrates when you touch it, it's not ready.

MAKE PERFECT WHIPPED CREAM

1. Use fresh, heavy cream. Chill the beaters and the bowl ahead of time. Keep the cream refrigerated until you're ready to beat it.

2. Add 1/2 tsp. pure vanilla extract and 2 tbsp. sugar—confectioners' or granulated—to each cup of cream.

3. Beat only until soft peaks form when the beaters are raised—don't overbeat.

MAKE PERFECT MERINGUE

1. Use a balloon whisk, hand beater, or electric mixer. If you use an electric mixer, be very careful not to overbeat the meringue, which can happen very quickly.

2. Separate the eggs when they're cold, but allow the whites to come to room temperature, because they'll whip up into higher, fluffier peaks.

3. Begin beating the whites in a glass or metal bowl that is absolutely clean and grease free. After 1 minute, beat in the cream of tartar and continue beating just until soft peaks form.

4. Gradually beat in the sugar, adding it around the edges rather than in the middle of the meringue, which would deflate it.

5. Continue beating until the meringue is high, smooth, and shiny. If the meringue is dry and grainy you've overbeaten it. To repair it, beat in 1 more egg white until the consistency is light and smooth and the meringue is shiny.

TOAST NUTS

1. Heat a small, cast-iron skillet over medium heat.

2. Place the nuts in the skillet and toast over medium-low heat, shaking the skillet constantly, until the nuts are evenly golden brown, 3 to 6 minutes, depending on the nuts.

3. Immediately remove the nuts from the skillet so they won't continue to brown.

MAKE CHOCOLATE SHAVINGS AND CURLS

1. It's important to use either white or milk chocolate, both of which are softer than semi- or bittersweet, and have it at room temperature.

2. Place a piece of wax paper on a work surface. Use a swivel-blade vegetable peeler. Hold a square of the chocolate in one hand over the wax paper, and pressing firmly, pull the peeler toward yourself along the bottom of the square until the chocolate curls fall to the paper.

3. Use the shavings and curls to decorate Tipsy Apricot Chocolate Cake (see index).

HOLLANDAISE SAUCE

¼ cup freshly squeezed lemon juice,
   room temperature
6 egg yolks, room temperature
1 tsp. salt

⅛ tsp. cayenne pepper
1 cup (2 sticks) unsalted butter,
   melted

   1. Pour hot water into a blender or the bowl of a food processor to warm it. Discard the water and add the lemon juice, egg yolks, salt, and cayenne pepper and run at high speed until smooth.

   2. With the motor on, slowly stream in the melted butter and continue to blend until thoroughly emulsified.

   Makes about 1⅔ cups.

CHICKEN STOCK

5 lb. chicken wings, backs, necks,
   and bones with some meat
   clinging to them
3 qt. water
2 medium onions, cut into chunks
2 large carrots, cut into chunks
2 celery stalks, including leaves, cut
   into large pieces

6 whole black peppercorns
4 sprigs fresh parsley
4 sprigs fresh thyme
2 tbsp. salt
1 bay leaf

   1. Combine the chicken pieces and bones with the water in a stockpot over high heat. When the stock comes to a boil, skim off the foam that rises to the top.

   2. Stir in the onions, carrots, celery, peppercorns, parsley, thyme, salt, and bay leaf. Reduce the heat to low, cover, and simmer until the meat is falling off the bones, 2 to 3 hours. Remove from the heat and allow to cool to room temperature.

   3. Strain the stock, discarding the solids. Skim the fat from the stock and use immediately or freeze for future use (see index). The stock will keep, frozen, for up to 1 year.

4. Store the stock in sealable plastic bags in 1-cup amounts so that you'll be able to use as much or as little as you need without defrosting all of it.

Makes about 2½ qt.

BEEF STOCK

4 lb. beef bones, preferably with
    some meat clinging to them, cut
    into 2 to 3" pieces
2 medium onions, cut into chunks
2 large carrots, cut into chunks
2 celery stalks, including leaves, cut
    into large pieces
2 garlic cloves, peeled and halved

2 tbsp. olive oil
3 qt. water
6 whole black peppercorns
4 sprigs fresh thyme
2 tbsp. salt
2 whole cloves
1 bay leaf

1. Preheat the oven to 450 degrees.

2. Arrange the beef bones in a single layer in a large roasting pan or baking sheet. Roast until lightly browned, about 15 minutes. Turn the bones over, add the onions, carrots, celery, and garlic. Sprinkle all with the oil and continue roasting until the vegetables are golden, about 20 minutes. Remove from the oven and place the roasting pan on the stove over medium-low heat.

3. Transfer the roasted bones and vegetables to a stockpot. Pour 1 cup of the water into the roasting pan and deglaze: cook, stirring and scraping the bottom until all of the browned bits have been dislodged. Pour this over the bones and vegetables.

4. Place the stockpot over high heat, add the remaining water, and bring to a boil. Stir in the peppercorns, thyme, salt, cloves, and bay leaf. Reduce the heat to low, cover, and simmer until the meat is falling off the bones, 2 to 3 hours. Remove from the heat and allow to cool to room temperature.

5. Strain the stock, discarding the solids. Skim the fat from the stock and use immediately or freeze for future use (see index). The stock will keep, frozen, for up to 1 year.

6. Store the stock in sealable plastic bags in 1-cup amounts so that you'll be able to use as much or as little as you need without defrosting all of it.

Makes about 2½ qt.

FISH STOCK

2 tbsp. vegetable oil
1 cup minced onions (about 1 medium onion)
4 lb. fish bones, heads, and trimmings from mild, non-oily fish

1 cup minced parsley
¼ cup freshly squeezed lemon juice
2 cups dry white wine
2 qt. water
1½ tbsp. salt

1. Heat the oil in a stockpot over medium heat. Add the onions and cook, stirring occasionally, until soft, 5 to 6 minutes.

2. Reduce the heat to low and add the fish bones and scraps. Sprinkle with the parsley and lemon juice. Cook, shaking the pot occasionally, until the bones begin to look translucent, about 5 minutes. Increase the heat to medium-low and add the wine. Cook, stirring occasionally, until the liquid has reduced by about half, 25 to 30 minutes.

3. Increase the heat to medium-high. Add the water and salt and bring to a boil. Cook at a brisk bubble until the stock has reduced by half, about 30 minutes. Remove from the heat.

4. Strain the stock into one or more containers, discarding all of the solids. Allow to cool to room temperature before refrigerating or freezing. Fish stock can be kept refrigerated for up to 2 days or frozen for up to 4 months.

5. When freezing, store the stock in sealable plastic bags in 1-cup amounts so that you'll be able to use as much or as little as you need without defrosting all of it.

Makes about 1 qt.

SHRIMP STOCK

Shells and heads from about 2 dozen shrimp
2 qt. water
2 lemons, quartered
1 large onion, coarsely chopped
1 stalk celery, including leaves, roughly chopped

½ tsp. salt
6 whole black peppercorns
4 large garlic cloves, peeled and halved
½ cup fresh parsley leaves and stems
4 bay leaves

1. Rinse the shrimp before shelling them. Combine the shells and heads with the water in a large pot over high heat.

2. Squeeze the lemons into the water and add the lemon quarters. Add the onion, celery, salt, peppercorns, garlic, parsley, and bay leaves, and bring to a boil. Skim off the foam that forms on the surface, reduce the heat to medium, and cook for 30 to 40 minutes.

3. Strain the stock into a container and allow it to come to room temperature. Use immediately, or divide into individual containers and freeze for future use.

4. Store the stock in sealable plastic bags in 1-cup amounts so that you'll be able to use as much or as little as you need without defrosting all of it.

Makes about 1½ qt.

Index